The discerning reader

The discerning reader

Christian perspectives on literature and theory

*Edited by David Barratt,
Roger Pooley, Leland Ryken*

APOLLOS

BakerBooks

A Division of Baker Book House Co
Grand Rapids, Michigan 49516

APOLLOS (an imprint of Inter-Varsity Press)
38 De Montfort Street, Leicester LE1 7GP, England

Baker Books
(a division of Baker Book House Company)
P.O. Box 6287, Grand Rapids, Michigan 49516–6287, USA

First published 1995

British Library Cataloguing-in-Publication Data
A catalogue record for this book is available from the British Library.

ISBN 0-85111-445-8

First published in the USA by Baker Books 1995
ISBN 0–8010–2085–9

Set in Palatino
Typeset in Great Britain by Parker Typesetting Service, Leicester
Printed in Great Britain by Clays Ltd, Bungay, Suffolk

Contents

About the contributors

David Barratt is former Senior Lecturer in English at Chester College, England, and Visiting Professor, University of North Carolina, Ashville, USA, and Chico State University, California, USA. His interests include gardening.

Elizabeth Clarke is Senior Lecturer in English at Westminster College, Oxford. Her forthcoming book, *'Divinitie, and Poesie, Met': Theology and Theory in the Poetry of George Herbert*, is to be published by Oxford University Press.

Rowland Cotterill is Lecturer in English and History of Music at the University of Warwick, England. His interests include Broadway musicals.

John Cox teaches English Literature at Hope College in Holland, Michigan, USA. He writes about early English drama, as well as Christianity and literary theory. His book *Shakespeare and the Dramaturgy of Power* (1989) responds to new historicist criticism of Shakespeare from a Christian perspective. He serves on the advisory board of *Christianity and Literature* and is associate editor for humanities of *Christian Scholar's Review*.

Valentine Cunningham is Fellow and Tutor in English Literature at Corpus Christi College, Oxford, and lecturer in English for the university. His publications include *In the Reading Gaol: Postmodernity, Texts and History* (1994) and *British Writers of the Thirties* (1988). He is currently working on a literary biography of Charles Dickens for Blackwell.

Elisabeth Jay is Head of English at Westminster College, Oxford. Her publications include *Margaret Oliphant – 'A Fiction to Herself'*:

A Literary Life (1995) and *Faith and Doubt in Victorian Britain* (1987).

U. Milo Kaufman was formerly Associate Professor Emeritus of English at the University of Illinois. His interests include tree-watching and science fiction. He has published *Heaven: A Future Finer than Dreams* (1981) and *Paradise in the Age of Milton* (1978). He is presently writing a book on heaven and the images of hope.

Donald G. Marshall is Professor and Head of English at the University of Illinois at Chicago. He has published numerous essays on literary theory and its history. He compiled *Contemporary Critical Theory: A Selective Bibliography* (1993). He has presented papers and participated in conferences and seminars at Wheaton College, Calvin College, Trinity Christian College, the University of Notre Dame, and elsewhere.

Kevin Mills is a church leader and youth worker whose interests include playing rock music. His book, *Justifying Language: Paul and Contemporary Literary Theory* is forthcoming from Macmillan, London.

Roger Pooley is lecturer in English at Keele University, England. He is Chair of the Literary Studies Group of the UCCF. His publications include *English Prose of the Seventeenth Century* (Longman).

Leland Ryken is Professor of English at Wheaton College, where he has taught since 1968. Author of over twenty books, his areas of expertise include literature in Christian perspective, the Bible as literature, Milton, the Puritans, and work and leisure. He is a frequent speaker at conferences and on college campuses.

John Schad is Lecturer in English at the University of Loughborough. He has published *The Reader in the Dickensian Mirror* (1992) and is editor of the forthcoming *Dickens Refigured*, to be published by Manchester University Press.

J. R. Watson is Professor of English at the University of Durham, England. With K. Trickett he is author of *Companion to Hymns and Psalms* (1988).

Donald T. Williams is an ordained minister in the Evangelical Free Church of America, and Associate Professor of English at Toccoa Falls College. His poetry and prose have appeared in such publications as *Christianity and Literature*, *Christian Scholar's Review* and *Mythlore*. His book *The Person and Work of the Holy Spirit* was published in 1994.

Introduction

Why worry about reading?

Since the Renaissance at least, literary education has had a central role in western societies, in the training of its young people and in the transmission of its culture. It is not surprising, then, that the values and content involved in the criticism of literature should be such a contested area. In our own time, 'English' has become the dominant form of literary education in universities and schools; and yet there remains an anxiety among teachers and critics (no doubt transferred to their students) about the status of their subject. So they have turned to other disciplines to provide a more secure, possibly scientific, basis for their practice – psychology, history, linguistics and so on. Or they have turned to belief systems, ways of explaining the world, such as feminism or Marxism, to give them a place to stand from which to construct their arguments about literature. This in turn has attracted criticism, both in Britain and America, from political and cultural conservatives who see education as a publically funded school for subversives. In Britain, we have a Minister for National Heritage who in Europe would be called a Minister of Culture; in America, the tradition of libertarianism is perpetually in tension with those who would prescribe what others should and (more often) should not read.

This book is not a political intervention on behalf of the forces of reaction ('The western tradition is mainly Christian, therefore . . .') or Christian minority rights ('We demand equal airtime with feminist, Marxist and psychoanalytic views'). Christians have traditions, not least because we believe that a bundle of documents composed two thousand years ago holds the key to what life is all about. Equally, Christians may sometimes feel like a suppressed minority, when Christian criticism gets virtually ignored by, for example, the latest Modern Language Association of America survey of English and American literary studies. Christian students sometimes feel similarly embattled as they are called upon to adopt theories and practices that seem, at least, to be hostile to their beliefs. This book is an attempt by their fellow Christians further along the line to help them think and write their way through that in a constructive way, not to retreat into silence or sloganizing.

Our first audience is thus students of literature, Christians, and those who want to know what Christians think about the major issues and some of the major texts faced by undergraduates and postgraduates on either side of the Atlantic. The idea of a 'discerning reader' is not simply that of the ideally responsive reader longed for by authors, but a measure of more than literary competence. In the New Testament, discernment is used in the context of the spiritual, of what is good and bad, and of a process of purity and maturity in seeing what the real purpose of an individual, or a community, or even God, might be. A reader who does not know the difference between a metaphor and a metonym, or pastoral and georgic, may still be in the foothills of professional reading; but there are more important differences, and they are not all listed in dictionaries of literary terms. Can a book deprave or corrupt, in the phraseology of the English obscenity laws? Can it improve the person who reads it? Is it any more than entertainment?

Our different authors bring varying Christian perspectives to bear; nonetheless, the book has an argument, a shape, and it may be helpful to see its outline as we conceive it.

The first half of the book addresses new and old theoretical approaches. The first two chapters form a pair – 'What does literature do?' and 'Canons' – asking what literature is. Although there is a strong post-Enlightenment, post-Kantian urge to approach literature from its intrinsic qualities, we argue that literature has effects. If we can be clear about that, we can see why what we read and study is important. The argument about what constitutes the 'canon' is not just about what we should regard as worth reading, and worth setting for school or college reading lists, but about minority rights and authority. It also brings up the parallel between reading literature and reading the Bible, and using them as privileged insights into the way we should live.

The third chapter, on the history of Christian poetics, investigates how Christians have thought about and practised literature.

Again, this forms a kind of pair with the fourth chapter. In view of the contemporary emphasis on the act of reading more than on the act of creation, Donald Marshall returns to one of the key concepts in the debate, the reading community, and asks what might constitute and distinguish a Christian reading community.

The succeeding three chapters pick up central features in the contemporary debate about critical reading. In 'The turn to history' John Cox discusses what underlies the current reconception of history as the place from which literature may be best understood. He looks at the relationship between Marxism and new historicism, and the limitations of 'an easily assumed atheism' when looking at the literature of past, ostensibly Christian, societies. In 'The woman's place' Elisabeth Jay discusses with sympathy and scepticism a number of feminist positions, recognizing that feminism is a broad political movement before it is a way of literary criticism. In 'Words and presences' Kevin Mills confronts what may seem the most radically anti-metaphysical (and therefore anti-Christian) tendency in theory, post-structuralism. He suggests that deconstruction can be adapted (though not without qualms) for the Christian to resist the value-free zone of the 'postmodern', in an original reading of Paul's distinction between letter and Spirit.

Leland Ryken's chapter on the Bible forms a kind of bridge between these theoretical discussions and the case studies which follow. For Christian readers, the Bible is a special case. How can it be read as literature, without devaluing its claim to be *the* authoritative book?

The case studies which follow are not simply examples of how Christian reading might proceed, but have been chosen to suggest responses to certain kinds of texts. U. Milo Kaufmann begins on a Christian text, *Paradise Lost*, which brings up the great questions about Christianity, and can be, for the Christian reader, more challenging than many openly atheist texts. J. R. Watson considers the Romantic rewriting of Christianity with particular reference to Wordsworth, and with a telling comparison of Blake and Isaac Watts. William Shakespeare, the endlessly debated, prescribed and performed, is the subject of Rowland Cotterill's chapter. In readings of *Richard III*, *King Lear* and *The Winter's Tale*, three particularly provoking texts for Christians, he asks key questions about Shakespeare's own Christianity as well as assessing the potential for a distinctively Christian reading of Shakespeare. David Barratt discusses what we originally considered 'a canonical humanist text', Hardy's *Jude the Obscure* – a text that confronts rather than ignores Christian ideas and Christian institutions. Finally, there are two studies of recent novels which link up with earlier chapters. Elizabeth Clarke investigates feminist readings of *The Handmaid's Tale*, with its critique of fundamentalism, and John Schad shows the metaphysical leanings of that early postmodern novel, Pynchon's *The Crying of Lot 49*.

David Barratt's bibliographical essay indicates some of the ways in which Christian criticism functions, and is an important resource for those who want to explore further.

We have (almost) taken for granted one key argument within Christianity – whether the arts are justifiable at all. What is the point of studying literature, when there are so many urgent calls on the conscientious person's attention? Many of us come from Christian traditions which were once iconoclastic, or would have had trouble stepping beyond the limits of *The Pilgrim's Progress* and versified psalms. What we have inherited from that tradition is not just a desire for truth-telling over deceit, but also a respect for the power of the imaginative word. If it is powerful, it can be dangerous as well as inspiring. It is the genius of literature to be persuasive in a distinctive way, to help us think our way into other positions, other possibilities. That means the reverse of passivity for the reader. Reading against the grain of the dominant literary culture may be the Christian's calling in many places; these essays show, too, that there is as much spiritual yearning as spiritual hostility demonstrated in literature and its criticism.

Part 1

Theory

1

What does literature do?

Roger Pooley

That sceptical Christian W. H. Auden asserted that poetry makes nothing happen, in conscious opposition to large Romantic assertions that 'poets are the unacknowledged legislators of the world' (Shelley), or that a poet has 'a greater knowledge of human nature, and a more comprehensive soul, than are supposed to be common among mankind' (Wordsworth).[1] Students of literature have often concurred, not least because of a culturally profound mistrust of those who assert their superiority to ordinary mortals. And what's wrong with humility as a Christian virtue? The bohemian notion of the artist as exempt from normal human responsibilities if only he or she will produce great art has often proved damaging to the artist, as well as those around him or her. Yeats reckoned that

> The intellect of man is forced to choose
> Perfection of the life, or of the work,
> And if it take the second must refuse
> A heavenly mansion, raging in the dark.[2]

We might prefer the painter R. B. Kitaj's remark: 'Art is not my life; my life is my life,' for the sake of everyone's well-being; and nothing is worth trading for a heavenly mansion.

There is no need to turn the writer into a separate species of humanity to recognize that literature does make things happen sometimes, even in public contexts – take the riots over *The Satanic Verses*, or the young men who committed suicide in imitation of Goethe's Young Werther. Nationalism needs a national literature – usually, like Shakespeare, co-opted into the role years later (a point Valentine Cunningham enlarges on in the next chapter).

The more obviously public and political impact of literature forms only one side of the answer. It ignores those individual readers who have been cheered up, consoled, depressed or excited by Aeschylus or Zola, *Adam Bede* or *Zuleika Dobson*; and there is also a problem, for lack of clear evidence, with the literature which might stop things happening, by bolstering the power of the *status quo*, like the monarchs eulogized by seventeenth-century court masques. That particular instance is an interesting paradox, because the art itself was often *avant-garde* – the first example of perspective painting in England is generally held to be Inigo Jones' design for a masque of 1605. What may seem revolutionary in the history of a genre may have the opposite effect in ideological terms. However, what is arguably the most revolutionary formal innovation of twentieth-century modernism, the interior monologue as in Joyce's *Ulysses*, may have had more impact, because it has taught us a different way of seeing ourselves, of being individuals. To ask if literature changes things, or simply responds to new situations, is a misleading choice; it does both.

Literature is, at one level, an inescapable feature of being human in community, though its function has varied considerably. The dominant position of 'English' in secondary and tertiary liberal education for example, is the creation of the last hundred years. Yet what culture exists that does not tell stories? Why do societies erect barriers of censorship around literary expression – characterized as pornography, blasphemy, or political dissidence – if it is impotent anyway? Or, for that matter, why promote it through prizes and selective patronage? Why did Jesus address his disciples in parables as well as commands and propositions?

1. Being human

My view is that literature is first an important *cultural* activity – that is, that it communicates in a particular way within and between individuals and communities, past as well as present. Its writing and reception can be variously cohesive, constructive or disruptive. It may be conceived as a leisure activity, as play, or as a practice of high moral or religious significance. It has a real if limited power to affect people. More than that, it has a *cognitive* dimension as well. We can know things through reading literature. In the words of the novelist Graham Swift, 'Fiction is not fact, but it is not fraud. The imagination has the power of sheer, fictive invention but it also has the power to carry us to the truth, to make us arrive at knowledge we did not possess and may even have felt, taking an empirical view of our experience, we had no right to possess.'[3] Literature is both *creative* and *mimetic*. A dramatist might create a new world or a new character which literally 'adds to the stock of available reality'. Shakespeare's Falstaff, for example, or the almost empty stage places of Beckett's plays are not without sources or antecedents; but they seem distinctive, like a new taste or a fresh idea. They rely on both audience expectation (convention, however disrupted; to be unconventional is to rely on expectations created by convention), as well as a correspondence with the world as we know it outside the literary experience, to make sense.

All these elements are most coherently understood within a Christian anthropology, by which I mean a Christian analysis of what it means to be human. This gives true weight to both the wonders and horrors of being human. Men and women are created in the image of God, which means they share his creativity, his capacity and desire for love, a sense of the infinite; and they are also fallen away from glory, and so torn between good and evil, destructive and alienated.[4]

At the level of creativity, Coleridge's famous definition of the imagination in *Biographia Literaria* explicitly parallels human and divine creativity, and emphasizes the secondary nature of human imagination. In his view, human imagination is less Promethean, stealing God's fire, than post-Edenic, struggling to re-create what is perceived as lost:

> The primary IMAGINATION I hold to be the living Power and prime Agent of all human Perception, and as a repetition in the finite mind of the eternal act of creation in the infinite I AM. The secondary imagination I consider as an echo of the former, co-existing with the conscious will, yet still as identical with the primary in the *kind* of its agency, and differing only in *degree*, and in the *mode* of its operation. It dissolves, diffuses, dissipates, in order to re-create; or where this process is rendered impossible, yet still, at all events, it struggles to idealize and to unify.[5]

There are difficulties with this, beyond those of Coleridge's own thought, in his drive to reconcile the self and nature. One might argue, like Nicholas Berdyaev, that 'the free power to reveal himself in creative action, is placed within man as a seal and sign of his likeness to God, as a mark of the Creator's image'; and yet be forced to recognize that there is a destructive, satanic 'creativity' as well.[6] Within creativity there is often an ambition reaching out to the infinite, which is both evidence of our eternal origins, and a reminder of our limits, mortal and moral.

At the level of mimesis, or realism in literature, there appears to be a stronger case for saying that scepticism and materialism are more likely motives than religion to tell the truth about reality. After all, isn't religion about the ideal, the possibility, rather than the reality of things as they are? The great nineteenth-century Realist manifestos stressed that they described life as it was rather than as it should be. Emile Zola, in an 1880 essay on 'Naturalism and the Stage', called for 'no more abstract characters in books, no more lying inventions, no more of the absolute; but real characters, the true history of each one, the story of daily life'. The counter-case is that the Christian gospels provide the most 'realistic' of sacred texts; that they stress the material rather than the abstract (Greek) nature of religious commitment; and that they inaugurate key features of the realist enterprise, even as they demand a committed response to those narratives.[7]

Those twin poles of describing what literature does, which go back to Aristotle, *poiesis* and *mimesis*, making and imitating, have been joined by a third, that literature is simply textual, a play of language that offers no window on to the world or the self. This post-structuralist position teases both common sense and religion by suggesting that any claim that language can present selfhood, or material reality, or truth, is metaphysical, that it requires an act of faith. (The phrase is 'the metaphysics of presence'.)[8] Difficulties with 'presence' will be familiar to Christians whose religion is based on a book regarded as authoritative; yet none of the books within it was written by Jesus. Indeed, the Jewish critic George Steiner has proposed in his book *Real Presences* that 'any coherent account of the capacity of human speech to communicate meaning and feeling is, in the final analysis, underwritten by the assumption of God's presence . . . the experience of aesthetic meaning in particular, that of literature, of the arts, of musical form, infers the necessary possibility of this "real presence"'.[9] Steiner thus recognizes how deconstructive reading challenges any certain epistemology, any straightforward passage from word to world. As Geoffrey Hartman, one of its major American practitioners, puts it, reading becomes an entirely self-referring, autonomous process: 'Reading itself becomes the project: we read to understand what is involved in reading as a form of life, rather than to resolve what is read into glossy ideas.'[10] This is more than a sophisticated version of the older critical dictum, that poetry is lost in paraphrase; it assumes that communication is indeterminate because incomplete. Yet we are still talking to each other. Language and its objects are not so easily torn apart.

Such a general account of what literature does might be accused of 'essentialism', that I am emphasizing the universal; whereas what we should address is 'difference': how history, class, gender, race and sexuality have been ignored or suppressed or marginalized in the name of a supposedly 'human' centre. Such recent critical titles or subtitles as *The Matter of Difference*, *The Discourses of Sexual Difference in Early Modern Europe* and *'Race', Writing and Difference* are indicative of such a shift of emphasis. What this contemporary discourse does not entirely acknowledge, though, is the extent to which this emphasizing of difference is still a prelude to some more universalizing gesture, that of a largely transhistorical feminism, for example.[11] The discourse of 'difference' derives in part from Saussure's characterization of language as a system of difference without positive terms, partly from a famous early essay of Derrida's; but it has become, quite properly, transferred into ideology, and thus itself subject to different kinds of questioning. The New Testament epistles, interestingly, take a parallel view of 'difference': that the differences between Jew and Greek, male and female, slave and free, humanity and God, all produce antagonisms which cannot be ignored, but that Christ has broken down the barriers. It could therefore be the calling of literature and its criticism to expose and break down those barriers, though not to 'transcend' them by itself, as if literature were a kind of alternative spirituality. A Martin Amis story has a famous novelist say airily: 'I don't think in terms of men or women. I think in terms of . . . people' – only to be savagely corrected by his old friend:

> Hey, how about being a spider, Gwyn, you Taff dunce? Say you get away with your life after your first date and look over your shoulder and there's the girlfriend eating one of your legs like it was a chicken drumstick. What would you say? I know. You'd say: I don't think in terms of male spiders or female spiders. I just think in terms of *spiders*.[12]

Ironically, it is the famous author who comes out with a vapid generalization; his friend Richard, the drunken hack, who tells the story which exposes its limitations.

2. Stories

The enjoyment of narrative starts early. It is one of our best ways of making sense of the world and ourselves. The bounds of 'literature' and even 'fiction' do not include anything like the totality. As I write, a battle rages within historiography about the role and status of narrative; there is a growing sub-discipline of 'narrative theology'; and even scientists, committed to the opposite of 'fiction', still follow their early Royal Society forebears in constructing reports of experiments according to a stylized narrative model. The idea that 'discovery' is the climax of a story, which according to Aristotle is a governing principle of the story in tragedy or epic, works just as well for William Harvey's account of the circulation of the blood in *De Motu Cordis*. Narrative is one of the crucial ways in which intellectual disciplines make sense of their material. For example, the historian and theorist Hayden White remarks that the 'value attached to narrativity in the representation of real events arises out of a desire to have real events display the coherence, integrity, fullness and closure of an image of life that is and can only be imaginary'.[13] This last word does not mean that White condemns such a move to narrativity; on the contrary, 'the function of imagination is the production of a specifically human truth', by testing a series of patterns ('typification') to see if they endow events with satisfactory meaning. As with much contemporary thinking, it is 'a truth' rather than 'the truth' that is expected. The postmodern condemnation of 'grand narratives' which explain everything has not blunted the desire to find contingent narratives which will explain something.

Narrative theology might also appear to be vulnerable to the criticism of accommodation, seeking, as T. R. Wright puts it, 'to combine confessional commitment with philosophical relativism'.[14] The key mode for theology of story is autobiography, because God's 'decisive story overarches, interprets, judges, sustains and calls forth our stories and is obliquely known to them'.[15] The commitment is less to a propositional or credal view of God (though it doesn't deny it) than to a process of finding God. Living a story, not just telling a story, is the way this works.

How does our experience of reading literary stories relate to this? The habit of reading stories as a leisure activity should not blind us to their importance. Fictions help construct our view of reality, if only temporarily or provisionally. The woman who reads pulp romances may be aware that they construct their readers as female rather than male, and that they are highly stereotypical in plot and character, yet she finds them useful as relaxation because they offer an alternative, rosier reality to the demanding one in which she lives. But are they not thereby offering a version of happiness, or of female power, by which the world is judged on the reader's return to it? Does 'better' literature do any better? Sometimes it does so by invoking such stereotypical romance figures and then changing, or altering them. So Aphra Behn makes the African slave Oroonoko the very image of a romance hero, brave, handsome and resolute in opposition to the supposedly more civilized Europeans who have enslaved him; and in her novel *Love Letters between a Nobleman and His Sister* she uses 'softness' to describe desirable men and women equally, thus undermining the usual divisions of sexual behaviour. And all this in the 1680s. A few years earlier, the Puritan writers Bunyan and Milton were, in their different ways, rewriting the concept of the heroic in the light of the Christian perception that God's strength is best apparent in human weakness. In other words, good literature works by making us re-examine the world as it is, and our conventions for under-standing the world as we experience it. It makes us look more critically at that reality – we call it 'realism', and Dickens' description of the realities of the worst boarding schools in *Nicholas Nickleby* put many of them out of business. It helps us to imagine alternative realities – the traditions of Utopia and fantasy create alternative worlds for the serious purpose of play as well as showing the gap between what might be and what is. Putting it in such baldly conceptual terms, however, does scant justice to the process by which a narrative works on us.

A common way of explaining this process is to invoke empathy. One cannot empathize with a concept; but one might find characters in a story and take their side, enter into their thoughts and feelings and see the world of the text through their eyes. In a novel this might be the storyteller as much as a central character. The virtue of empathy, as opposed to sympathy, is that it requires us to enter into the experience of someone else, not necessarily someone we would agree with or even like. It is one of the justifications of literature as moral education, seeing the world through fresh eyes. The problem with empathy is that it involves a suspension of the critical faculties. With attractive stage villains we can get caught up in what Peter Womack calls the 'savage euphoria' of an audience. All too often we forget that when Aristotle recommended tragedy as a purgation (catharsis) of our emotions of pity and fear, he regarded those emotions as dangerous in excess, not to be indulged in an orgy of empathy. Still, put the emotional chocolate box to one side, and the experience of literature, not just the story-based sort, can be a way of seeing and feeling beyond ourselves and our usual horizons, a mental practice for being good Samaritans. Equally, it can be a way of recognizing ourselves, of giving voice to a half-perceived feeling, and thus being able to place it within a wider scheme of things. George Eliot shows how this emotional truth can be linked to a discursive truth in her account of Dorothea Brooke on disappointed honeymoon in Rome:

> She was humiliated to find herself a mere victim of feeling, as if she could know nothing except through that medium: all her strength was scattered in fits of agitation, of struggle, of despondency, and then again in visions of a more complete renunciation, transforming all hard conditions into duty. Poor Dorothea! she was certainly troublesome – to herself chiefly; but this morning for the first time she had been troublesome to Mr Casaubon.[16]

Here are the social and moral constraints on feeling, of 'duty' (famously described by the agnostic Eliot as absolute), deftly named as that interweaving of social imposition and internalized desire. Following the French psychoanalyst Jacques Lacan, critics have argued that such writing is constituting a 'subject', a particular conception called the individual who is prepared for 'subjection' to law and society while convinced that his or her 'subjectivity' guarantees an internal space of freedom. In a curious way this critique of the metaphysics of western liberal humanism echoes the opening of Calvin's *Institutes*, which recommends introspection, not because the individual will find a sphere of freedom and plenitude within, but because the devil is within, and the individual will recognize the need of God's salvation from such disastrous inner subjection. As so often, we can see Eliot working through a secularized version of spiritual dilemmas, within the Romantic tension of individual freedom *versus* social constraint. If we want to hold on to a notion of literature as knowledge, perhaps we should regard it as a process, a critical process of emancipation from the blunt simplicities of 'empathy' towards some more dialogic engagement with texts.

Literature is not just an invitation to feel. We might approach it from another view and see it as a persuasive instrument. All sorts of literary forms are arguments. Hamlet's soliloquies can be read as essays in persuasion rather better than as outbursts from his own tortured psyche. John Berger argues at the beginning of his story 'Boris is Buying Horses' that 'Sometimes, to refute a single sentence it is necessary to tell a life story.'[17] Stories, though, are a rather special form of argument. Berger says in his 'A Story for Aesop' that 'The story becomes a story because we are not quite sure how much life's experience of itself (and what else are stories if not that?) is always sceptical.'[18] Even when a story seems to be an illustration of a proposition, story and proposition have a habit of pulling apart, of opening up in ironic distance. An earlier homage to Aesop, Robert Henryson's *Morall Fabillis*, are particularly provoking in this way. Yet what is opening up between story and proposition is still an argument. Arguments need to be argued with as well as respected, analysed and plundered for one's own. So it is with literary texts.

3. Moral positions

Should moral arguments come into literary criticism, though? There is no lack of high moral tone in the history of literary criticism. Here is Samuel Johnson *versus* realism, for example, in a tradition of literature as pleasant moral instruction that goes back at least to Horace:

> It is therefore not a sufficient vindication of a character that it is drawn as it appears, for many characters ought never to be drawn; nor of a narrative, that the train of events is agreeable to observation and experience, for that observation which is called knowledge of the world will be found much more frequently to make men cunning than good. The purpose of these writings is surely not only to show mankind, but to provide that they may be seen hereafter with less hazard; to teach the means of avoiding the snares which are laid by Treachery for Innocence, without infusing any wish for that superiority with which the betrayer flatters his vanity; to give the power of counteracting fraud, without the temptation to practise it; to initiate youth by mock encounters in the art of necessary defence; and to increase prudence without impairing virtue.[19]

As a defence of the Christian humanist position on literary education, it has strength and subtlety; but, like many moral statements about literature, it is vulnerable to charges of restrictiveness. The key to this Christian humanist position, though, is not so much what it leaves out as how it concludes. Sidney, in the *Apology for Poetry*, and Johnson, notably in his comments on the last Act of *King Lear*, prefer plots that end with a provisional last judgment. Such a dream of justice is common to such genres as utopian fiction and the detective story, and the degree to which such fictional worlds display their moral certainties is an important diagnostic tool for the critic. Agnostic writers such as George Eliot sometimes seem more anxious to administer justice to their creations than more ostensibly Christian writers such as Ben Jonson. For them, there is no other last judgment to await.

Historically, Johnson's moral analysis was superseded by the belief that the best art has a life of its own – 'A poem should not mean/but be', in Archibald McLeish's 1926 formula – and that its formal, aesthetic qualities are what should be admired and made the basis of judgment. This promised, for the young academic discipline of English, an area of objectivity. The discussion of beauty might still be fatally compromised by questions of taste – is literary criticism any more reliable than wine-tasting? asks Terry Eagleton at the opening of his polemic survey of *Literary Theory*. The image of epicene dons selecting poets for the syllabus along roughly the same lines as the claret for their cellars has an irresistible appeal for the iconoclast. Poetry and wine do have things in common, though – pleasure, variety and subtlety – and discourse about them both can be precise up to a point, but then gets impressionistic just where quality judgments become most important. Eventually, though, they have to be distinguished. For one thing, poetry can discuss wine, but wine cannot talk about poetry, though some poets have claimed that it could inspire it. And, despite the best efforts of some writers, literature is incurably semantic. It means things, at all sorts of levels, with a marvellous complexity and an equally marvellous plainness.

That intricacy or multiplicity is what unites a wide range of otherwise mutually opposed views of what literature is like. It makes literature teachable and discussable: 'Have you seen the way this episode or stanza works if you look at it from this angle?' It has meant that the academic literary establishment has tended to favour difficult texts, demanding a heroism of interpretation on the part of its readers. The twentieth century did not invent 'difficulty', or even the special cachet that comes from being able to understand an obscure poem. What is new is how complexity has taken over the role that beauty had in earlier thinking about art. The problem comes when we try to decide if there is, in W. B. Yeats' phrase, a 'mere complexity', which is ultimately triviality, because that involves a judgment which is not simply intrinsic.

At this point, however, Christian criticism should not immediately ally itself with 'high seriousness', against the current orthodoxy favouring the idea of literature as sophisticated play. Erich Auerbach argued that the New Testament produced a new kind of literature which completely upended the classical standards of decorum. Briefly, classical rhetorical criticism (a largely prescriptive rather than descriptive approach) said that a high style was appropriate for high subjects, defined in social terms as well as religious. A low, or plain, style was appropriate to lower-class characters and everyday subjects. However, when Jesus said that eternal salvation could be gained by giving someone a cup of cold water or visiting a prisoner (Mt. 25:34–40) the distinction between high and low could no longer be maintained. The incarnation brings the high and low, the bodily and the sublime, together.[20] So, Thom Gunn's marvellous poem 'Considering the Snail' (with its echo of Jesus' invitation to 'consider the lilies') could not be regarded as trivial because snails are trivial. But one might still ask whether the thought, or the language, is adequate to the subject. Brendan Kennelly's *The Book of Judas* invites that sort of judgment, with its insistent courting of bathos in the brave attempt to produce the authentic, contemporary voice of Judas. Consider the end of 'An Absorbing Theme', on the way writers have investigated Judas' suicide:

> Pathetic efforts! I should, I suppose, have been offended
> By such feeble scrutiny of my character in action
> But I realise most men manage only
> To talk about themselves and their simple
> Obsessions. I am completely myself. That's why
> I inspire such helpless imitation. Consider
> The incidence of teenage suicide, for example.
> What mind can grasp the ignominy of the pimple?[21]

Careful of the quick dismissal; this is the dramatized voice of Judas, not the poet. But what precisely is the uneasy laugh about the pimple doing? Is it looking for the easy laugh of bathos? Or is there a reflective quality to it?

In asking such questions, I am doing instinctively what a reader trained in the last forty years would do: looking for the complexities, the multiplicities, of a text. According to this practice, what is bad about a bad text is its banality. There are no rich ambiguities in its images, its syntax, its meaning. The case for a moral reading of literature based on complexity rather than a code of morality was most influentially made, in this century, by F. R. Leavis out of D. H. Lawrence. This is Lawrence in a 1925 essay on 'Morality and the Novel', contrasting the novel with religion, philosophy and science with their desire to nail things down to a stable equilibrium:

> But the novel, no! The novel is the highest complex of subtle interrelatedness that man has discovered. Everything is true in its own time, place, circumstance and untrue outside of its own place, time, circumstance. If you try to nail anything down in the novel, either it kills the novel, or the novel gets up and walks away with the nail.

The collaborative process that Leavis describes as the main process of criticism, rather than the appeal to 'standards' of a literary Weights and Measures Office, comes from a similar stance. At the time, and subsequently, Leavis was criticized for his unwillingness to reveal the abstract standards by which he proceeded to judgment – and there have been many who have supplied them by inference, as a kind of exposé. After some decades in which coming clean, theoretically, has been unavoidable, we can see that the Lawrence/Leavis position is close to the anti-foundationalist position prevalent in much thinking in the humanities today. Its central thesis has been reformulated by Stanley Fish as follows:

> When we act impartially . . . we do so 'by our lights', which means that we act within and as an extension of an interpretative and therefore partial notion of what being impartial means.[22]

The assumption that truth is made, not found, thus has a longer history than post-structuralism. Richard Rorty, one of the major anti-foundationalist philosophers, dates it back to the French Revolution, and some think it goes back to the Sophists of ancient Greece. Rorty also makes considerable use of fiction, for example those 'which dramatize the conflicts between duties to self and duties to others', and in doing so attempts to get rid of the moral *versus* aesthetic distinction that still haunts the discussion of literature. Instead, he proposes the simpler question: 'What purposes does this book serve?' As an evangelizing liberal, Rorty naturally makes the classic liberal distinction between the public and private, the way in which we live with others, and the way in which we become ourselves. Then, revealingly and helpfully, he remarks that only Christians and a few others 'for whom the search for private perfection coincides with the project of living for others' make the two sorts of questions come together.[23] The suggestion, then, is that the apparently conflicting languages of beauty and morals, private and public, ought not to be ultimately divided. In one way, the key Lawrence word, relatedness, returns.

I am very happy for Rorty's question, 'What purposes does this serve?' to be the first the discerning reader should ask of a text, whether it be a poem or, indeed, a critical reading of that poem. As he notes, 'relaxation' might be as appropriate an answer as some more strenuous purpose. But, as we noted earlier in the discussion of romance, even escapist texts serve wider purposes. Chesterton's *Father Brown* stories were posited on the human knowledge one might gain from the confessional. An acute sense of human sinfulness might produce a murder mystery as much as it does Donne's Holy Sonnets, and the echoes of the Book of Common Prayer in P. D. James' crime novels (*Devices and Desires*, for example) alert us to the origins of the darkness in her world of darkness (and, in *The Children of Men* at least, redemption). The division between 'novel' and 'entertainment' in the novels of Graham Greene is not a division between those where the author's Christian, Catholic vision is clear and those where it is not. Christian literature, like Christian criticism, is not Christian only when it is being serious.

What, though, of the texts of transgression, those we call pornography and blasphemy? This is where a sharper division between the liberal humanist and the Christian reader might obtain.

It is probably a caricature to say that the Christian perspective in the arts comes into focus only when we want something banned – we are found policing the boundaries of the acceptable rather than leading the *avant-garde*. The experimental nature of recent Christian poetry should give the lie to that, from Hopkins and T. S. Eliot to R. S. Thomas and Les A. Murray. Yet a protest against transgression will make the headlines, and 'Good book cheers up several people' will not. The transgressive power of literature, whether in erotic, or political or religious terms, is often testified to by censorship. It is often a sign that those in authority recognize the impact of literature.

Censorship in Freudian thinking has a profound internal source, and a vehement denunciation is sometimes a sign of an unresolved inner conflict. Davenport-Hines links it to projection, 'whereby emotions, vices, and qualities which an individual either rejects or refuses to recognize himself are expelled from the self and relocated in another person and persons'.[24] Thus, he and others argue, an attack on the expression of homosexuality is due to homophobia, the fear of a repressed or potential homosexuality in oneself, cloaked under an appeal to nature or Scripture. An analysis of Christianity as denying the freedom of both sexuality and art emerges in various other ways. When R. S. Thomas castigates Protestantism as the 'adroit castrator of art' ('The Minister'), he is making a similar association of art with a forbidden erotic realm.

We might want to stand outside Freudian analysis and say that the system is self-reinforcing: it can cope with any kind of denial as a repressed agreement. The Christian conviction that the sexually dissolute will not be part of God's kingdom might govern our feelings about the literature that tackles such issues; but so should Christ's continually embarrassing habit of dining with 'sinners', breaking up a hypocritical party who wanted to stone a woman taken in adultery, and accepting the tearful devotion of a prostitute. Christianity is not simply, inhumanly, proscriptive. Moreover, as Freudians and, even more, Foucauldians recognize, policing the erotic boundaries is itself productive as well as protective, and repression may re-channel energies in ways it might not intend. Donald Davie's characterization of the non-conformist aesthetic in *A Gathered Church* shows how a Christian suspicion of art can have a distinctive, creative effect. In particular, he shows how the theological term *kenōsis*, the self-limitation of Christ's divine power at the incarnation, can translate into a Christian aesthetic. He cites André Gide on Mark Rutherford: 'His art is made of the renunciation of all false riches.'[25] The poets of Communist Russia and eastern Europe had a comparable experience. Tom Paulin's droll poem 'Where Art is a Midwife' has the Communist censors going on day-release classes on literary criticism so that they can recognize a metaphor when they see one:

> The types of ambiguity
> Are as numerous as the enemies
> Of the state.[26]

The state control of art under censorship has precise artistic effects. It is not an adequate justification for repression; but it does point to the virtues of discipline.

The wisdom of retrospect enables us to ask another question. For Roland Barthes, at least, censorship is also promotion of what is not censored; and what has that usually been?

> True censorship . . . does not consist in banning . . . but in unduly fostering, in maintaining, stifling, getting bogged down in (intellectual, novelistic, erotic) stereo-types, in taking for nourishment only the received word of others, the repetitious matter of common opinion.[27]

Barthes is articulating a feature of the last hundred years or so, the notion of the serious artist as the forbidden, the disruptive artist, the figure who points to the banality and dishonesty of the *status quo*. 'More than half of modern culture depends on what we shouldn't read' wrote Oscar Wilde; Joyce and Lawrence both saw their work as promoting a true morality as against the false, repressive morality of their home countries which they left in reproachful exile. In *Dubliners*, Joyce claimed to be writing a chapter in the moral history of his nation. His printer objected to the description of a woman who 'changed the position of her legs often' in one of the stories, 'Counterparts'. When Joyce replied in exasperation that he had told a far more sordid story in 'An Encounter', the printer promptly objected to that, too. Standards of what is suggestive and objectionable change over quite a short period with almost comic effect for us now.

As we have seen, Lawrence took the high moral tone, even as his writing was being censored for its sexual explicitness. For example:

> In life there is right and wrong, good and bad, all the time. But what is right in one case is wrong in another . . . Right and wrong is an instinct: but an instinct of the whole consciousness in a man, bodily, mental and spiritual at once. And only in the novel are *all* things given full play, or at least, they may be given full play, when we realize that life itself, and not inert safety, is the reason for living.[28]

This is characteristic Lawrence, torn between the Christian insights of his nonconformist upbringing (humanity is body, mind and spirit; living, not burying one's talent, is what counts in ultimate terms; deciding between right and wrong is a constant necessity), and yet stymied into relativism because he can see no God as source or judge.

Valentine Cunningham notes how both Joyce, in *Finnegan's Wake*, and Lawrence, especially in *Sons and Lovers*, reserve a particular textual violence for the Bible, which he interprets as 'a struggle to silence, nullify, annihilate, the prime father and his textual fatherings'.[29] The Modernist desire to write the ultimate, inclusive book, a kind of new Bible – *Ulysees*, *A la recherche du temps perdue*, Pound's *Cantos* – is an ambition echoed in the inclusive sprawl of the postmodern novel. This is the other side of modern literature's transgressive urge, to replace an outworn decorum by getting everything in, and in doing so to forge a new, contingent, individualist metaphysics. For those who are still close to their religious origins, such a move might even be seen as blasphemous, as Salman Rushdie's risky questioning of Islam in *The Satanic Verses* was taken; though there is a distinctively verbal emphasis in the Judeo-Christian definition which makes it different.[30] The instinct to call for banning art hostile to Christianity seems to me not just misguided, as in the examples of Martin Scorcese's film about Christ and the prosecution of *Gay News* for a poem about the crucifixion, but to misunderstand the implication of Jesus' own response to being accused of blasphemy himself.[31]

Although the relation between the graphic and the verbal is complex, one reason for Christian difficulties over screen violence and sex is a lack of understanding of how artists see their role. The idea that a steady pushing back of the bounds of decorum is a good idea goes back to Wordsworth's Preface to the *Lyrical Ballads*, or the Goncourt brothers on realism; one of the main Romantic and Modern ideas of truth-telling in art is that the writer should tell the truth about what has been repressed, from above and within. By an obvious, if illogical step, every breaking of the bounds can be seen as desirable. It is that step we need to question.

A Christian will need to avoid transgressing; but after rigorously examining what the true boundaries are. Opting for banality may deny the way in which the God of the Bible often turns into his own iconoclast, like Jesus, fulfilling prophecies while confounding expectations of how they were to be fulfilled. Oliver O'Donovan remarks that counsel 'is the church's most characteristic form of address to the individual, because it respects his status as one whom God also addresses directly, and whose particular decisions are partly hidden from public gaze'.[32] This does not mean that there is no authoritative truth, but simply that it stands above both church and individual, and each has a responsibility to interpret and obey.

So what is the difference between pornography and the biblical erotics of the Song of Songs? Is it one of exploitation, of rendering what is human merely instrumental? The strength of the feminist argument against pornography is not that it is transgressive, but simply that it reinforces more explicitly the use male-dominated society makes of women routinely. The scientifically debatable link between pornography and rape is less important than the obvious cultural continuity. Making violence sexy is what Bret Easton Ellis, top-shelf magazines and videos and *Macbeth* have in common. What they do not have in common are the seeds of their own discussion. Answerability is a Christian as well as a liberal standard.

Banning, or restricting to an inevitably self-selected élite of the adult, intelligent, and so on, is dependent on a number of things, not least a shared sense of values which is increasingly insecure in British and American society. To the Christian student worried about such things I would suggest four principles, which are to a certain degree in tension.

First, develop a culture of debate within Christian circles. I would advise against not reading a particular book within a course, or one that has been recommended; but it needs to be talked about, so as to get some shared sense of its effect. Second, adopt the principle of 1 Corinthians 10:23–24, that what damages the weaker person in my group is a more important consideration than my Christian, artistic or creative freedom. Third, take up the argument of Philippians 4:8, that whatever is just, pure and lovely deserves thinking about. The list includes 'virtue', in Paul's time the best that the pagan world had to offer. The converse is that thinking on the opposites will have an opposite effect. Finally, we need to be aware of the consequences of the displacement of God to the individual mind and will that is so much a feature of modernity. In Colin Gunton's words:

> An attempt to wrest from God the prerogatives of absolute freedom and infinity leads to the inversion of Pentecost and what is in effect a new babel. 'Post-modernism' represents that Babel perfectly, because when each speaks a language unrelated to that of the other . . . the only outcome can be fragmentation.[33]

Gunton's argument is that created beings, like their God, have their true being in relation. This gives him a theological basis for the role of culture:

> The distinctive feature of created persons is their mediating function in the achievement of perfection by the rest of creation. They are called to the forms of action, in science, ethics and art – in a word, to culture – which enable to take place the sacrifice of praise, which is the free offering of all things, perfected, to their creator.[34]

4. The religion of literature: or, can literature do what religion does?

There is a large body of literature *about* religion and *expressing* religion – from the devotional poetry of Herbert and Crashaw to the exploratory or critical, such as the novels of 'Mark Rutherford', whose *Revolution in Tanner's Lane* is one of the most searching accounts of the relation between nonconformity and politics in the nineteenth century. A modern readership also needs to be more alert to the literature which *assumes* a religious viewpoint without taking religion for its subject, such as the crime novels of P. D. James or the poetry of Les A. Murray. They are Christian writers, but even within anglophone literature the other great religions have made their mark; for instance Sufism (mystical Islam) on the novels of Doris Lessing, or Buddhism on the poetry of Gary Snyder. There is a misleading assumption that the Middle Ages or the seventeenth century were ages of faith, when Christianity was reckoned to be a public truth; then came the Victorian period, which was an age of doubt, and then . . .? The problem with that evolutionary model is that one could compile an enormous list of twentieth-century Christian writers, and it is misleading to call them marginal – T. S. Eliot and Graham Greene, John Berryman and J. R. R. Tolkien, Tim Winton and Jack Clemo. These are all writers who take Christian doctrine, or living, or institutions into their art at a deep level.

There is, however, a larger claim, which is nothing less than literature *as* a religion, or at least a substitute for its most important doctrines and practices. We might characterize it as the overvaluing of literature.

Top of the list would be creativity. As we have seen, Coleridge described the imagination as 'a repetition in the finite mind of the eternal act of creation in the infinite I AM' (*Biographia Literaria*,

1817), and thus moved the writer from being the imitator of God's creation to being the imitator of God. However, we should beware of making Romanticism the historic villain, of making the crucial move of elevating the artist from craftsman to priest and prophet. The notion that the artist has some kind of link with the divine is inherent in the notion of inspiration, and present in some of the classical writings about art, for instance Plotinus in the *Enneads* or Longinus *On the Sublime*. What is the guarantee of inspiration? Is it the beauty, or the truth, of the utterance?

The modern religion of art, and particularly poetry, has no god to guarantee, or underpin, except the poetry itself. The case of Wallace Stevens is instructive here, because he seems to have pursued the analogy between religion and art to the point where it becomes substitution. His long meditative poem 'Notes Towards a Supreme Fiction' is the culmination of this process, as he asks what qualities a religion might have, while acknowledging that it will be a 'fiction', a creation rather than a description or revelation of what is the case about the world, God and humanity. 'Aesthetic creeds,' he says in an essay, 'like other creeds, are the certain evidences of exertions to find the truth,' and then goes on to quote Henry James on the significance of art 'which makes life, makes interest, makes importance'. Makes, not recognizes, nor imitates. 'The world about us would be desolate except for the world within us', comments Stevens, claiming that the consolations of art are like the consolations of religion.'[35]

This idea began as a reproach to organized religion. Matthew Arnold, seeking to counter Puritan 'Hebraism' with the 'sweetness and light' of 'Hellenism', argues that the uncultured Christian has shrunk Christianity:

> Whenever we hear that commonplace which Hebraism, if we venture to inquire what a man knows, is so apt to bring out against us, in disparagement of what we call culture, and in praise of a man's sticking to the one thing needful, – *he knows*, says Hebraism, *his Bible!* – whenever we hear this said, we may, without any elaborate defence of culture, content ourselves with answering simply: 'No man, who knows nothing else, knows even his Bible.'[36]

Arnold is still arguing from within Christian culture, like Coleridge; but he is advocating a position in which the pursuit of culture and the pursuit of godliness are not just compatible but interchangeable.

At the root of this kind of move is a notion of literature as tapping into some kind of transcendence through the privileged subjectivity of the writer – the metaphysics of selfhood, if not God. The artist becomes a saint, especially in his confrontation with death. The art may survive, as an alternative to heavenly immortality. If we are not careful, the artist becomes greater than the saint; as George Steiner, not entirely approvingly, voices it:

> At a dread cost of personal means, at a risk more unforgiving of failure than any other – the saint, the martyr, know their elected destination – the artist, the poet, the thinker as shaper, seek out the encounter with otherness where such otherness is, in its blank essence, most inhuman.[37]

This vision of the artist as metaphysical hero manages to undervalue and misunderstand martyrdom and, Faustianly, celebrate damnation. As Steiner notes, and laments, deconstruction has targeted such transcendent ambitions, and his project is to try to reinstate them. It may be that the religion of art needed an appetite for absolutes; the fluidity, the boundary-crossing mobility, of postmodern art admits, at best, a New Age syncretism. Yet the appetite for inclusiveness that these characteristically big postmodern novels such as *Gravity's Rainbow* have is still evidence of a heroic desire to rewrite the world.

Literature, then, may still be conceived as an act of gratuitous creativity which echoes that of a divine creator. As the poet-artist David Jones puts it, 'man is a creature whose end is extra-mundane and whose nature is to make things and that the things made are not only things of mundane requirement but are of necessity the signs of something other'.[38] This other-worldly dimension does not make this world unimportant or uninteresting. Flannery O'Connor, the Catholic novelist and short-story writer from the southern USA, warns that 'Fiction is about everything human and we are made out of dust, and if you scorn getting yourself dusty, then you shouldn't try to write fiction';[39] though she still argues that the Christian novelist lives in 'a larger universe', which contains the supernatural. One can see this happening most spectacularly in the novels of Susan Howatch, a 'bestseller' rather than a literary writer. The novels written after her conversion to Christianity are noticeably more ambitious in their attempt to contain spiritual realities more or less absent from her earlier work. 'You make us for yourself', confessed St

Augustine to God, 'and our hearts find no peace until they rest in you.'[40] The religion of literature, and religion in literature, both exemplify that analysis of human restlessness.

Glass manufacture has improved since George Herbert's day, but his analogy still has much force for the discerning reader and writer. We are missing the point of something designed to be transparent if we concentrate on its opacity:

> A man that looks on glasse,
> On it may stay his eye;
> Or if he pleaseth, through it passe;
> And then the heav'n espie.
> ('The Elixir')

If the world is charged with God's glory, the poet and the critic alike are called to recognize it, celebrate it, and interpret it.

2

Canons

Valentine Cunningham

'Who would've thought it? Literary immortality a protection racket.'

He mouthed his cigar obscenely. 'Come off it, kid. There's no immortality in this business. You want twenty years, even forty, we can arrange it. Beyond that, we'll have to renegotiate terms at the end of the period. Sooner or later there's going to be a, whaddaya call it, reassessment. We send a guy down, he does an appraisal, figures the reputation's not really earned, and bingo you're out. Maybe you'll get a callback in fifty years or so. Maybe not.'

I shook my head. 'You guys play hardball.' I laughed but I was scared.

'You see what we did with James Gould Cozzens?'

'Who?'

'Exactly . . .'

It is in these terms that the spoof literary gumshoe of Henry Louis Gates, Jr – the heavyweight champion of US black literary studies – encounters the Organization, fixers of literary reputations, the mafia running the literary canon.[1] In another parodic fictional venture into the canonicity ballpark Sandra Gilbert and Susan Gubar, doyennes of US feminist criticism, gleefully imagine the reactions of the North American literary establishment and its enemies when a text – rumoured to be one of the Great Books of All Time, Plato's *Symposium* it might even be – is threatened with execution, tied up by culture thugs on a railway track down in Boondock, Indiana. All of them veterans of canon wars of recent times, and on the winning side in the struggle to expand the syllabus to include black literature and many more women than heretofore, these three critics can afford their jest.[2]

Other, more established, fictionists are far less amused by the news from the canon front. Saul Bellow, for instance, object of mounting criticism for white élitism, chauvinism and Euro-centrism – the black writer Brent Staples has attacked him for making the black characters in his novel *Humboldt's Gift* (1975) so 'sinister' – toughly resists threatened relegation from the first division of the American novel with counter-attacks against what he calls cultural Stalinism ('we can't open our mouths without being denounced as racists, misogynists, supremacists, imperialists or Fascists').[3] John Updike is another very white male novelist. He has the narrator of his *Memories of the Ford Administration* (1992), history professor Alf Clayton, strike pre-emptively against the loathsome Brent Mueller and 'his anti-canon deconstructionist chic' ('He was contemptuous, dismissive, cocky, and a great hit with the students; he played to them with a televisable glibness and catered to their blank, TV-scoured brains by dismissing on their behalf the full canon of Western masterpieces, every one of them (except *Wuthering Heights* and the autobiography of Frederick Douglass) a relic of centuries of white male oppression, to be touched as gingerly as radioactive garbage').[4] *Wuthering Heights* was, of course, written by a woman, Emily Brontë, and Frederick Douglass was a black American slave. In Updike's hectic and gloomy view, only such writers are safe on the current canonical battlefield. But he and Bellow are clearly well advised to be worried. For the canons seem to be falling, one by one.

1. The meaning of canon?

The canon issue has become the hottest of critical hot potatoes. At every point it offers challenges not just for reading in general but for Christian reading in particular. To be sure, just what is meant by 'canon' in current literary-critical debates is by no means certain or agreed, and canon discussions slide glibly and happily from sense to sense – from great canons to temporary and lesser ones, from canonical books to canonical meanings and interpretations. But the polarities are pretty clear. Broadly speaking, when 'the canon' is invoked – whether approvingly or through clenched teeth – a list of the world's Great Books, the Classics, the historically acknowledged masterpieces, is usually in mind. What is being appealed to is the essence of what F. R. Leavis dubbed The Great Tradition, that is, those very great texts of the Greco-Judeo-Christian, or western, world which until very recently it was thought all educated men should have read, or at

least be cognizant of – Homer, Plato, the Bible, Dante, Shakespeare, Milton, that kind of thing. They are the texts that used to
appear regularly on Great Books courses in the colleges of the
USA – ministers and agents of culture as Matthew Arnold defined
it: 'a pursuit of our total perfection by means of getting to know,
on all the matters which most concern us, the best which has been
thought and said in the world'.[5] When, on the other hand, 'a
canon' or 'the *x* canon' gets invoked, some list of much less
potency is usually in play – individual or partisan or partial lists
of texts, thought to be good for the moment, or for some
pragmatic or practical occasion (my own personal list of the
books I like or approve of most; the syllabuses of required reading
set by particular teachers, universities, examination boards; lists of
approved writings that serve some particular sectional critical
interest such as the 'female canon', the 'feminist canon', the 'post-
colonial canon', and so on).

The now famous six kinds of canon suggested by Alastair
Fowler patrol, roughly, this opposition: on the one hand the *official*
canon, the classics 'institutionalized through education, patronage, and journalism'; on the other, the *personal* canon, subsets of
which are the *selective* canons of the formal curricula of
educational institutions and the *critical* canon (those works subject
to repeated discussion by literary scholars). Fowler's *potential*
canon (the entire corpus of written material) and his *accessible*
canon (all the works actually available for inspection) make a kind
of frame for the entire canon-making business. Tinkerings with
Fowler's categorization only confirm the larger canonical polarities. Wendell Harris, for instance, adds the sense of canon
usually applied to the Bible ('a closed, uniquely authoritative
body of texts') and the *diachronic* canon (the 'glacially changing
core' of books recognized as essential reading), but these are
simply features of what is usually meant by *the* canon. As for
Harris's *pedagogical* canon, *nonce* canon, and *truly popular* (non-
academic) canon, these are clearly part of the less clamant
canonicity which *a canon* usually signifies.[6]

Everything that touches texts here also applies to the related
department of canonicity, namely reading and interpretations of
texts. And at first blush the two great canonical extremes, the
universal and the nonce, might seem rather far apart. Commonly,
however, there is considerable commerce or overlap between
them. Nonce lists usually imply some claim on status larger than
the merely incidental. At the very least, nobody wants students to
waste their time by reading utterly worthless stuff. Even so-called

Rubbish Theory does not imply that its subject-matter is really rubbish. When what some observers account rubbish is taught – genre fiction (detective stories, crime novels, SF, magazine fiction) or comics or TV programmes or video or rock lyrics – it is usually with the aim of proving it of some telling cultural significance, and certainly of much more importance than conservatives or parents or the older generation have thought. Most promoters of nonce canons hope, whether openly or just in their hearts, that their choices will be recognized as truly meritorious, get promoted on to some more widely accepted list, move up from being thought good by me to being thought good, or even the very best, by others. And in recent times the loud makers of new canons (feminist, black, queer, and so on) have tended to promote their textual clients and their readings not as meeting some occasional interest or pragmatic educational need but as open bids for room among the great texts and the standard interpretations.

2. *Canon and power*

But whether it is an all-time World Series Great Book, what the publishers Penguin or Signet or the Oxford University Press mean by a Classic, a *Hamlet* or a *Robinson Crusoe*, say, or some utterly established reading of such a text ('Hamlet delays'; 'Robinson is a Protestant individual marooned in the bourgeois capitalist plight'); or whether, at the other extreme, it is simply a question of the reading list that happens to have been set by Professor Y for her course this semester, or the readings of Professor Z recently floated in some learned journal or tried out on his seminar and that you need to repeat in order to pass the exam, canonicity is always characterized by one large shared feature – it implies, reflects, builds on authority. You, the student, the critical client, the Christian in the pew, the reader in the bookshop, had better read these books, heed these views. These canons make demands. They wield power. They are instruments of power. These are the books that people agree demand to be read because they are self-evidently what Matthew Arnold labelled the best ones. Their intrinsic power is established, and by the fiat of extrinsic powers. For these are the books that some established authority, power, state, institution or other strong agency – the church, a church, the university system, a college, an examination board, a teacher, a faculty – demand to be read by the believer, the citizen, the reader.

Canons – texts and interpretations – are instruments of literary power. They are a big stick wielded over readers. Which is what the concept of canon has implied since the word's inception. Canon comes from *kanōn* in Greek, meaning a *reed* or *rod*, a *stick* in fact, used as a measuring instrument. A ruler. It thus comes to mean *rule* or *law*. The Christian church early on adapted the word for its own rules and decrees, and throughout its history the idea of canonicity has stuck close to this beginning association with Christian regulation (church laws are still known as canons and church law as canon law). Very early in its history *canon* came to be used for legislation of any kind, for any legal regulation or edict, and for any general rule or fundamental principle or formula (such as in maths). Early on, too, *canon* got applied to the collection or list of the books of the Bible that were accepted by the Christian church as inspired and genuine and thus to be submitted to as regulators of faith and practice. It took time for the word to be transferred to a list of secular texts (the *Oxford English Dictionary* records 'Platonic canon' occurring only in 1885) but the step was clearly inevitable.[7] The progress of the word *canonical* was similar. At first *canonical* meant practices and ideas that were in keeping with ecclesiastical, or canon, law. It quickly came to mean anything which is prescribed, authoritative, excellent, orthodox, standard. So the canonical went on from meaning particular interpretations of the Bible and of Christian theology as endorsed by the Councils and governing bodies of churches, to include any standard reading or interpretation, especially one accepted by some powerful secular institution such as a university or the profession of teachers of literature.

The secularizing application of canonicity, away from churches and towards secular institutions, has been a steady feature of canon life. But throughout all its history canon has had to do with the setting of boundaries and limits, maintaining borders, with authorization, prescription, strictness, order, statedness, and thus with the promotion of claims to excellence as well as orthodoxy, obedience, conformity. Canons are about gatekeeping. They are border patrols, gamekeepers. They keep some texts, readings, ideas, out, and fence others in.[8] Canonicity comprises texts and readings that have binding force. Canons are, as Gerald Bruns put it of the Hebrew Torah, or Books of the Law, texts which are 'forceful in a given situation'.[9] Canonicity asserts hegemonies, élitism, centre against margin, rightness *versus* error, light *versus* darkness, us against them, orthodoxy against heresy, that which is properly belonging to us *versus* that which is improperly theirs, otherness, what is out there, the Other. Canons are thus vital instruments of whatever powers there happen to be, secular, political, ecclesiastical, pedagogical.

Canons are central to what Michel Foucault has described as the discourses of power. Canons have served, and do serve, whatever ideology happens to be current: nationalist, patriarchal, capitalist, white, colonialist, Stalinist, feminist, gay, and so on and on. From Plato to NATO, so to say, canons have promoted the stories and the histories of the presently powerful: of men as opposed to women, whites as against blacks, Europeans against Africans and Asians, powerful settlers against helpless indigenous, the English against the Germans, always the victorious over the defeated. Modern English literature, for example, was brought into schools and universities as a main instrument of British national education after the First World War to displace what the routed Germans stood for, namely study of the Greek and Latin classics. What is more, Shakespeare was reclaimed as ours again, not theirs, and promoted as the emblem of an Englishness uninfected by the barbarism of the Germans who had tried to take over the interpreting of Shakespeare. Shakespeare, Milton, Shelley: these English authors would be taught as representing, in the words of George Sampson, English for the English. And this is the way canons tend to get instated – by the victorious, those who win the war and the argument.[10]

The power of the canon, by its nature tending towards authoritarianism and exclusivity, obviously makes for tyranny, as even Cardinal Newman recognized. It is a short step from Newman's praise of the classical authors as 'those whose thoughts strike home to our hearts . . . who are the standard of their mother tongue, and the pride and boast of their countrymen' and 'who have the foremost place in exemplifying the powers and conducting the development of [a] language', to his recognition that canons can acquire overweening power. 'In Literature . . . there is something oppressive in the authority of a great writer, and something of tyranny in the use to which his admirers put his name. The school which he forms would fain monopolize the language, draws up canons of criticism from his writings, and is intolerant of innovation.'[11] And since oppressions, tyrannies and monopolies inevitably provoke resentment and resistance, the canon wars of recent times are utterly understandable. The old patriarchal canon or canons incite resistance from women, the imperialist canon is opposed by those who speak for once subaltern people and texts, the centrist list is countered with one comprising formerly marginalized or excluded texts, those texts and readings branded heretical get touted as a proper neo-orthodoxy, and so forth. Old canon force, the old canonical forces, are met by neo-canonical force, as the syllabus shifts from, say, Western Lit. to Westerns as Lit.[12] Once upon a time there was T. S. Eliot's *After Strange Gods: A Primer in Modern Heresy*,[13] chasing out D. H. Lawrence and Thomas Hardy in the name of Anglican Christian orthodoxy. Now there is Lillian S. Robinson proclaiming 'Treason Our Text: Feminist Challenges to the Literary Canon'. And, of course, overhanging all such encounters, resistances, turf wars, is the inevitable suspicion, more or less loudly put by radicals and encouraged by American right-wing antagonists of developments in the humanities since the Second World War, that the promotion of *the* canon or any insistence on the Classic, on Great Books, on Shakespeare and his kind, is *per se* a patriarchal, Eurocentric, heterosexual, logocentric, Judeo-Christian plot, the attempted hegemony of the dweller in DWEMSville, the dead, white (and dead-white) European males, whose day ought to be over. A sort of totalitarianism, in fact, which 'canon-busting' needs to erase. Or, as the Stanford University students marching against the old Western Civilization requirement are rumoured to have put it: 'Hey hey, ho ho, western culture's gotta go.'[14]

3. The fluidity of canon

Much of the recent rhetoric against the tyrannies of the canon – which in practice keeps coming down to arguments about what should be imposed on readers in the institutions of education – has been excessive. While emphasizing that canons are always constructed, always made by human agency, always reflective of current ideologies and inevitably shifting over time, the polemic has also played up the hegemony of the canon, the resistance to change of the institutions, especially the academic ones, that keep up canonical texts and readings. But as Gerald Graff has put it, 'Canon-busting is nothing new'[15] The old order, the institutions in place, the old men, always put up a fight, but changes do keep occurring. The canonical has never managed to remain a totally closed shop.

The history of Christian canonicity is a clear case in point. The Roman Catholic Church insists on the canonicity of the apocryphal books of the Bible. The Protestant churches relegate them with more or less strictness. Athanasius and Augustine led the struggle to fix the canon of the New Testament as twenty-seven texts – definitively excluding the *Didache*, the *Shepherd* of Hermas, and the *Wisdom of Solomon*; definitively including Hebrews, James and Jude. The Syrian National Church was among those not readily convinced. For a long time it stood out against the book of Revelation and some of the general epistles, at the same time preferring the second-century *Diatessaron* of Tatian, a harmonization of the gospels, to the four separate gospel texts. They did eventually cave in, but the East Syrian Nestorian Church never did, and they still hold to a twenty-two-text New Testament (no 2 Peter, 2 and 3 John, Jude or Revelation). The New Testament of the Ethiopian Church, by contrast, is still thirty-eight books strong – including Hermas, two epistles of Clement and the so-called *Apostolic Constitutions*.[16] Not dissimilarly, authoritative canonical interpretations of Scripture have altered massively across the ages. Development in doctrine was heralded by Cardinal Newman as the special glory of the Roman tradition.[17] He was countering the familiar Protestant line on the fixed and final authority of Scripture. But of course Protestantism, while loudly upholding the principle of the givenness of the Word, the *sola Scriptura*, the open text whose meanings are utterly manifest to the simplest reader, has spread and developed ever since the Reformation in a continuous history of competing biblical readings and rereadings, a proliferating set of re-orderings and re-emphasizings of meaning, each one of which has in turn been canonized and remained canonical for some group, some sect, some church, some time. Discovering and insisting on new light on the old texts has always been precisely the rationale of the forever splitting and dividing Nonconformist churches.

But this sort of interpretative fluidity is the very nub and essence of canonicity. A distinctive feature of the Classic, the high canonical text, is that it can go on being read and reread, can continually provoke and accommodate new readings, and new readings which, furthermore, then become canonical in turn. So, as Frank Kermode put it in his classic study *The Classic*, the Classic 'retains its identity' but nonetheless continually changes.[18] The history of the Christian tradition's dealings with the Bible is as good an illustration as any of the paradoxical openness within a guarded closeness that survival in the canon or a canon requires. And if what is canonical within the Christian church, which gave us canonicity in the first place and is for many still the model of hard canonicals and closed canons, has in fact never stayed wholly fixed in stone, how much more malleable and shifting, even fissiparous, has canonicity been in the world of academic and secular textuality. Thus English literature pushes its way in as a substitute for Greek and Latin literature. Then universities open the door to very modern English literature and to European literature. Oxford has hung on to the canonicity of Anglo-Saxon literature; Cambridge rejected 'philology' as one more of the specialisms of the Germans defeated in the First World War. While the world's universities went steadily modern, Oxford held out against the study of twentieth-century English literature until 1970, but after that allowed anything at all published in the English language academic house-room. And so it goes. In the early part of this century, T. S. Eliot fights for the Metaphysical Poets and the School of Donne, while Virginia Woolf fights for the women who had been silenced and occluded by the men who used to draw up the lists of the good and the best. Now no English poet is more canonical than John Donne, and, inspired by Virginia Woolf, feminist critics have recovered and instated whole hosts of women onto the syllabus, into the canon. Fanny Burney is now as secure as Laurence Sterne, Sarah Fielding as her brother Henry. Roger Lonsdale's *Eighteenth-Century Women Poets: An Oxford Anthology* (1989) unearths, confirms and reaffirms numerous lost and forgotten women. They are already crowding over from the woman-canon into the larger canon of English poetry. And similiar work is being done all over the academic world, especially for women and black writers, especially those blacks now known as African Americans, but also for Caribbean, Asian, Chicano/Chicana writers, as well as for Chinese Americans, 'Native Americans', and the rest. The British writer most read in British universities after Shakespeare is now probably Angela Carter. Just as secure in American universities are black women writers such as Alice Walker and Zora Neale Thurston.

Maps of such changes are the great Norton Anthologies – all at once mere markers of canonical shift, registering what is being taught in the USA, and also makers of canons, for inclusion there is already a kind of canonization. The glossy Norton advertising brochures spell out the wares offered by the latest editions (reminder, if any were needed, that there is cash in canoneering): seven new women writers in the Fourth Edition of the *Norton Anthology of American Literature*, greatly expanded entries for women such as Adrienne Rich, three new African-American writers, increased space for the African Americans Langston Hughes, Gwendolyn Brooks, Frederick Douglass, and five new Native Americans. Radicals once demanded of the canon, the syllabus and the university, 'Where were the blacks?', 'Where were the women?' The answer now is: everywhere, on nearly every list, in nearly every seminar.[19] The newest canon arrivals are female, black, queer; the oldest canon members are being actively politicized, genderized, queered. And across the whole historical range of texts. It is not just the Renaissance that is enjoying a 'queering'.[20] 'Is there a woman in this text?' It was thought only a little while ago to be a fairly daring question to ask.[21] Now the presence of a woman, a black, a gay, or any other kind of marginalized, repressed or subaltern person is among the many standard items to look for when first approaching a text.

Carolyn Heilbrun anticipated that feminism would help literary criticism overcome the dullness of its old routines, and these canon expansions have undoubtedly been the cause of great critical excitement.[22] Literary study cannot be said to be dull as the canon's doors are barged open. It cannot, either, be said to be always fair, at least not fair on some of the older authors, older readings, and so also on the older maps of literary history, the older versions of cultural history, which the latest practices and criteria squeeze out, nullify, marginalize, and make less canonical, or even uncanonical altogether. There are losers as well as winners in the canon wars. Graduate students in Britain have, apparently, almost deserted the eighteenth century in favour of Angela Carter.[23] Kate Millett's *Sexual Politics* (1969) started a marked decline in the old centrality D. H. Lawrence enjoyed in the critical reign of F. R. Leavis. Radical and feminist reaction to the publication of Philip Larkin's *Selected Letters* (1992) got him crossed off numerous lists almost overnight – for his 'throwaway derogatory remarks about women, and arrogant disdain for those of different skin colour and nationality'.[24] And such exclusions are real and may become permanent. The Right, especially in the USA, is undoubtedly exaggerating when it suggests that the existence of the once Great Books, the old essential textuality of the European tradition, and thus Americanism itself, are utterly threatened. And Gilbert and Gubar and Henry Louis Gates are right to scoff at such jeremiads. And Stanley Fish – one of the favourite targets of much conservative American complaint – is of course right to point out that Chaucer, Shakespeare, Milton and Pope are required reading even at his own Duke University, whose members have been accused by Dinesh D'Souza (author of the notoriously whingeing *Illiberal Education*) of demonstrating 'open contempt for the notion of a "great book"'.[25] But still the new canon-making must work, as the old canon-making did, to the detriment of some books, some readings, which once enjoyed security of tenure in the canon. Any opening of the canon is also a closing of the canon.

Stanley Fish's stance is in principle pragmatic and liberal.

> Think of the prime exhibits: Stanford University, which has been accused of gutting its Western Civ requirement in face of demands by rabid multiculturalists. In fact the change that has been made in a multitrack, multi-sectioned course prevents no-one from teaching the standard list of Great Books, while opening up a space for those who want to leaven the traditional list – still very much intact as a core – with some texts from alternative cultures. The change, in short, is in the nature of a modification that leaves much of what was in place before exactly as it was.[26]

But though 'much' may still be in place, by definition 'much' then is not; 'very much intact' is not wholly intact. As feminists and other neo-canonists have recognized again and again, canon warfare does not mean simply a liberal inclusionism but poses a threat to the traditional canon, to Homer and *Moby Dick* and all the rest. This may simply be a question of room on this year's syllabus. It may be the result of some more aggressively minded new broom ('either a given woman writer is good enough to replace some male writer on the prescribed list or she is not').[27] Either way, T. S. Eliot's gently wise urgings on the way the arrival of the poetic newcomer wholly alters the extant tradition are to the point:

> The existing monuments form an ideal order among themselves, which is modified by the introduction of the new (the really new) work of art among them. The existing order is complete before the new work arrives; for order to persist after the supervention of novelty, the *whole* existing order must be, if ever so slightly, altered; and so the relations, proportions, values of each work of art toward the whole are readjusted.[28]

4. Canon and value

What is evidently at stake in canonicity arguments and man-oeuvres is what has been fundamentally at stake in every discussion of any text whatsoever at any time: namely, what literature is about; what it is for; what it is to be valued for; what in effect are the meanings, the values, the truths it deals in. Every canon debate raises – or begs – questions of value: what constitutes quality; what grants books, texts, worth; what makes this item worth reading, makes it good, better, best; and if you think that you can tell quality, will anyone else be convinced by your case, your criteria, especially tomorrow and the day after? There are of course many sceptical voices raised, for example Barbara Herrnstein Smith's, dismissing value questions as irrelevant or as so impossible of answer as not to be worth broaching.[29] But the value questions will not be shooed away, not least because the criticism and teaching of literature always involve persuading others – readers, students, deans of faculties, heads of department, funders of research, buyers of books – that a text, and this text rather than some other one, is worth investing time and money in. Even the noisy American neo-pragmatists, Stanley Fish and Richard Rorty, who profess to believe textual meaning and value entirely personal and utterly contingent upon what happens to be pleasing to the individual reader (useful truth; roll-your-own value; whatever is, is right), still cannot help acknowledging the necessity of valuation in reading.[30] And there is no canonicity debate that is not built on that necessity.

Which is not to say that the value debate is finally resolvable. It rumbles on and on, its polarities exactly cognate with polarities of canonicity. On the one hand: is this text valuable because it has, in the words of Dr Samuel Johnson, risen 'to general and transcendent truths'?[31] On the other: is it valuable because of some more limited merit, true to the experience of a particular section of society, of some interest group, or well illustrative of some historical phenomenon or moment: the life of inner-city blacks, say, or of white western females or New England Puritans? Thinking of the historical criterion, Matthew Arnold invoked *adequacy* (does Virgil 'represent the epoch in which he lived in all its fulness, in all its significance'?).[32] Recent critics talk a lot about a text's *relevance* to this or that student group. For its part, universality has undoubtedly come under the same modern frown as the Great Books idea it served – though the Down My Way argument of a Lisa Jardine (her department majors in works by women Asian and Afro-Caribbean writers and non-British writers in English because, she says, its students 'are for the most part neither Anglo-Saxon nor male')[33] looks rather miserably poky. It certainly does not confront the feeling widespread in almost every quarter that one point of reading is to introduce you to difference, otherness, new things, to take you out of your small corner, out of yourself. Similarly, it tends to obscure the fact that among professed sectionalists there is often a strong feeling that the locally relevant text has more than local relevance, that it is good for men and whites to read this black woman's work, which is also truthful about women and blacks as more than just locally based or narrowly viewed persons (as, for example, factory operatives, Londoners, bourgeois, Americans, or even members of that large and messy entity the human race).

The nature and level of transcendence implicit in ordinary canonical arguments are always going to be debatable. For his or her part, though, the Christian reader will inevitably share Dr Johnson's interest in transcendent truth. The Christian (like the Jewish and Islamic) reader comes to all of life with a belief in transcendent truth and truths, and, most pertinently for his or her activity as a reader, this is a belief that transcendent truth is available through text, through reading – in the first place, of course, transcendent truth through Christ the Word and the Word of God, the set of texts known as the Bible. But faith in The Big Book lends itself very readily to a not dissimilar faith in books as such. Christian logocentrism, founded in highly canonical texts, in fact in the ultimate and foundational canonical Big Book, the Bible, leans naturally towards canonicity and towards Big Canonicity. It is everywhere recognized, and rightly so, that the old European canon was deeply implicated in the history of Christianity, that it embodied Christian values and assumptions, and that the very idea of canon is imbrued in the history and the question of those particular values.

In the wars over canonical texts and interpretations it comes as no surprise, then, to discover Christian writers and meanings constantly challenged precisely for what is thought to be amiss with old canonicity – exclusiveness, authoritarianism, racism, patriarchy, homophobia. The sweep of Molly Hite's denunciations is characteristically broad: western culture, Jesuits, God himself (a 'large Jesuit') are all male oppressors of women and John Donne's poetry registers the nasty submission all these males prescribe ('God as exemplary rapist, I learned, is a constant in all Western cultures').[34] Christian readers have constantly to weigh the justice or injustice of such charges and to test the history they both state and imply. But even when and if proven, none of them is enough, by itself, or even cumulatively, utterly to discredit any text and cause it to be written off. Certainly none of such things detracts *per se* from the possibility of John Donne's poems being read, whether for reasons of some large truth or of some local significance. It is commonly the case that the nastiest texts, politically speaking, are good reads for any or all of the reasons that make a book pleasing or captivating. What is more, the politically irksome features of a text for the modern reader – the Christian patriarchalism, say, of *Paradise Lost* – may be the very aspects that give it value as a document in the thought of its time. And, of course, although there will probably be few Christian readers for whom Milton's doctrine of women is orthodoxy itself and part of what they value as the transcendent truth and Protestant Biblicism of the poem, that male-centredness interferes very little, if at all, with the claim of the poem to be dealing with less disputed 'general and transcendent' Christian truths such as evil, its origin and nature, human fallenness, and so on. But whatever the disagreement among Christian readers over detail, no Christian reader would, I imagine, wish to allow *Paradise Lost* to be shunted out of the canon without a fight, at the heart of which would be a contention for the very possibility that Christian texts, and so texts in general, might be bearers of transcendent truth. Certainly the faith in transcendent and universal truths cannot easily be abandoned without an essence of the Christian faith being given up. And beyond all this, of course, and in quotidian practice, the Christian reader and teacher have exactly the same rights as anyone else to claim a sectional interest, and to appeal to the particular relevance of certain texts to the Christian, and to insist, on the mere equal-opportunities grounds others claim, on a continuing place in an opened, or re-opened, canon.

The Christian's claim on canonicity is always, of course, going to be bigger than that. The Christian claim is that the nature of the Christian story and the set of old books called the Bible is very close to the heart of what gets you a place in *the* canon. Big stories are the ones that matter, and the biggest stories matter most of all. The Christian story is that the Bible and Christian theology offer the greatest stories ever told, the grandest narratives of all.[35] And if all interpretation is based on a faith that a text may speak, as it were, from the dead, that the author you cannot see may yet be heard; if, in other words, the meaning may be made present, may come forth, like Lazarus, from the dead (because, as Maurice Blanchot has put it, all reading-acts are an exhortation, in Christ's words to Lazarus, to 'come forth' from the dead: *Lazare, veni foras*), then the texts of the religion centred on belief in resurrection, on real presence, on the manifestation of the Word within the word, are getting very close indeed to the utter centre of the reading matter.[36]

Cause for Christian triumphalism? Yes, but . . . A wise, or wised-up, Christian criticism knows that the bearing of Christian witness, the conveying of or dealing in Christian truth, are by no means the only test of a writing's quality. There will continue to be much orthodox but low-grade Christian writing. It is hard to stick up for Abraham Cowley's biblical epic *Davideis* or Edwin Atherstone's *The Fall of Nineveh*. The writings of good Christian Charles Williams can still seem deplorable on grounds of sheer bad writing. It was even the truths of *Paradise Lost* themselves that troubled Dr Johnson: a good epic in his book would simply not handle the unbearably aweing story of the Fall ('The good and evil of eternity are', he claimed in his *Life of Milton*, 'too ponderous for the wings of wit'). By the same sort of token, Christian critical wisdom also recognizes that the paganism, unorthodoxy, atheism, wordliness, even the blasphemy of a text will not be enough by itself to debar it from the highest canonical place. Dante's theology compelled him to put the classical heroes and writers, Aeneas and Hector, Plato and Aristotle, Cicero and Seneca, into Hell, but he invented the most comfortable First Circle limbo for them because their canonical status remained for him untouched by their paganism. The 'old Adam' smells rank, as Newman put it, in Homer, Ariosto, Cervantes and Shakespeare, but still they are 'the masters of human thought, who would in some sense educate' us.[37]

And if the Christian leanings of a text are never the last word on its merits, then neither does Christianity guarantee the last word in interpretation, not least in readings of the biblical classic. Readers of T. S. Eliot will need no reminding of Lancelot Andrewes' captivation by the paradox that the eloquent word, both the Word as Christ and the Word as Scripture, is also the *verbum infans*, the unspeaking word of the infant Christ, the incarnated deity in the manger. Sound theology reminds us that only God sees and knows everything, *sub specie aeternitatis*, only he possesses the truth about transcendent truth, and that we humans only ever see through a glass darkly, speculate in the midst of enigmas – *per speculum in aenigmate*, as the Vulgate text of 1 Corinthians 13:12 has it. Just so, the very ground of the Classic's survival, its perpetual re-readability, logically carries with it the corollary of some perpetual unreadability. That which will come clear only to future readers is by definition unclear now. Christian reading knows that while it is proper to hope for the truth of a text, to strive for it with might and main and to have 'nothing but the truth' as one's hermeneutical wish, the 'whole truth' of texts is necessarily going to evade the interpretative grasp. So the Christian reader's position, on canonicity as on meaning in general, is neatly summed up in a biblical proposition about faith which Stanley Fish arrestingly co-opted as a text for the proper moral attitude of the reader before the text, and as the fine expression of his own and all other readers' ultimate humble reading faith: 'Now faith is the substance of things hoped for, the evidence of things not seen'.[38]

3

Christian poetics, past and present

Donald T. Williams

The story of Christian poetics – that is, of Christians thinking consciously *as* Christians about the nature and significance of literary art – is the tale of a movement struggling almost in spite of itself to come to grips with its own doctrine that human beings are created in the image of God. The faith was born into a pagan culture and has survived into a secular one which shows signs of returning to paganism. The church has perforce used the languages, the markets, and the forms of the surrounding culture. It has transformed them and been transformed by them. In the West, as the faith and the culture grew up together, this process has at times made them all but indistinguishable. But the relationship has always been ambivalent. 'What has Athens to do with Jerusalem?' asked Tertullian; and the answers, while legion, have never been simple or easy.[1]

Specifically, Christians have struggled to apply to literature the general New Testament principle about being in the world but not of it (Jn. 17:11–16). They were rightly wary of a culture based on idolatry – hence of its literature – hence of literature in general. But they could not escape the literary foundations of their own origin, or the fact that they, and all humankind, were created in the image of one who expressed his inmost nature from the beginning as the Word. This tension gives rise to the seeming contradictions of their collective response: condemning literature as dangerous at worst and a waste of time at best, while producing some of the greatest poems the world has ever seen. And in the process, a few of them have found in the *imago Dei* the only coherent explanation of why the human race is, for better or worse, a tribe of incorrigible makers.

1. *The beginnings: Augustine*

St Augustine, the most profound and articulate of their early spokesmen, is in his own writings a microcosm of their larger, continuing discussion. As such he requires extended treatment. The negative side is more well known. In Book I of the *Confessions* he seems to look back on his study of Virgil with nothing but regret for lost time. The exercise of imitating his poetic lies (*figmentorum poeticorum*) was 'mere smoke and wind'; Augustine's time would have been better spent on God's praises in Scripture than such 'empty vanities'; his labour on them was in effect nothing more than a 'sacrifice offered up to the collapsed angels'.[2] He had wept for Dido who killed herself for love, while staying dry-eyed over his own spiritual death, but now thinks of his enjoyment of her fictional sorrow as madness (*dementia*).[3] In Book III he confesses that when he attended theatres in his youth he 'sympathised together with the lovers when they wickedly enjoyed one another'.[4] To enjoy in tragedy that which one would not willingly suffer in reality is 'miserable madness' (*miserabilis insania*). Literary experience does not lead to virtue because true mercy is practical. The emotional catharsis of the theatre, though, is a sham, for by it one is not 'provoked to help the sufferer, but only invited to be sorry for him'.[5]

The complaints are the familiar ones which would be repeated again and again throughout history. The fictions of the poets are lies; they are a waste of time, distracting us from more profitable pursuits; and they are an enticement to evil. Yet even as we read these passages, we cannot believe that for Augustine they tell the whole story. Where, we ask, would the felicitous style of the *Confessions* have come from if he had never studied the classics from the standpoint of rhetorical analysis? And where would he have found such a perfect concrete example for his point about the ironies of misplaced human emotion had he remained ignorant of the dolors of Dido? Indeed, if we just keep reading, we find that there is more to Augustine's view of literature than at first meets the eye.

Even in the *Confessions* we find hints of factors in Augustine's upbringing which help explain the vehemence of his negative statements and nuance our understanding of their significance. His education was rhetorical and sophistic; he was trained, in other words, to be a lawyer, a professional maker of the worse to appear the better reason and a teacher of others to do the same. He was taught to scour the classics for examples of eloquence which could be used cynically to win court cases with no concern for the truth. And in this eloquence his 'ambition was to be eminent, all out of a damnable and vain-glorious end, puffed up with a delight of human glory'.[6] It is little wonder then that in his post-conversion reaction he felt compelled to resign that profession and ended up at times appearing to toss out the baby of literature along with the bath-water of sophistry. Yet even the very terms of his rejection testify to the power of words well used.

It is evident on every page of his writings that Augustine was impacted for the good by his classical reading in spite of his cynical teachers and his own scruples, and sometimes he is not unaware of it. The pagan Cicero's *Hortensius* was a major influence leading to his conversion to Christ. It 'quite altered my affection, turned my prayers to thyself, O Lord, and made me have clean other purposes and desires'. It had this effect, he interestingly notes, because he made use of it not to 'sharpen his tongue' but 'for the matter of it'.[7] He had, then, moments in which he recognized something of value even in pagan literature, something which the abuses which also exist ought not to deter us from seeking. Elsewhere he expounds the principle implicit here and defines explicitly what the something is:

> We [Christians] should not abandon music because of the superstitions of pagans if there is anything we can take from it that might help us understand the Holy Scriptures . . . Nor is there any reason we should refuse to study literature because it is said that Mercury discovered it. That the pagans have dedicated temples to Justice and Virtue and prefer to worship in the form of stone things which ought to be carried in the heart is no reason we should abandon justice and virtue. On the contrary, let everyone who is a good and true Christian understand that truth belongs to his Master, wherever it is found.[8]

Literature – even pagan literature – conveys truth and is therefore not to be despised. Unfortunately, the balance is provided by lesser-known treatises such as the *Christian Education*, leaving the negative impression of the *Confessions* unchallenged for most readers. Even in the *Confessions*, learning to read is a good thing, and even eloquence as such is admitted not to be inherently evil: 'I blame not the words, which of themselves are like vessels choice and precious; but that wine of error that is in them.'[9] Clearly, the studies Augustine seems to reject have enhanced his ability to write the book in which he seems to reject them. The rationale for their use is worked out in the *Christian Education*.[10]

How can Christians make use of the products of an idolatrous culture? In pagan learning, error and superstition are to be rejected. But pagan learning also included the liberal arts, which are servants of truth. 'Now we may say that these elements are the pagans' gold and silver, which they did not create for themselves, but dug out of the mines of God's providence.' Therefore, it is proper for Christians to 'take all this away from them and turn it to its proper use in declaring the Gospel'.[11] Even the infamous art of the rhetorician (we should remember that through the Renaissance poetry was considered a species of rhetoric) is in itself morally neutral and capable of being used in the service of truth; therefore, 'we should not blame the practice of eloquence but the perversity of those who put it to a bad use'.[12] This being so, Christians have not only a right but also an obligation to learn and employ the art of rhetoric. Since it is 'employed to support either truth or falsehood, who would venture to say that truth as represented by its defenders should take its stand unarmed?' The result of Christians abandoning the field would be that falsehood is expounded 'briefly, clearly, and plausibly', but truth 'in such a manner that it is boring, . . . difficult to understand, and, in a word, hard to believe'.[13]

In spite of eloquently expressed doubts, then, Augustine articulates a defence of Christian appropriation of and production of literature on the model of spoiling the Egyptians (see Ex. 11:2–3; 12:35–36). It is a limited and pragmatic approach: literature is valued for the truth (probably, for Augustine, propositional truth) it contains, and the arts which produce it are valued for the ways in which they can help us understand the Scriptures and proclaim the gospel. But it is a place to begin, and it adumbrates possibilities which would be developed later. When he says that art makes truth plausible and its absence makes it 'hard to believe,' it is difficult not to hear the phrase resonating with Coleridge's 'willing suspension of disbelief which constitutes poetic faith', and to see C. S. Lewis' magnificent attempts to make Christian truth believable by making it imaginable looming on the horizon. It would be to consider too curiously (not to mention anachronistically) to consider so, as concerns Augustine's meaning. But perhaps in retrospect we can see the seeds of later developments already embedded there.

2. Medieval and Renaissance periods

Augustine set the terms of the discussion and defined the tension which would characterize much of it down through the years. In the Middle Ages, criticism was mainly practical, focused on grammar, the classification of rhetorical tropes, and so on.[14] Meanwhile, Christian writers wrestled with the issues in practical terms, embodying their Christian vision of the world in concrete images and moving stories. The *Beowulf* poet struggled with the relationship between his Christian faith and his Teutonic heritage and made a grand synthesis in which the heroic ideal was enlisted in a cosmic war of good and evil.[15] Dante and Langland created concrete images which incarnated Christian doctrines allegorically so that they could bid their readers to 'come and behold, / To see with eye that erst in thought I roll'd'.[16] Anonymous lyricists captured the emotion of their faith in musical lines of beauty and simplicity. Chaucer gave us a humane and sympathetic portrait of 'God's plenty', and then felt obliged to retract most of it before his death in a passage which still embarrasses his admirers and shows the Augustinian tension to be yet unresolved.[17] By the time of the Reformation, some serious polarization had set in.

Luther said that Reason was the devil's whore, but he also asked why the devil should have all the good music and noted that literary study equipped people as nothing else does to deal skilfully with Scripture. Calvin applied the new grammatico-historical exegesis to secular writings and Scripture alike, and increased the number of quotations from Plato, Seneca and Cicero in the *Institutes* proportionally to the size of the work in each edition.[18] Ironically, some of his followers would take Augustine's doubts about the value of secular literature, untempered by his more positive perspectives, and run with them to extreme and sometimes almost hysterical lengths.

These objectors have been characterized, not entirely fairly, as Puritan. While Puritans took the lead in the drive to close the theatres, for example, not all who were sympathetic to the Puritan cause or the spiritual values they represented were in agreement with these objections. Nor could all who raised them be classified, without anachronism, as Puritans. We find it as early as in that old humanist and gentle pedagogue Roger Ascham, who even as he praises the virtues of the (Greek and Latin) classics, inveighs against 'books of chevalry', warning that 'Mo papists be made by your merry books of Italy than by your earnest books of Louvain,' and railing particularly against Malory's *Le Morte D'Arthur*, 'the whole pleasure of which book standeth in two special points, in open manslaughter and bold bawdry'. In Malory, 'those be counted the noblest knights that do kill most men without any quarrel and commmit foulest advoulteries by subtlest shifts'.[19]

When the Puritans do sound this note, even their later, more moderate spokesmen such as the usually sensible Richard Baxter (seventeenth century) sound extreme. Baxter advises Christian readers to read first the Bible, then books that apply it. If there is any time left, they may turn to history and science. But they must beware of the poison in 'vain romances, play-books, and false stories, which may bewitch your fancies and corrupt your hearts'. He buttresses such attacks with arguments: 'Play-books, romances, and idle tales' keep more important things out of our minds; they divert us from serious thoughts of salvation; they are a waste of valuable time. Finally, he asks in a rhetorical flourish, 'whether the greatest lovers of romances and plays, be the greatest lovers of the book of God, and of a holy life'.[20]

We have heard it all before. But now it is Augustine one-sided, without the balance of his more mature reflections. It cannot be called an advance, but such sentiments did perform one useful service: they provoked a reaction. It came from a Puritan who did not fit the caricatures. His name was Sir Philip Sidney, and what he wrote could be called an advance indeed. He called it *The Defence of Poesy*. It raised the discussion to heights which have seldom been reached again.

3. *The Renaissance: Sir Philip Sidney*

Responding in general to such scruples as we have noted and in particular to Stephen Gosson's *School of Abuse* (1579), Sidney wrote his *apologia* in the early 1580s, though it was not published until 1595. In it, he not only gives a thorough and brilliant refutation of the enemies of 'poesy' (by which he means imaginative literature, whether in prose or verse) but also lays out a comprehensive vision of its place in the larger structure of learning and the Christian life. He leaves no stone unturned, appealing in luminous and eloquently cadenced prose to poesy's antiquity, its universality, and its effectiveness as a mnemonic device and as an enticement to and adornment of what his opponents consider more 'serious' studies. In the process, he makes many of Augustine's positive points, distinguishing the right use from the abuse of literary art. He appeals to the example of Jesus and other biblical writers, who told stories (the parables) and wrote beautiful poetry (the Psalms, Song of Songs, *etc.*). But Sidney is not content merely to win a grudging admittance for literature to the curriculum; he will not stop until he has won it the highest place of all.

Sidney takes it for granted, along with his opponents, that the purpose of education is the acquisition not of knowledge only but of virtue as well. So then: the moral philosopher tells you the precepts of virtue, what ought to be, but he does it so abstractly that he is 'hard of utterance' and 'misty to be conceived', so that one must 'wade in him until he be old before he shall find sufficient cause to be honest'. The historian, on the other hand, tells a concrete story we can relate to; but he is limited to what actually has been and cannot speak of what ought to be. The one gives an ideal but abstract precept, the other a concrete but flawed example. But 'both, not having both, do both halt'.[21] How then do we get beyond this impasse?

> Now doth the peerless poet perform both: for whatsoever the philosopher saith should be done, he gives a perfect picture of it by someone by whom he presupposeth it was done; so as he coupleth the general notion with a particular example. A perfect picture, I say, for he yieldeth to the powers of the mind an image of that whereof the philosopher bestoweth but a wordish description, which doth neither strike, pierce, nor possess the sight of the soul as much as the other doth.[22]

By combining the virtues of history and philosophy, the poet then becomes the 'monarch' of the humane sciences, the most effective at achieving their end, virtuous action. He can give us better role models – and negative examples too – than can be supplied by real life in a fallen world. 'Disdaining to be tied to any such subjection [to nature], lifted up by the vigor of his own invention', he makes in effect another nature.[23] He has the freedom to do this because he is created in the image of the Creator. Greek and English rightly agree in calling the poet (from Greek *poiein*, to make) a maker, for people are most like God the Maker when they create a world and people it with significant characters out of their imagination. The very existence of literature, then, even when it is abused, is a powerful apology for the Christian doctrine of humanity and its creation in the image of God. Therefore, we should:

give right honor to the heavenly Maker of that maker, who, having made man to his own likeness, set him beyond and over all the works of that second nature: which in nothing he sheweth so much as in poetry, when with the force of a divine breath he bringeth things forth surpassing her doings.[24]

Here then is finally a profoundly Christian understanding of literature which does not merely salvage it for Christian use but finds the very ground of its being in explicitly Christian doctrine: creation, the *imago Dei*, the 'cultural mandate' to subdue the earth. Christians alone understand why human beings, whether 'literary' types or not, are impelled to make, tell and hear stories. When Christians also do so, they are not so much spoiling the Egyptians as recovering their own patrimony. That is why we not only learn from literature but enjoy it: it delights as it teaches. And it conveys its kind of truth through the creation of concrete images which incarnate or embody ideas which would otherwise remain abstract and nebulous.

Subsequent criticism, both Christian and secular, has confirmed Sidney's emphasis on the significance of the concrete image as an important way in which literature communicates. And the most profound moments in Christian reflection on literature since have simply followed up on hints Sidney gave us: that the principle of incarnation is why images communicate so well; that the *imago Dei* is the key to our identity as poets as well as human beings. It is no exaggeration to call Sidney's *Defence* the fountainhead of modern Christian poetics. Those who do not begin with it are condemned to reinvent the wheel or to drag their load without one.

While Sidney gave us the foundation, there is yet a lot that can be built on it. Seventeenth-century devotional poets such as Donne explored the ability of unexpected metaphors to express the paradoxical mysteries of Christian truth and experience. George Herbert struggled to reconcile sparkling wit and simplicity in the service of edification, finally bringing his 'lovely metaphors' to church 'well dressed and clad' because 'My God must have my best – ev'n all I had'.[25] Poets such as Herbert increasingly looked to Scripture to provide both a justification for their writing and a model for how to pursue it.[26] Milton, following Spenser's example, looked to both biblical and classical models as he created images of truth, virtue and vice (from Sabrina to the Son, from Comus to Satan) which function in precisely Sidneyan terms.[27]

4. John Milton

Milton also buttressed Sidney's case with some powerful arguments of his own. The end of learning, he said, is to 'repair the ruins of our first parents by regaining to know God aright, and out of that knowledge to love him, to imitate him, to be like him' by acquiring 'true virtue'.[28] This reinforces and expands Sidney's point that the end of learning is virtuous action. While we are in the body, our understanding must 'found itself on sensible things', and education must follow that method – which helps to explain the importance of concrete images for acquiring both understanding and virtue. The well-rounded Renaissance education Milton recommends then includes 'a well-continued and judicious conversing among pure authors digested'.[29] The salutary effects of literature then come only from a life-long habit of living with the minds of thoughtful and creative people in their books.

It is because of their connection with the mind of the author that books have such power, Milton explains, in a passage which essentially extends one of Sidney's points: if human beings are the image of a creative God, books are the image of such people.

> For books are not absolutely dead things, but do contain a potency of life in them to be as active as that soul whose progeny they are; nay, they do preserve as in a vial the purest efficacy and extraction of that living intellect that bred them . . . [Hence] as good almost kill a man as kill a good book: who kills a man kills a reasonable creature, God's image; but he who destroys a good book kills reason itself, kills the image of God, as it were, in the eye.[30]

It is the 'seasoned life of man' that is 'preserved and stored up' in books.[31] Part of what Milton valued in a good book then was contact with the mind of an author rendered otherwise inaccessible by distance or time. Such contact is precisely what much modern criticism insists we cannot have. Perhaps a secular worldview inevitably leads to a universe in which a text is merely a playing field for the reader's own intellectual athleticism. Perhaps only a Christian view (such as Milton's) of the *imago* descending from God to author to text can preserve the writing of literature as an act of communication. Perhaps Christians have too easily accepted the dominance of reader-centred approaches when their own tradition could provide the basis for a more humane alternative. At any rate, Milton's language and its theological grounding may offer one reason Christians still tend to be more sympathetic than other modern readers to author-centred approaches such as that of E. D. Hirsch.[32]

Milton also strengthens the rationale for refusing to ban literature on the grounds of its potential for abuse. His arguments against government censorship of some books tell equally against those who would eschew all books lest they be corrupted by them. Such attempts to bury our heads in the sand are smothered in terms of their own goals because virtue that is preserved only thus is 'but a blank virtue, not a pure'. In the real world after the fall, as in the literary worlds which represent it, good and evil are so intertwined that the responsibility of discernment cannot realistically be avoided. As a result,

> What wisdom can there be to choose, what continence to forbear, without the knowledge of evil? He that can apprehend and consider vice with all her baits and seeming pleasures, and yet abstain, and yet distinguish, and yet prefer that which is truly better, he is the true warfaring Christian.

This is so because we 'cannot praise a fugitive and cloistered virtue, unexercised and unbreathed, that never sallies out and sees her adversary, but slinks out of the race'.[33] Spenser's Guyon is a positive role model of uncloistered virtue who makes his author a better teacher than Scotus or Aquinas. Thus Sidney's poet defeats the philosopher and the theologian. But even when a text promotes error, discernment is better than blindness, and 'books promiscuously read' can help prepare us for life. If they do not, the fault lies not in the book but in the reader. Anyone who tries to avoid corruption by avoiding books only becomes a citizen of Mark Twain's Hadleyburg.

5. The modern era

The eighteenth and nineteenth centuries saw advances in our understanding of literature, but few of them came from Christians speaking specifically as Christians. Dr Johnson's observation that staying power – 'length of duration and continuance of esteem' – is the ultimate criterion of literary greatness has stood the test of time itself, while his dictum that nothing can achieve such stature but 'just representations of general nature' has not.[34] Wordworth's attack on poetic diction, Coleridge's insights on the role of the imagination, and Keats' concept of negative capability have enriched our appreciation of the range of possibilities in literature. Arnold showed us how literature and its criticism could help us to see things as in themselves they really are and to discern the best that has been done and thought, but he succumbed to the post-Darwinian scepticism of his age so far as to make poetry more a substitute for faith than its servant.

In the twentieth century, the New Criticism focused constructively on the details of the text and sought to define the kind of knowledge literature offers in contradistinction to that which comes from the sciences, concluding that it was knowledge of human experience.[35] On the other hand, its imbalanced emphasis on the autonomy of the text ironically opened the door to deconstruction and other essentially anti-literary ways of reading. Christians participated in, benefited from, reacted against, and were influenced by many of these modern movements, but made few contributions to them that were motivated by their distinctively Christian worldview as such.

In the meantime, a number of Christian thinkers from various traditions were profitably pursuing the idea that literature is a form of natural revelation parallel to the cosmos, conscience, and so on. Jesuit priest Gerard Manley Hopkins held that Nature is 'news of God', and sought in his poetry to embody the 'inscape', the inner unity of being which a particular created thing has, for 'I know the beauty of our Lord by it'.[36] Conservative Protestant theologian A. H. Strong saw art giving testimony to 'the fundamental conceptions of natural religion'; neo-Thomism emphasizes art as a form of natural revelation; and liberal Protestant theologian Paul Tillich attempted to correlate 'the questions posed by man's existential situation, expressed in his cultural creations' with the answers of the Christian message.[37] Michael Edwards is the best of the recent writers in this vein. 'Literature occurs', he says, 'because we inhabit a fallen world. Explicitly or obscurely, it is part of our dispute with that world.'[38] If the heavens declare the glory of God (Ps. 19:1) and the invisible things are understood by the things that are made (Rom. 1:20), then the things made by the creative member of the creation ought in a special way to bring the truths embodied in creation into focus. An eye that knows where to look should then be able to find in the recurring themes and structures of human literature (whether written by believers or not) an apology for and an elucidation of biblical motifs. As Edwards puts it,

If the biblical reading of life is in any way true, literature will be strongly drawn towards it. Eden, Fall, Transformation, in whatever guise, will emerge in literature as everywhere else. The dynamics of a literary work will be likely to derive from the Pascalian interplays of greatness and wretchedness, of wretchedness and renewal, of renewal and persisting wretchedness.[39]

6. *Inklings and friends*

To my mind, the most interesting contributions to Christian poetics in the twentieth century came from a group of friends centred in Oxford, in mid-century, who, consciously or not, harked back to Sidney's themes and brought them to their fullest development. In 1938, J. R. R. Tolkien gave a lecture at St Andrews University which was later published as 'On Fairy Stories'.[40] In it he provides a full critical vocabulary for Sidney's idea of the poet as maker made by the Maker: sub-creation for the process, primary creation for God's making, secondary creation for the poet's created world:

> Although now long estranged
> Man is not wholly lost, nor wholly changed.
> Dis-graced he may be, yet is not dethroned,
> And keeps the rags of lordship once he owned:
> Man, Sub-creator, the refracted Light
> Through whom is splintered from a single white
> To many hues, and endlessly combined
> In living shapes that move from mind to mind.[41]

While the doctrine of sub-creation was created to explain certain features of fantasy literature, it is applicable to many other genres as well. Even in the most 'realistic' fiction, the writer creates a world, peoples it with characters whose actions give its history significance, and determines the rules of its nature. And usually there will be a hero, a villain, a conflict, and some sort of resolution (which Tolkien called *eucatastrophe*), so that the secondary world echoes the primary creation in more ways than one. The hero, at great personal sacrifice, defeats the villain, rescues the damsel in distress, and they ride off into the sunset to live happily ever after: this basic plot we keep coming back to is salvation history writ small, as it were. As Edwards says, literature is 'drawn' towards a biblical reading of life. Tolkien explains why: 'We make still by the law in which we're made.'[42]

In 1941, Dorothy L. Sayers provided a detailed analysis of that creative process in *The Mind of the Maker*. She developed the relevance of the *imago Dei* for understanding artistic creation in explicitly trinitarian terms. In every act of creation there is a controlling *idea* (the Father), the *energy* which incarnates that idea through craftsmanship in some medium (the Son), and the *power* (which proceeds, *Filioque*, from the Father and the Son) to elicit a response in the reader (the Spirit). These three, while separate in identity, are yet one act of creation. So the ancient credal statements about the Trinity are factual claims about the mind of the Maker which can be shown to be literal truth about the mind of the maker created in his image. Sayers delves into the ramifications of these ideas for writing and reading, using numerous literary examples, in what is one of the most fascinating accounts ever written both of the nature of literature and of the *imago Dei*. While some readers may feel she has a tendency to take a good idea too far, *The Mind of the Maker* remains an indispensable classic of Christian poetics.[43]

C. S. Lewis never produced a major statement on literary theory from an explicitly Christian standpoint to rival Tolkien's or Sayers', but he gave us a constant stream of practical criticism from an implicitly Christian stance and a number of provocative essays that deal directly with the relationship between Christianity and literature. Probably best known is the essay 'Christianity and Culture',[44] superficial readings of which have given rise to the notion that Lewis had an 'anti-cultural bias'.[45] Actually, he was making the point that idolization of culture (including literature) corrupts and destroys culture – a point he made more clearly in later essays.[46] In 'Christianity and Culture' he was engaged in the Augustinian task of defending the *innocence* of literary pursuits; in later writings he expanded his view of the positive *value* of reading.

In the first place, literature enlarges our world of experience to include both more of the physical world and things not yet imagined, giving the 'actual world' a 'new dimension of depth'.[47] This makes it possible for literature to strip Christian doctrines of their 'stained-glass' associations and make them appear in their 'real potency',[48] a possibility Lewis himself realized in the Narnia series and the space trilogy. Then, too, literature can have something of the significance that Lewis denies it in 'Christianity and Culture' through the creation of positive role models and the reinforcement of healthy 'stock responses': life is sweet, death is bitter, and so on.[49] 'Since it is likely that [children] will meet cruel enemies, let them at least have heard of brave knights and heroic courage.'[50] Finally, literature can cure our provincialism and fortify us in the 'mere Christianity' which has remained constant through the ages, if we do not limit ourselves to the books of our own age.[51] That literature will do these things is uncertain – much modern literature tries not to – but the literature of the ages *can* do so if we receive it sympathetically. In *An Experiment in Criticism* Lewis shows us how to do just that, in a book that demonstrates the possibility of a sane, reader-centred criticism which would not exclude the authority of the author.[52]

7. *Other voices*

No one writer had more influence on modern thinking about literature than T. S. Eliot, whose conversion brought him back from the wasteland of modernity to dance at the still point of the turning world. Two major themes from his criticism compel our attention here. The first was a constant in both his modernist and Christian periods, though it makes best sense when grounded in the Christian worldview: the importance of rootedness in the literary *tradition* of the West for both intelligent reading and original writing. Many modernists and postmodernists tend to dismiss the 'dead writers' – or at least their ideas – as irrelevant because 'we know so much more than they did'. 'Precisely,' Eliot replied, 'and they are what we know.'[53]

The second theme is the relation of *content* and literary value. Here, Eliot gradually moved from an early aestheticism in which he tended to rigorously separate the two toward an appreciation of the fact that ultimately literary greatness is inseparable from the value of the ideas expressed or implied. In 1927 he said that, from the standpoint of poetry, Dante's system of thought was 'an irrelevant accident'.[54] Just two years later he recognized that Dante's 'His will is our peace' was 'literally true', and that 'it has more beauty for me now, when my own experience has deepened its meaning, than it did when I first read it', concluding that appreciation of poetry could not in practice be separated from personal belief after all.[55] By 1935 he was calling for literary criticism to be 'completed by criticism from a definite ethical and theological standpoint',[56] and for Christians to produce both such criticism and also literary works themselves whose content was 'unconsciously Christian'.

A final important voice for twentieth-century Christian poetics belonged to an American local-colour writer, the self-styled 'hillbilly Thomist', Flannery O'Connor. Like Tillich and Edwards, she believed that great literature deals with ultimate concerns which are essentially theological; Like Lewis, but in a totally different manner, she removed stained-glass associations so that the 'action of grace' could be seen in new contexts with new power. In a small but powerful body of fiction she made the American South an image of the human condition seen in profoundly Christian terms. Her letters and critical writings are loaded with practical wisdom on how to embody the anagogical vision in concrete images which can speak to the modern reader.[57]

Conclusion

Where, then, has this brief history of Christian thinking about literature brought us? Cary rightly notes that 'the modern critic who wants to deal with literature from a Christian standpoint has not found direct precedent in the literary criticism of the past 150 years, which constitutes what is inevitably the critical milieu for him'.[58] The Christian giants we have surveyed in the twentieth century definitely stood outside the mainstream. They all had roots sunk deep in a venerable and humane tradition which goes back to the ancients through Milton and Sidney, and thus they preserve a way of reading and writing which has been able to resist the ideological fragmentation and de[con]struction which has followed the breakup of the hegemony of New Criticism.

In the pages of journals such as *Christianity and Literature*, explicitly Christian wrestling with literary questions continues. It represents a range from futile efforts to accommodate modernist and postmodernist perspectives to virile and living heirs of the truly evangelical tradition descending, as I have argued, from Sir Philip Sidney. By grounding literary activity in a specifically Christian understanding of human nature, that evangelical tradition can give a coherent explanation of why people make worlds out of words and of the ways in which those worlds are valuable.

Perhaps being reminded that there *is* a unique and distinctly Christian tradition of poetics could help us tap into its power once again. In America, evangelicals produce too many cheap imitations of Lewis and Tolkien on the one hand, and too many saccharine historical romances on the other. While such writers as Walter Wangerin, Jr, and Calvin Miller have produced some interesting creative work, and such writers as Leland Ryken, Gene Edward Veith and Michael Bauman have produced some incisive criticism, there is no-one on the scene with the power of a Lewis, a Tolkien, a Sayers, or an O'Connor – much less a Milton. But the tradition which gave us those writers can give us more. As Francis Schaeffer reminded us, 'The Christian is the one whose imagination should fly beyond the stars.'[59]

Suggestions for further reading

A more specialized companion piece to the present essay is my ' "Thou Art Still My God": George Herbert and the Poetics of Edification', *Christian Scholar's Review* 19/3 (March 1990), pp. 271–285. There I give detailed treatment to Herbert's wrestling with these issues and attempt some practical applications of his conclusions for Christian writers at the end of the twentieth century. More bibliographical material is to be found in the final chapter of this book.

4

Reading and interpretive communities

Donald G. Marshall

Jean-Honoré Fragonard's *A Young Girl Reading* (*c.* 1776)[1] shows a teenage girl wearing a yellow dress in left-facing profile, reading a book of a size that fits comfortably in her hands. The carriage of her body is upright without stiffness. Her facial expression is alert without strain, poised at an Aristotelian mean between intense concentration and slack vacancy. Of her physical environment, we see only the comfortably cushioned chair on which she is seated, and she seems unselfconsciously absorbed, unaware of being observed.[2] There is no indication of what kind of book she is reading, but from the whole atmosphere, we may guess that despite the prevalence of religious reading in the eighteenth century, she is reading a novel – engaged in 'free' reading, reading 'for pleasure', as we say in instructive phrases.

This portrait represents not only a young woman but our very notion of reading, especially of reading literature. There are many earlier pictures of readers, but usually of identifiable figures reading for a discernible purpose. We see Jerome in his study translating Scripture. We see Erasmus working on his manuscript. We see the Virgin studying the passage in Isaiah that is about to be fulfilled.[3] But the girl in this picture is an anonymous member of the middle or – more likely – upper-middle class. Nor is her gender arbitrary. The novel came into its own in the eighteenth century in close relation to the increasing number of female readers.[4] The reader as portrayed here enjoys the autonomy of the self but not self-centredness (or 'narcissism', as the psychoanalysts call it), for the reader's self is fully engaged with something beyond the self – the book. The reader is disengaged from the public realm of economic or political concerns and withdrawn even from the domestic sphere.[5] But that disengagement puts the reader at the service of the imaginative world she is projecting and sustaining through the means of the book. Given the conditions of women's lives in the eighteenth century, this may be the only sphere in which she can exercise her autonomy. What she is enjoying is the imaginative power that belongs to, in fact is the defining characteristic of, a human being simply as a human being.[6] The self enjoys losing itself in reading, and this moment of stopped time, lost time, suspended animation, completely suits the painting as still life.

Yet, in a longer historical perspective, this representation of reading seems both revolutionary and questionable. It was not the custom in antiquity to read silently. A striking memorial to that fact is a statue carved around 540 BC by the sculptor Aristion, and recently re-joined to its base, which bears an inscription and had been found already in the eighteenth century. The statue shows a young woman, named Phrasikleia, her right arm held alongside her body, her left forearm held across her chest, her left hand holding a closed lotus blossom.[7] As Jesper Svenbro interprets it, the lotus blossom represents the fame of the girl's family. Having died young, she cannot carry on that fame by bearing children. Instead, she attracts viewers who read aloud the inscription which reveals her name. The meaning of the memorial statue 'blooms or rekindles whenever its inscription is read aloud'.[8] Fame requires an actual presence in the real world, and consequently, the statue will achieve its end only when the name rings out in 'the living world of sounds'.[9] For the Greeks, 'reading meant *reading aloud* . . . Their relation to the written word might perhaps be compared to our attitude to musical notation: not everyone can read music in silence, and the most common way to read it is by playing it on an instrument or singing it out loud to hear what it sounds like'.[10] Analysing Greek inscriptions in which the inscribed object is referred to as 'I', Svenbro concludes that the reader of these inscriptions is understood as having 'lent his voice, relinquished it . . . It belongs to what is written: the reading is part of the text'.[11] The reader with his voice is 'the sonorous instrument of what is written'. Hence, the text's 'listeners' are not its readers, but the 'individuals who are listening to the reading'. The reader disappears in the service of mediating between the text and whoever hears it read aloud.

Where the normal practice is to make a silent text resound for an audience, the silent reading Fragonard portrays is an anomaly. Almost a thousand years after Phrasikleia's memorial was carved, Augustine recorded his surprise at seeing Ambrose, Bishop of

Milan, reading a text silently. The first explanation that occurs to Augustine is that Ambrose does not want to be interrupted: Ambrose admits anyone without being announced to enter the room where he is reading, and if a visitor hears something obscure or perplexing in the text Ambrose is reading, he might ask Ambrose to stop and expound it.[12] The privacy that made solitary silent reading a normal practice emerged only gradually in the course of the seventeenth century.[13] It was late in the nineteenth century before silent reading drove out the ancient practice of reading aloud in the home, workplace, or public gathering place. Those who listen may do so because they are illiterate, but they may be able to read and simply prefer the experience of sharing with other persons in a common imaginative experience, as we may still prefer going to a cinema or a concert, even though video and audio recordings make films and music available in solitude. One who reads aloud serves others by making the text accessible to them in a way that simultaneously affirms them as a group.

1. The solitary reader

The contrast between our modern picture of a reader as a separate individual involved in a solitary transaction with a text and the older assumption that the reader effaces himself to let the text reach the ear of its audience has further implications for our understanding of interpretation. For it makes a great deal of difference whether an individual is seen as seeking the meaning of a text for himself or, on the contrary, in order to connect a text which arises from a past community with a present and future community of other readers. Yet, the picture of the isolated self reading and attempting to understand a single text, so that reference to other readers comes in only after individual under-standing has been achieved, is deeply ingrained in all of us. Its presuppositions and implications are thoroughly matter-of-fact for us, so that trying to imagine and think through other possibilities is a source of surprising ideas we may not quite know what to do with in practical terms. That constitutes both the difficulty and the value of such an investigation. Let us now reflect further on both terms in the relationship – the reading self and the text – in order to bring out some of these ideas that will have to be taken into account if we hope to develop a more adequate understanding of what 'reading' involves.

We can gain a great deal of help in reflecting on our picture of the reading and interpreting self from Charles Taylor's *Sources of the Self.*[14] I do not wish to overlook the originality of Taylor's thinking in this book, but the book's chief value for my purpose here is that it brings together in a comprehensive and systematic way ideas that have emerged in many recent books on the way the 'self' is understood in modern culture and on the way that understanding developed historically. As Taylor describes it, the key characteristic of the modern 'self' is 'inwardness'. I cannot summarize here all the aspects of this idea or all the key moments in its historical emergence. But I want to bring out three strands Taylor articulates: one is scientific/epistemological, one is religious/moral, and one is social/political.

Certain texts by the French philosopher René Descartes[15] have served repeatedly to exemplify for historians of culture the key moment in the development of the scientific and epistemological understanding of the self. The religious wars of the early seventeenth century provided an appalling demonstration for Descartes of his contemporaries' inability to achieve certainty and consensus on matters of the highest importance. 'From my childhood,' Descartes says, 'I lived in a world of books'.[16] But at the end of his studies, he found himself filled with doubts and errors, and 'resolved instead to seek no other knowledge than that which I might find within myself, or perhaps in the great book of nature'.[17] But having travelled and observed the world, he finally decided to examine his own ideas and try to sort out true from false. Confined by winter weather and lacking company, he meditated all day 'alone in a warm room'.[18] He hit upon four rules defining a method for achieving truth: first, never accept as true anything he did not recognize as certainly and evidently such; second, divide every difficulty into as many parts as possible in order to solve it; third, think in an orderly way from simplest to most complex; and finally, enumerate so completely and review so generally the results attained as to be certain nothing was omitted.[19] But even this method will not work without a starting point that is absolutely certain. To find this starting point, Descartes decided to reject everything he could possibly doubt. But he found remaining one thing he could not doubt, namely, he who was doubting was something. He thus found his starting point, which he formulated in the famous words, 'I think, therefore I am.'[20]

Descartes thus makes the isolated self the beginning and ground of any inquiry that could achieve certainty. Instead of grasping an objective order in the world, the self disengages itself from the natural and human world, confines itself to clear and distinct ideas, and pursues a carefully regulated method of analysis and inquiry to achieve reliable results. This is Descartes' prescient picture of modern science. The scientific enterprise involves a vast collectivity of individuals who pursue researches over decades and centuries. But in a paradoxical way, the enterprise is strictly individualistic in the sense that every achieved result must in principle be verifiable by any scientific researcher. Though the laws of science often bear the names of their discoverers, there is nothing like 'individual genius' to mark them in the way that, say, a poem of Keats is recognizable by its unique and irreproducible style.

As applied to the interpretation of works of literature, this way of thinking about the self directs our attention to the problem of finding a method the self can follow to achieve a reliably correct interpretation of a poem or other literary work. The transaction appears to take place between the reading self and the text, and the question is what sort of knowledge about a poem an interpretation can claim to be. What makes this picture seem so plausible is that it does in fact match our modern practice of reading in isolation and, in that situation, we do seek some way of dealing with the work so as to assure that our understanding is true, and that it can count as knowledge. We see that individual readers come up with quite different interpretations, and even experts disagree not only about particular interpretations but even about what method of interpreting to follow. Like Descartes, we may be tempted to reject the library-full of irresolvable critical disputes and seek a single method that will make us sure we correctly understand what we read.[21]

A second strand in the modern self is the religious and ethical claim to autonomy. This impulse is clearly at work in the Reformation principle that all individuals must work out salvation for themselves.[22] Individuals must be personally and strongly committed to God, must have a direct and personal relation with Jesus, and must assume personal responsibility for their own sins. Luther found particularly offensive the idea that individuals could purchase 'indulgences' from the church. The idea behind this practice was that the church as a collective body accumulated merit with God (the treasure of the church) through the prayers and good deeds of holy persons. This merit accrued not only to the individuals who performed the deeds but to the church as a corporate body, just as the whole person gains merit through the good deeds the person's hand performs. The officials of the church had the power to dispense this accumulated merit to individuals who had committed some offence, and an offering in gratitude could only increase the merit the sinning individual might gain.[23] In this conception, the corporate body of the church outweighs the individual. But the Reformation insisted that God's relation was with each Christian rather than the corporate body of the church, even though the church undoubtedly had an indispensable role to play in the individual's salvation.

The Reformation emphasis on individual responsibility could, however, undermine the religious dedication that motivated it. Critics of Christianity in the eighteenth century complained that the idea that Jesus had died for our sins made no sense. How, they insisted, could one person – and an innocent person at that – atone for the sins committed by individuals, including ones not even born yet?[24] These critics were just pushing to its conclusion the idea that all individuals have to assume responsibility for themselves.

The emphasis on the individual believer emerged also in views of the interpretation of the Bible. Scripture had in it everything needed for salvation, and Scripture made its message abundantly clear. If there were difficult passages in Scripture, they could be understood through the clearer passages: Scripture was self-interpreting. The long tradition of the church did not guarantee it an autonomous authority, and indeed, errors and corruptions might have crept in over time. What was needed was not so much mastery of the tradition. Rather, each believer had to have access to the Scripture and had to confront God's Word directly, praying with confidence that God would grant the grace of understanding.

If we bring this perspective to the interpretation of a poem, the issue is less one of knowledge than of taking responsibility for one's understanding. Whether my view is correct or not, I must reach some understanding of a poem for myself, and I must sincerely and faithfully state that understanding. It is not acceptable for me merely to repeat someone else's idea, however penetrating or insightful it may be. There is, of course, the risk that the surest way to prove my autonomy will be to pursue a novel, unprecedented interpretation and to stress its difference from every other view. The repetition without examination of conventional ideas may turn into its mere opposite, an eccentric or 'antinomian' originality that has become an end in itself. Moreover, if my personal under-standing of a poem is the end-point of reading, then the reading and study of literature have nothing to contribute to our relations to our fellow human beings – the core of ethics.[25]

Finally, the conception of the self as isolated also has important implications for social and political life. The classical liberal theory that individuals are absolutely prior to political organization leads to attributing to individuals rights which must be respected by even the largest majority as well as by any government, whatever its form. For political decisions to be legitimate, each individual must have the opportunity to participate on an equal basis with every other. Society should cultivate the widest possible tolerance and minimize the imposition of collective values that restrain individuals. A political system or a social order is legitimate only to the extent that it makes it possible for individuals to pursue their own purposes, choices and lives.

The sense that the individual must be liberated from restrictive social orders carries over into literary interpretation. Authority figures, whether individual teachers or organized groups of professional literary critics, easily come to be seen as conspirators imposing their views on individual readers. Their authority is exercised simply on behalf of their own interests or the interests of the dominant group they serve. Even taste, which seems like a personal and immediate response, can be exposed as socially constructed, more or less deliberately shaped so as to internally enslave the individual to a dominant group.[26] All such imposed schemes need to be exposed, demystified, and broken, so that individuals can be liberated to pursue their own unfettered reading of literary works.

It is obvious enough that social and political individualism can be carried to extremes which destroy the very society on which the individual's survival depends. At the same time, it seems impossible to deny that there exist some exclusions or discriminations in the social body and in the study of literature which would be difficult to justify on reasoned and evidentiary grounds. Christians have, after all, joined other groups in protesting against their exclusion from the mainstream, demanding to have their own values represented to them in the works they study, and claiming the right to resist the imposition of alien values on them or even the forced exposure to advocacy for such values. We are all so saturated in the language of individual rights that we would have immense difficulty making sense of our world without that language.

2. *Reading amid a cloud of witnesses*

I do not pretend to have presented a balanced view of the modern conception of the isolated, inward self. I have tried to point to some of the features that make the idea appealing or even compelling for us. But I have also expressed reservations at every point. If we return to the two poles in our individualist picture of reading, namely, the reader and the text, we can consider first the reader. It is obvious that we have *learned* to read and that means that we have been taught by others. Instruction involved, implicitly and explicitly, orientation toward particular texts and textuality in general. Much more than learning to decode marks on a page, we were learning what reading various texts in various ways could do for us: inform, entertain, provoke thought. What students in literature courses are studying is, precisely, how to read – whether Milton or Emily Dickinson or novels or other works. Sometimes the weight of instruction can seem a burden that comes between the reader and the text. But honest reflection will usually discover that our freshest and apparently most spontaneous insights arise because we have fully absorbed sophisticated skills of reading, not despite those skills. We have internalized an activity that retains at every point the traces of its social origin. Where the custom is for a group to listen to a text read aloud, understanding what is read is more obviously social, for comments and interpretation emerge from the discussion that spontaneously breaks out. As Noakes observes, 'only a very highly trained and experienced reader can raise in solitude the range of questions likely to be generated by a group'.[27] By the time we are adults, we cannot erase our experience as readers, make ourselves *tabulae rasae*, when we approach a text. If we could accomplish such a feat, we would eliminate along with everything else our capacity to read and understand. As the critic Gerald Prince put it, 'We read because we have read.'

On the other side of this presumed dyadic relation, the text also appears as isolated and self-subsistent. And this is true whether we speak about 'the text itself' as object or think of it as mediating our access to its author's meaning. Yet this picture leaves out a great deal. Reading a text – let us say, a poem – is so ordinary a part of our experience that we do not often ask how it happens that we are reading this particular poem. Any large college library contains hundreds if not thousands of volumes of poetry in English written over many centuries. Most of them are not read by anybody at all any more, or at most by only a few people. Living poets write a great deal, and there are dozens of magazines which publish nothing but new poems. Out of this huge mass of past and present poems, how did we arrive at this one?

Even a contemporary poem comes to us through the decisions and deeds of editors, printers and distributors. It takes an immense social machinery to bring to a reader any work of literature. That machinery is moved by the economic reality of the position such works occupy in our culture. We participate in assigning that position when we regard works of literature as worth the effort and expense of acquiring, reading and understanding. Once we read them, we may find them entertaining or edifying or instructive, but first we must *find out* about them by hearing from a friend, a teacher, or one of those organs, such as book reviews or specialized magazines, which help us navigate the ocean of printed material around us. Paradoxically, our sense of the poem as an isolated text is almost a defensive fiction that screens out a background reality too large and complex for us to keep in mind as we read.[28]

Our encounter with older works of literature adds even more layers. Typically, we come to an older poem in school, probably in college. A teacher asked us to read it and we found it in a book, perhaps such an anthology as Valentine Cunningham mentioned in his chapter on the canon, the *Norton Anthology of English Literature*, or perhaps in a selection of the author's poems. This poem was already there, waiting for us, and somebody – usually teachers, including the teachers who put the books together – for some reason wanted us to read it. When we come to such a poem, there already cling to it many choices based on differing purposes by various people. Many, if not all, of those choices have never been directly explained to us. Those who worked cooperatively and formed the whole social process that brought this poem to us were interested in it, presumably because they thought it showed something. Even if they simply liked it, they picked out this poem to show something they liked, the sort of thing they liked, and they wanted to invite others to like too.

Their care for it extended to bringing it to us in this precise form. When we scratch the surface of most texts, the sweat if not the blood of its editors oozes out. The text of a Shakespeare play, assembled from several early printed versions, each with defects; the poems of Emily Dickinson, their original form still being recovered after early printings revised and altered them; texts from Qumran (the Dead Sea Scrolls), pieced together like a jigsaw puzzle out of manuscript fragments and then edited, corrected and translated from difficult and obscure ancient languages – these are only a few examples of the dedicated scholarly effort, often lasting over many generations and still ongoing, through which a text we may take for granted was established and brought to us.

Nor should we overlook the price of that transmission. Christians are not alone but are certainly among those who risked or even gave up their lives merely for possessing a copy of their Scripture. To the thoughtful reader, the pages we read are sometimes tinged with the blood of martyrs. But transmission can also be joyous. Nehemiah 8 tells the moving story of the scribe Ezra's restoration to the Jews of their written law after their return to Jerusalem from Babylonian exile. All who can understand, men and women alike, gather in a public place. When the scroll is unrolled for the reading, they stand, shout 'Amen!' to Ezra's blessing, lift up their hands, bow and prostrate themselves, and listen with rapt attention. Even though Ezra explains that the day is holy and they should not mourn or weep, they do in fact weep with reverent joy. This vivid and powerful scene in which reading is embedded in the historical life of a community is still relevant to our greatly different situation. The historical process which comprises the decision of which works to include in the Bible, its transmission from generation to generation, and the passionate and continuing debates over its text are not an 'extreme case' (again, a point Valentine Cunningham makes), but only exhibit in its amplitude a process which goes on, usually with less intensity, around virtually every text of significance to some body of readers.

Thus, examination both of the reader and of the text uncovers a cloud of witnesses instead of an encounter between two isolated and autonomous beings. And it is precisely in this discovered community that Christianity can find one point of relevance to criticism. For Jesus' 'new command' is that we 'love one another' (Jn. 13:34). Paul insists that we are all members of one body and that Jesus is its head (1 Cor. 12:12–31; Col. 1:18). John tells us that we cannot sincerely love the God we have not seen if we do not love the brother or sister we do see (1 Jn. 4:20–21). Yet, I think an honest Christian in our day will have to admit to feeling a tension between the obvious Christian insistence on the community of the faithful and the sense that religious belief is, as we readily say, a 'personal commitment'.[29] The question is whether it is possible to achieve within the individualistic framework of modern life a conception of the community, and more specifically of the church, that does not simply 'balance' the claims of self and society. How do we displace the opposition into terms that do justice to the good we perceive in the individual, the community loosely conceived, and the more concrete and organized body which is the church, without imposing an unavoidable and presupposed conflict between self and society?[30]

3. Interpretive communities

I believe we can gain a great deal of help in answering this question from Josiah Royce's *The Problem of Christianity*,[31] a series of lectures published in 1913, and in particular from his conception of 'interpretive communities'. Royce was not thinking in these lectures of reading, whether of secular or religious texts. His question was, 'In what sense can the modern man consistently be, in creed, a Christian?'[32] or, as he carefully reformulates it, 'When we consider what are the most essential features of Christianity, is the acceptance of a creed that embodies these features consistent with the lessons that, so far as we can yet learn, the growth of human wisdom and the course of the ages have taught man regarding religious truth?[33] He considers whether, within the modern world, it is possible to understand the individual and the community in a way consistent with specifically Christian ideas, and his answer is that we can do so once we understand society as consisting of individuals standing in interpretive communities, of which Christianity is one.

I am starting, so to speak, from the other side – from reading as an activity of interpretation – and trying to work toward an adequate conception of the community which is adumbrated when we rediscover the social dimensions of reading. But obviously, Royce's view has a particular interest for Christian students of literature, in so far as it helps them connect their interest and work as readers with their Christian faith. I will not claim at this point that Royce's is the only adequate way to conceive this community. But I do claim that his view is sufficiently impressive that alternative conceptions will lack intellectual seriousness to the degree that they ignore or fail to consider it.

Royce focuses on three insights which, the Christian community has felt, emerged under the guidance of the Spirit as interpretations of Jesus' teachings: that membership in the spiritual community of the church was necessary to salvation; that the individual is burdened by a guilt which the individual cannot escape by his own effort; and that through Jesus' atonement for human sin and guilt, individuals are enabled to unite themselves with the divine spiritual community and thus to gain salvation.[34] It is these doctrines which are a special challenge to the modern mind.

To begin with the first idea, community means more than a collection of individuals: it is a group animated by a certain spirit, expressed in a variety of ways and works.[35] Such a community, Royce argues, 'when unified by an active indwelling purpose, is an entity more concrete and, in fact, less mysterious than is any individual man . . .'[36] 'Loyalty' is 'a spirit of active devotion to the community' thus conceived.[37] As the loyal reflect on loyalty, there arises 'a consciousness of the ideal of a universal community of the loyal'.[38] Ideally, such a community in its purposes will be worthy of the loyalty of all human beings and all will belong to it. This community is not actual, but a task and a challenge; to act as if it existed and in a way aimed to cooperate in its emergence is 'to win in the highest measure the goal of individual life . . . what religion calls salvation'.[39]

From community, Royce turns to the individual. He begins with the fact that instinctual impulses cooperate with stimuli from the environment to build up in the individual habitual actions – forms of conduct. Along with them emerges a consciousness of these forms of conduct, springing from the critical tension that arises when we compare our own conduct to that of other human beings.[40] Thus individualism and collectivism grow and intensify each other as there emerge 'vast organizations of collective power'.[41] This double allegiance cannot be resolved without a transformation in the relation of individuals and their conduct to the reality of the collectivity. The collectivity must change into community, and the individual must achieve 'an essentially new type of self-consciousness, – the consciousness of one who loves a community as a person', in short, what Royce terms 'loyalty'.[42]

In the ordinary view, Royce observes, the development of the modern world – characterized by such features as complex and vast forms of social organization, a sophisticated awareness of the self as the focus of the responsibility and authority for knowledge and for moral action, and the creation of science as a collective enterprise for achieving reliable knowledge – all seem to conflict with Christianity, which emerged in an earlier society with a now outmoded anthropology and epistemology. But Royce's examination of the three central ideas in Christianity leads to the claim that, on the contrary, 'the Christian doctrine of life is the expression of universal human needs, – and of the very needs upon whose satisfaction the very life of every social order depends for its worth and for its survival'.[43] These needs can never be removed by material progress or political reform. In fact, vast social changes 'will inevitably mean vast social tragedies',[44] which will call for precisely the Christian answer to the problem of human life.

Modern culture has produced an acute awareness of the separation of the individual, individuated by feelings, thoughts, and personal actions. But on the other side, it has produced equally acute awareness of the realm of social cooperation and of social processes and actions in relation to which individual persons seem 'almost helpless instruments'.[45] How can we conceive the relation between them? Royce begins by observing that a crowd is no community, but a mere aggregate of individuals. A community 'is essentially a product of a time-process':[46] it has a past and a future, and 'its more or less conscious history, real or ideal, is a part of its very essence'.[47] But the same is true of the individual, who is not 'just a flash of consciousness' in the present instant. Rather, 'my idea of myself is an interpretation of my past, – linked also with an interpretation of my hopes and intentions as to my future'.[48] Royce then asks the key question: 'Can many different selves, all belonging to the present time, possess identically the same past as their own personally interesting past life?'[49] The answer seems undeniably that not only can they, they have done so repeatedly and ordinarily. Community thus depends 'upon an interpretation of the significance of facts'[50] – not only past acts, but present acts as related to them and as pointing toward a future.

A community is something practical, 'a being that attempts to accomplish something in time and through the deeds of its members'.[51] It needs as its members persons who understand their own lives as extended time-processes.[52] But secondly, such members must be linked together by communication, which presupposes that they do not merely 'melt together',[53] but remain distinct. And third, each member must have at least some remembered and some hoped-for events in common with all the others.[54] The coherence of the community is thus rooted in the common memory and shared interpretation of definite events, and that memory and interpretation will be sustained by acts of commemoration and in the stream of communication. The substance of the community's life consists in common deeds, that is, deeds undertaken cooperatively by its members.

Royce proposes a method to attain the goal of assuming 'responsibility for and to the life of the community'.[55] He argues that a community 'depends for its very constitution upon the way in which each of its members interprets himself and his life'. Moreover, 'a self is a life whose unity and connectedness depend upon some sort of interpretation of plans, of memories, of hopes, and of deeds'.[56] But what is an interpretation? Interpretation – the process by which we know our neighbour's mind – is what we seek in all our social and spiritual relations'.[57] Interpretation is a triadic relation: the interpreter interprets a sign (a person, a text, anything which expresses mind) by producing another sign which is itself addressed to another person and calls for further interpretation. The interpretive process is thus temporal – a person interpreting a past to the future – and endless, broken only by the death of a particular participant or of the whole group of participants linked by interpretive communication. Ideally, this interpretive process would link all signs and all persons as interpreters of signs into a single community in which each interpreter would take his or her place without any blurring or blending, and yet in clear articulation. This social order Royce calls 'a Community of Interpretation'.[58] Every act of interpretation aims 'at an ideal event, – the spiritual unity of our community'.[59] Interpretation thus reveals its ethical and religious significance.[60]

4. Resisting and rebuilding communities

A sense of Royce's relevance to the practice of criticism can be gained, I believe, from examining Patrocinio Schweickart's rethinking of reader-oriented critical theory from a feminist perspective.[61] Schweickart asks how reader-response criticism might be changed if one thinks of the reader as specifically female. She summarizes the response reported by female readers, both amateur and expert, to texts written by men, texts which take for granted that the male perspective is universal, that of humanity as such. As she analyses her own response to D. H. Lawrence's *Women in Love*, what emerges is a woman's resistance to this assumption and to the exclusion or distortion of her own experience and identity in male-written texts. But not only this, even more subtly and more damagingly, the positive values of autonomy and love are coded in the text so as to invite the reader's identification with male figures. Both the negative and the positive reactions of the female reader to many (not all) masculine texts 'immasculate' her.[62]

What we encounter here is the characteristic moment of the modern assertion of the self. The authority of a socially valued work is rejected, and the self's right to its freedom and self-responsibility is asserted. The moment of individual liberation, however, leaves the self in a vacuum over against the demystified text. What is illuminating is that Schweickart continues by examining the response of a female writer to a female-written text, Adrienne Rich's 'Vesuvius at Home: the Power of Emily Dickinson'. Schweickart finds three key moments in Rich's reading of Dickinson. The first is a defence of Dickinson against 'patriarchal misreadings that trivialize or distort her work'. Second, Rich actually visits Dickinson's home in an effort to understand her text as the expression of her actual, highly concrete existence. This effort is inherently limited by Rich's historical distance from Dickinson, but that apparent limit is transformed by a third moment, Rich's own personal voice in the essay. For this is not a merely antiquarian quest, but aims at a connection, the establishment of a living context or tradition 'that would link women writers to one another, to women readers and critics, and to the larger community of women'.[63]

In the movement of Schweickart's argument, it seems to me, we encounter in miniature the tension I have been trying to trace within modern culture. For the liberation of the individual in all his or her concreteness to avoid an absolute isolation, it is indispensable to recover an understanding of the self as joined in a genuine community. That community arises out of sharing with other members of the community a relation to a common past and to a future goal. This does not lead to any blurring of identity: Rich is, as Schweickart says, a visitor, who must neither intrude nor appropriate what belongs to Dickinson. What checks the danger that Rich will simply project her own subjective notion on to Dickinson is not any power of Dickinson herself to refuse that projection but rather in another direction: Rich's relation to her own time and to the living members of her interpretive community. Here, 'we can think of validity not as a property inherent in an interpretation, but rather as a *claim* implicit in the *act* of propounding an interpretation', and hence as offered to and 'contingent on the agreement of others'.[64] Thus, 'feminist reading and writing alike are grounded in the interest of producing a community of feminist readers and writers, and in the hope that ultimately this community will expand to include everyone'.[65] This hope may fail, but in it lies the universality of the experience of the reader Schweickart insists must be concretely specified, a universality which is generated by and which preserves difference.

I do not claim that Schweickart would agree with me, but I

believe her line of thought can strike a responsive chord for a Christian. The negative and reactive moment in which the individual reader's self is liberated is also a moment of isolation in which the individual is constricted to a language of complaint – at exclusion or victimization. The isolated self has no grounds for believing that its responses are anything but idiosyncratic. The cure for this danger is not, however, a purely technical method through which the individual joins a complex collectivity as a merely impersonal member, equivalent to every other. It is rather the discovery of an interpretive community, which can be grasped only in loyalty, love and hope. This seems to me consistent with Royce's account. It does not follow that Schweickart's line of thought is implicitly Christian, or that there is a distinct Christian criticism. What may follow is a claim that is actually stronger: that the social order implicit in every genuine community of interpretation finds its adequate model only in the Christian understanding of the church.[66]

5

The turn to history

John D. Cox

Having established the validity of reading and interpreting literature Christianly, we need to look in the next three chapters at contemporary theories which aim at generating particular interpretations.

1. The material base

Some literary theorists have recently turned to history as the appropriate site for understanding literature, though they do so with varying emphases and under various banners: neo-Marxism, New Historicism, cultural materialism, among others. One motive for turning to history is an open rejection of the so-called New Criticism, which prevailed in the middle of the century. New Critics emphasized the apparently timeless (*a*historical) aesthetic qualities of writing. To capture those qualities, an important New Critical theorist, W. K. Wimsatt, chose the phrase 'verbal icon' to describe a literary work. What he meant by it was 'a verbal image which fully realizes its verbal capacities', both pictorially and as 'an interpretation of reality in its metaphoric and symbolic dimensions'.[1] Wimsatt put the emphasis, in other words, on the formal qualities of literature, not on the 'reality' they interpreted. In fact, it is 'heresy', wrote Cleanth Brooks, another New Critic, 'to refer the structure of the poem to . . . something outside the poem', including history.[2] Some theorists see an analogy between this New Critical conviction about the formal qualities of literature and the deconstructive preoccupation with the *language* of literature. Defending deconstruction against the turn to history ten years ago, J. Hillis Miller sounded remarkably like formalists forty years earlier, when he insisted in his 1986 Modern Language

Association presidential address that the only legitimate site for theorizing is language itself.[3]

The recent turn to history, however, is more than a rejection of formalism; it is also a *return* to history, for New Criticism was itself reacting against pedagogical and critical practice that treated literary works as the phenomena of 'objective' history. This 'old' literary history was inspired by Hegel and rooted in nineteenth-century notions of 'scientific' history and national destiny. It located a given work in a given author's life in a given national tradition, with its various periods, styles, and political influences. 'Political' in this case meant the major events in public life, dominated by those who held political power (*cf.* chapter 2, Valentine Cunningham's discussion of national canons). The multi-volume *Cambridge History of English Literature* is a foremost example of this approach to literature through history. Published in 1907 in fifteen volumes, this huge work was authored, in effect, by a committee of scholars whose aim was to create a definitive statement of knowledge about its subject, like the contemporaneous eleventh edition of the *Encyclopaedia Britannica*.

The recent return to history in literary theory, then, is to something quite different from the *Cambridge History*. It involves a reconception of history, strongly influenced by Marxist tradition and by previous developments in literary theory, including feminism, deconstruction and reader response. Deconstruction's 'linguistic turn' has in fact left its mark on the return to history, in that critics no longer seek an 'objective' account of literature in the past, because 'objectivity' itself is now recognized as a culturally specific ideal of the Enlightenment. 'Only from history in thought, the theory of history, was it possible to account for the historical religion of reading', writes Louis Althusser, a leading Marxist theorist: 'by discovering that the truth of history cannot be read in its manifest discourse, because the text of history is not a text in which a voice (the Logos) speaks, but the inaudible and illegible notation of the effects of a structure of structures.'[4] Althusser is not directly discussing literary theory here, but his comment invites comparison with Derrida's rejection of 'logocentricity' in modern discourse (that is, discourse from the Enlightenment to postmodernism). Both Derrida and Althusser reject the presumption that a text (either about fiction or about the past) contains the truth as if it were a fish to be contemplated through the walls of a transparent tank, and both use 'the Logos', borrowed from Greek and Christian thought, as a metaphor to stand for 'the truth'. For both theorists, the truth evades a confident search for positive certainty; rather, it is 'inaudible and illegible', in Althusser's phrase.

But Althusser affirms something else as well, something that distinguishes the return to history from deconstruction, as well as from the old literary history. He affirms 'a structure of structures', of which the text of history is an effect. Althusser's affirmation recalls the famous image that Marx uses in the Preface to *A Contribution to the Critique of Political Economy*, distinguishing a 'foundation' and 'superstructure' in cultural history:

> The general conclusion at which I arrived and which, once reached, became the guiding principle of my studies can be summarised as follows. In the social production of their existence, [people] inevitably enter into definite relations, which are independent of their will, namely relations of production appropriate to a given stage in the development of their material forces of production. The totality of these relations of production constitutes *the economic structure of society, the real foundation*, on which arises *a legal and political super-structure* and to which correspond definite forms of social consciousness. The mode of production of material life conditions the general process of social, political and intellectual life. It is not the consciousness of [people] that determines their existence, but their social existence that determines their consciousness.[5]

Let us consider a particular example of Marx's claim (and Althusser's, following Marx): the culture of the southern United States before the Civil War of 1861–65. The 'mode of production' in the South (the 'foundation' in Marx's metaphor) was a slave economy: without slavery, the economy of the South would collapse, and eventually did collapse. Yet the 'legal and political superstructure' was the liberal democratic ideology of the Enlightenment, around which the United States had been founded, overlaid in the South with the trappings of English country gentility and the discourse of Victorian morality. In the language of Marx's analysis, the 'consciousness' of the culture (its 'superstructure') did not determine its social being; if it had, slavery would have been impossible, because slavery is incompatible with the liberal democratic affirmation that 'all men are created equal', as abolitionists repeatedly pointed out. Rather, the social existence of the South (the 'foundation', slavery) determined its consciousness, which was an elaborate tissue of evasion – appropriately called a *'false* consciousness' when the system was affirmed by slaves themselves, as it sometimes was. The 'Logos' that Althusser denies is, in effect, an autonomous 'consciousness', floating free of the economic and social facts of the culture, whereas 'the truth' of history is in the 'inaudible and illegible' 'foundation'.

Despite similarities, where materialist theory and deconstruction part ways, then, is in the Marxist assertion that a material reality indeed underlies ideological appearances, and that the relationship between the two is determinative. For the materialist critic, unlike the deconstructionist, literature therefore has a significance beyond language itself, and that significance is the economic and social base that gives rise to literature as a manifestation of social consciousness, a culture's 'superstructure'. From a materialist perspective, Miller confirms this distinction by rejecting it, for he thereby reveals the essentially idealist nature of his enterprise. Language itself is the only reality we know, he argues in his presidential address, and 'the concept of the material is therefore not a solution but a problem'.[6]

The job of historical materialist literary criticism is to expose the conscious, or ideological, aspects of a text as products of its cultural base. In doing so, it proceeds very differently from the old literary history, which did not look beyond the ideological superstructure; in effect, literary historians assumed that they could find the 'Logos' ('the truth of history') by identifying a literary work with the consciousness of its culture, particularly an aesthetic consciousness. Much the same could be said of New Criticism and other varieties of formalist analysis that post-structuralists reject. Such idealist projects are encompassed in the sarcastic irony of Marx's story in *The German Ideology* (originally directed at Hegel's followers) about a man who was concerned that so many people drown all the time: finally deciding that the problem was gravity, he went about trying to convince people that gravity did not exist, in order to save them from drowning.[7] For the materialist critic, paying attention to a culture's 'superstructure', without attending to its base, is to deal in the same kind of folly. 'The philosophers have only *interpreted* the world, in various ways,' Marx says in the Eleventh Thesis on Feuerbach, 'the point is to *change* it'.[8]

Critics who have returned to history have done so with varying degrees of commitment to Marxism, but common to all of them is an affirmation of 'materialism', understood in the Marxist sense as the determining circumstances of a culture. Important among explicitly Marxist critics are Terry Eagleton in Britain and Frederic Jameson in the United States, who endorsed Marx's call to change the world as the aim of literary pedagogy. Gerald Graff and Frank Lentricchia prefer to be called 'socialist', because their commitment to liberal democracy inclines them to avoid the stigma that has attached itself to Marxism in totalitarian regimes. In Britain, Jonathan Dollimore and Alan Sinfield have been publishing broadly Marxist criticism under the label of 'cultural materialism', which they borrowed from Raymond Williams. In the Foreword to *Political Shakespeare*, for example, they write in Marxist terms that ' "materialism" is opposed to "idealism": it insists that culture does not (cannot) transcend the material forces and relations of production'.[9] Dollimore also begins *Radical Tragedy* with a polemical introduction that rigorously engages Althusser.[10]

Less rigorously indebted to Marx is New Historicism, which has grown rapidly since 1980, mostly in the United States, and has followed the lead of Stephen Greenblatt in taking its inspiration from Michel Foucault and social anthropologists such as Clifford Geertz and Victor Turner rather than Marx. 'Cultural *poetics*', an alternative label to 'New Historicism', suggests a different emphasis from 'cultural *materialism*', though both proceed in quasi-Marxist fashion to uncover the 'real' cultural commitments of texts, no matter what their explicit ideology might be. Stephen Greenblatt's recent book, for example, called *Marvelous Possessions*, interprets a series of early modern travel narratives, from John Mandeville to Bernal Díaz, as revelations of European viciousness and rapacity, despite the trappings of Christian civilization.[11] Though Greenblatt does not put it this way, he could be said to be uncovering the material 'base' of competitive power that underpins the travel writers' 'superstructure', their explicit, *conscious* awareness and affirmation of cosmic order and manifest destiny in whose name they conquered the New World.

2. *Christianity and the material base*

In a Marxist estimation, Christianity is a prime example of cultural 'consciousness': it is a keystone in the 'superstructure' that western culture has built up to disguise its 'base', the truth of history. In fact, Christianity is the religion Marx was really thinking of when he wrote in the Introduction to *Contribution to Hegel's Philosophy of Law* that 'religion is the *opium* of the people'.[12] What he means in that passage is that religion functions in exploitative social systems to enable their victims to endure suffering, but religion also prevents the exploited from understanding the system that exploits them and therefore from doing something to change it. For Marx, Christianity thus functions just as Hegelian philosophy does: both impede material or structural changes that promote social justice. Both, in other words, try to save people from drowning by convincing them that gravity does not exist. This function of Christianity can also be seen at work in the antebellum American South, at least in imaginative form, for it was immortalized by Harriet Beecher Stowe in the title characters of *Uncle Tom's Cabin*.

But the antebellum American South is not, of course, what Marx had in mind in his trenchant analysis of western culture. He probably learned what he knew about slavery from reading Hegel's theory of the master-slave relationship, not from observing it at first hand. Rather, his interest was in what he did see, namely industrial capitalists' exploitation of workers in early nineteenth-century England, and it is the heritage of this particular interest that has made his ideas so compelling to some people and so controversial to others. For Christians, I want to suggest, Marx and his tradition are both compelling *and* controversial, and it is necessary to consider both aspects of his legacy before considering specifically how a Christian who is also a literary critic might respond to literary criticism's recent return to history.

How, then, could Marxist tradition possibly be compelling to Christians when it dismisses Christianity as a mere product of cultural 'consciousness'? For one thing, what makes historical materialism compelling is what it tells us about ourselves as social beings. We do indeed appear to be shaped (or 'constructed', as the sociologists like to say) by our social and economic context. Numerous social factors contribute profoundly to our identity – to our being one kind of person rather than another: language, customs, race, food, geography, habits of dress, family relations, gender roles, economic expectation, social class. None of us can escape these shaping influences as we grow up, and even if we expand our awareness, we cannot do so infinitely, for we retain the indelible imprint of cultural particularity. The impact of African culture on the culture of the modern United States would not be as profound as it is if cultural identity could be completely eradicated, for slave owners did everything they could to assimilate their slaves forcefully to the dominant culture.

Second, as Marx observed, we are largely unconscious of the

factors that shape us socially; they are scarcely present to our minds, unless we put our minds specifically to identifying them, as he tried to do. They are the medium that sustains our particular identities, as water sustains the fish that live in it. Nothing makes us more aware of the factors that unconsciously shape us than being removed from them. Suddenly introduced to a very different culture, we are literally like fish out of water, unable to understand the language, constantly confronted with incomprehensible customs and expectations, gasping at alien behaviour, dying for the context in which we feel at home, where things seem 'natural', where people do things the way they 'ought to be done'.

Third, the shaping forces of our material circumstances often contribute in complex ways to structural social injustice, as Marx pointed out. Slavery in the United States is a striking example, but much closer to our own experience is apartheid in modern South Africa, which bore many resemblances to what was happening in the United States 150 years ago. In the case of South Africa, the economic base has not been outright slavery but capitalism, and Marx's critique of capitalism significantly has appealed much more strongly to the black majority who suffered from apartheid than to the white minority who profited from the system. The elaborate defence of apartheid – intellectual, legal and political – indeed resembles the conscious 'superstructure' that Marx describes. With a remarkable internal coherence of its own, it floated free of the material circumstances in which it flourished, generated by structural injustice while providing an apparently autonomous explanation of the system's 'necessity' that was credible only to those whom the system favoured.

Fourth, the materialist social critique is compelling to Christians because it helps us see how Christianity is often used to defend unjust social structures. Racism is again a pertinent example. In both the antebellum American South and modern South Africa, racial injustice was defended in explicitly Christian terms, and the defenders were often faithful churchgoers. Frederick Douglass, who escaped from slavery in Maryland, observed that in his own experience Christian slaveholders were far more vicious than their unbelieving counterparts. Douglass recalls that after one of his masters was converted at a camp-meeting, the slaves hoped their master would emancipate them or at least treat them better. But in fact he became much worse after his conversion than before: whereas he had once relied only on his own depravity to justify inhuman cruelty, he now turned to the Bible and the support of local preachers, intensifying his cruelty in the confidence that he was piously justified in doing so.[13] The defence of apartheid in South Africa was conducted in explicitly Christian terms, carried out in divinity school departments of theology, and sustained by a minor publishing industry in learned journals and scholarly monographs.

All these points and more comprise a case for Christians to pay close attention to the materialist critique. But in paying attention, and in acting accordingly, we need to remind ourselves what compels us to do so. For the complex set of observations that Marx originated is not itself autonomous, self-evident, self-justifying, or scientifically positive; if it were those things, it would be, in its own terms, the product of superstructural self-consciousness.[14] Rather, it is a product of history understood in a particular way. And the way materialist tradition understands history is not, finally, what compels Christian assent. Rather, what compels our assent to materialist observations about social justice is what we affirm as Christians, and what makes Marxist tradition properly controversial for Christians is the materialist assessment of Christianity. Let me explain this assertion by briefly describing Christianity's relationship to history in two ways: first, with regard to history in Christianity, and second, with regard to Christianity in history.

3. History in Christianity

What Christians affirm is explicitly indebted to a religious tradition inherited from ancient Israel: Jesus was a first-century Jew in Palestine, and he was profoundly shaped, like his first followers, by Jewish belief and tradition. Christianity's historical debt to Judaism is not incidental; it is central to Christian affirmation, and it is itself an adaptation of the Jewish tradition that Christianity affirms. For the Hebrews were alone among peoples of the ancient world in having a religion of history, and in the fullness of time they bequeathed that characteristic to Christianity. Though both Christianity and Judaism confronted serious challenges from the pointedly ahistorical philosophy of the Greeks, neither completely surrendered its essentially historical quality. Both continued – and continue – to affirm the origin of human history in the uniquely creative power of God, the continuance of God's saving presence in history, and the anticipation of history's fulfilment in a time of God's choosing.

The mark of ancient Israel's orientation to history is in the narrative form that much of the Hebrew Scriptures eventually assumed: the story of God's creative power and initiative in the very beginning of all things and of how God remained faithful in spite of humankind's faithlessness. For God moved redemptively in the lives of Abraham, Isaac, Jacob, and their descendants, freeing them from the degradation of slavery in Egypt and bringing them to a land that God had promised and prepared. The story continues in God's faithfulness to the people of Israel, even when Israel made the profoundly symbolic and literal choice to follow a human king, rather than simply to honour Yahweh as her king. God's nurturing and supportive presence remains at the centre of Israel's story even in the midst of political power struggles for succession, even when the kings reject God, the nation of Israel is defeated politically, and the people God had chosen to be God's own people are scattered over the earth.

Like the Hebrew Scriptures, the Christian Scriptures also take a largely narrative historical form, continuous with their predecessor. Specifically placed in Roman-occupied Palestine during the reign of Augustus Caesar, the birth of Jesus continues, fulfils and definitively redirects the historical faithfulness of God to Israel. The gospels interpret the ministry and mission of Jesus as one of priest, prophet and king, meeting the expectation of ancient Israel and radically redefining that expectation at the same time. The narrative is not merely episodic and additive; it is directional and purposeful, redolent with hope and the saving promise of God, not only for Israel but for the whole human race. In this narrative, immediately after the ascension of Jesus, the Holy Spirit manifests God's self among Jesus' followers at Pentecost, and Peter tells a story that interprets the life, death and resurrection of Jesus (Acts 2:1–36). The narrative continues in the establishment of churches among non-Jews, concretely revealing the promise of God in Jesus, who acted definitively with redemptive power on behalf of all human beings and indeed of the creation itself, which God had made to serve a good plan and purpose.

The end of the Christian story is open, like history itself, but its direction is clear: God continues to act faithfully in history through the church. This is the group of those whom God calls, as God called ancient Israel, to respond obediently and hopefully to God's saving promise. They are called not to a national destiny, like Israel's, but to the imitation of Christ, in whose life, death and resurrection they discover redemptive meaning and purpose for their lives, their communities, and the creation. This discovery is open to people of every language, as demonstrated at Pentecost and in the missionary activity of the early church. In so far as it is open to every language, it is also, by necessity, potentially open to

every cultural particularity, through which God works to transform the world in the light of the story Jesus fulfilled and initiated,
until his coming again, which will be the definitive end point and
culmination of the Christian story and of human history alike.

This brief review of what Christians affirm about history is not
meant to answer rational historical analysis with pious cant; it is
designed to show why Christians are compelled both to affirm
and to dissent from the materialist critique. As John Milbank has
pointed out, Marx promulgated a historical metanarrative, with
its own inherent sense of purpose and system of values.[15] This
metanarrative is important to Christians in so far as it tells us
things about ourselves that we need to know. What enables us to
recognize our need to know them, however, is not the materialist
metanarrative itself but our *own* metanarrative, outlined in the
paragraphs above. For Christians, too, history is suffused with
purpose, but that purpose is not inherent or positivistic; it is
enabled and revealed by God. We cannot therefore either discover
or disprove it through empirical analysis and research. For the
Christian story affirms the transcendence of God:

> my thoughts are not your thoughts,
> my ways not your ways – it is Yahweh who speaks.
> Yes, the heavens are as high above earth
> as my ways are above your ways,
> my thoughts above your thoughts.
>
> (Is. 55:8–9)[16]

God's purpose is hidden, discoverable only in part and provisionally through the construction of every believer's own story in
dialogue with God and in faithful interaction with the body of
believers. 'Now we are seeing a dim reflection in a mirror', writes
Paul, in his discourse on Christian love, 'but then we shall be
seeing face to face. The knowledge that I have now is imperfect;
but then I shall know as fully as I am known' (1 Cor. 13:12).

The transcendence of God, however, does not mean that the
God of Abraham, Isaac and Jacob, the God who raised Jesus from
the dead, is a product of superstructural class consciousness. On
the contrary, the story of Israel and of the Christian church
repeatedly tells how God takes the side of the poor and
oppressed. It is not therefore a story that justifies power and
success, like the self-serving stories of kings and emperors in the
ancient Near East, or of divine-right monarchs in early modern
Europe, or of self-made millionaires who profited from the

industrial revolution and its aftermath. In Israel's story, God chose a people because God loved them, even when they were enslaved and had no land of their own; God did not choose them because they were wealthy, powerful, and socially and politically dominant. The exodus covenant identifies God to Israel as the one 'who brought you out of the land of Egypt, out of the house of slavery' (Ex. 20:1). The prophets repeatedly admonish the kings of Israel not to be confident in their own strength but only in the blessing of God, and the narrative traces the cause of national collapse in the kings' failure to heed this admonition. The stories about Jesus similarly make clear that he is a peasant, born to a labouring family. His kingship consists not in power, wealth and social prominence but in a life of obedient trust and humility before God, as he suggests in his parables of the kingdom. Moreover, this way of living is not a resignation to the power of evil, including the evil of social injustice; rather, it is the only possible means by which society can be redemptively transformed, as yeast makes a loaf rise, or salt flavours a meal, or a lamp banishes the darkness, or a tiny mustard seed grows into a tree.

In fact, Christians might well be said to affirm what Nicholas Lash calls 'Christian materialism'.[17] Acknowledging that Marx would have found such a phrase to be sheer nonsense, Lash nonetheless questions the materialist assumption that theological discourse is necessarily 'idealist' in character. For one thing, it is not necessary for Christians to subscribe to 'historical quietism', to the assumption that evils must simply be endured until God removes them. Jesus was not such a quietist, Lash points out. 'He acted out his unswerving trust in his Father in a manner which indicated that he supposed there to be that which, if it was to be done, had to be done by him'. Again, Lash argues, it is not necessary for Christians to subscribe to the assumption that 'there are, or can be, events or situations in which the experience of God is *unmediated*'.[18] That is, where Christians acknowledge the hand of God, they do so in events and situations – in the concrete, material stuff of human life – not in anything *separate from* human life and experience.

4. Christianity in history

Despite Christianity's affirmation that the definitive meaning for human history lies in the mission and ministry of Jesus, it is obvious that world history involves a great deal that has nothing whatever to do with the death of an obscure Jewish peasant in first-century Palestine. Moreover, where the church *has* played a part in social and political institutions, it has too often been a dismal failure, falling far short of what it is called to do and often contributing instead to suffering and social injustice. Marx's observations about religion would have no force if there were no truth to them at all. Yet their force is compelling whenever we look at particular examples, such as the ecclesiastical exploitation of peasants during the Middle Ages, the religious wars of the sixteenth and seventeenth centuries, the failure of Christian witness against the rise of National Socialism in Germany, or, in the modern industrialized West, the mainline churches' pursuit of wealth and social prestige to the neglect of the poor.

But dismal failure is not the whole story. In the process of recovering and telling the Christian story, we need again to take our cue from our own metanarrative, not from the metanarratives of others. Since I have mentioned slavery several times, let me take it briefly as an example, for the Christian story is by no means one of consistent and mindless exploitation of slaves. Virtually everyone now recognizes the social institution of slavery itself as an evil, but the recognition took a very long time, and Christianity played a major part in its fruition. While the New Testament itself says nothing contrary to slavery as a social institution, it follows the example of the Old Testament in establishing guidelines for the appropriate treatment of slaves (Ex. 21:1–11; Lv. 25:35–46; Dt. 15:12–18; Phm. 1–25). Paul says extraordinary things to Philemon regarding his runaway slave, Onesimus: treat him 'not as a slave any more, but something much better than a slave, a dear brother' (Phm. 16). Such admonitions do not encompass the kind of thing Frederick Douglass's Christian master did to him. In medieval Europe, uprisings by enslaved peasants were inspired by hope in the promise of the gospel. Sometimes, to be sure, this hope took dubious theological form, but in many cases (particularly in the English uprising of 1381), the hope of serfs was ignited by Christian preaching, which denounced the exploitation of the poor from every social level, even though preachers did not recognize serfdom itself as an evil. Parliament's emancipation of slaves in the British Empire eventually came about from a variety of factors, but by no means negligible among them was a career of persistent political activism by William Wilberforce, an evangelical Christian and a Member of Parliament for forty-five years. Evangelicals such as Charles Grandison Finney and Theodore Weld were similarly outspoken among abolitionists in the new United States, helping to found the influential American Anti-

Slavery Society in 1833, the same year that Parliament passed legislation to free slaves in all territories under British dominion. Like many other folk songs from the antebellum American South, the stirring slave hymn, 'Go down, Moses', draws its inspiration from the story of Israel, evoking God's liberation of slaves in the past to encourage the hope of African slaves in the United States during the time of inspired hope and severe repression following Nat Turner's rebellion. The legacy of Christian anti-slavery movements continues into the present, having made itself felt in the American civil rights movement of the 1960s and in the ongoing involvement of African-American churches in political action. In short, in the complex story of recognizing slavery as a moral evil and eradicating it as a social institution, Christians played key roles, and their own story is therefore an important corrective to the materialist story that Christianity is necessarily the idealist product of a socially exploitative superstructural consciousness.

A more complex and difficult issue is still with us, in the form of capitalism itself, which inspired Marx's original insights. On this issue, too, Christians have been, and continue to be, deeply divided, and their division is precisely the point.[19] If Christianity were no more than a bad-faith justification for exploitative concentrations of capital and power, no Christian voice of any importance would be raised against capitalism. But in fact many such voices have been raised, from nineteenth-century Catholic advocates of socialism such as Maurice Blondel to the prophetic observations of a recent writer in the Anabaptist tradition, Ron Sider.[20] My point here is not Marx's – that capitalism is an institutional social evil like slavery; I want simply to emphasize that the Christian story qualifies the claim of the materialist metanarrative about religion. On the other hand, the Christian story also qualifies claims of a certain kind made by advocates of capital. Francis Fukuyama's recent book, *The End of History and the Last Man*, for example, makes claims about history that the Christian affirmation of God's transcendence cannot countenance.[21] Christians affirm that the future is radically open to God's initiative, which is neither disclosed nor foreclosed by the apparent vindication of free-market economies in the collapse of the Soviet Union. Capitalism's 'freedom to choose' cannot be equated with freedom in Christ, while consumerism, competitive acquisitiveness, and ever-expanding economies arguably encourage another kind of materialism that is hard to square with the gospel.

5. *Christianity and the turn to history*

Christian literary critics are called to be faithful to their own story, just as Christians are called in any other vocation. This means they are obliged to wrestle with what their story means in the context of their discipline, and to teach and write in light of what they believe. The return to history thus offers both an opportunity and a risk. The opportunity derives from Christianity's own commitment to history and concrete human situations as the appropriate site for God's redemptive action and self-revelation. For this commitment is constantly threatened by the pressure of success that emanates from wealth, power and social status, even in interpreting literature, and the turn to history is salutary in reminding us of that threat.

Consider E. M. W. Tillyard's little book *The Elizabethan World Picture*, for example, which was enormously influential for many years in the study of English Renaissance literature.[22] It is unusually imaginative, learned and insightful, but severely limited by its idealist assumptions. In fact, *The Elizabethan World Picture* was actually an offshoot of a longer and more scholarly book called *Shakespeare's History Plays*, which ironically (for a history of history plays) devotes almost half its pages to 'background' and a good proportion of that to 'The Cosmic Background'.[23] Tillyard's emphasis on 'cosmos' and 'picture' suggests where his real interest lay – not with history but with a static image of perfect order that recalls Wimsatt's choice of 'icon' to describe a literary work. As a consequence, what Tillyard claimed about the Elizabethans has a strong class bias that favours a tiny fraction of the most powerful, wealthy and socially privileged members of England's population in the late sixteenth century. To be sure, this was the most influential fraction, but it is by no means the only part of the population that has left a witness to itself, and – most important – Shakespeare did not belong to it, nor are his history plays exclusively about it, with the possible exception of *King John*. Shakespeare was certainly influenced by the upper class, but to claim that his plays manifest only aristocratic interests and concerns is pointedly to ignore the plays' remarkable social diversity and points of view. Tillyard's insistence that Elizabethan culture emphasized static order above all else is self-evidently upper-class: those who possess power and social prestige are most likely to be drawn to ideas about the world not really changing, because such ideas preserve the *status quo*. Such a critique of Tillyard is decidedly 'materialist', but nothing in it is anti-Christian; on the contrary, it may well offer Christian critics an opportunity to affirm their own story more richly and more truly than they can when working with an idealist paradigm.

On the other hand, Christians face a risk in the return to history. This risk consists in taking the materialist metanarrative, rather than our own story, as our starting point. While no-one can see history or the creation as God does, Christians need to see things differently from the way they are seen by those who are not Christians; that is, Christians need to see their own story, not only in terms of their individual dialogue with God (as in Augustine's *Confessions*), but also in terms of their culture. The way Christianity manifests itself in the history of English literature will therefore look different to a Christian from the way it looks to a Marxist, and Christians have an obligation to describe their angle of vision – always subject to correction, of course. As Milbank points out, 'If theology no longer seeks to position, qualify or criticize other discourses, then it is inevitable that these discourses will position theology: for the necessity of an organizing logic . . . cannot be wished away'.[24]

To take an example in this case, consider the organizing logic behind Stephen Greenblatt's analysis of Shakespeare's history plays, in a landmark essay called 'Invisible Bullets'.[25] This essay has been criticized chiefly for its grim thesis that religious political oppression generates its own subversion in order to contain and suppress it; for this thesis is so hopeless about social resistance in early modern England that it virtually denies any possibility for social change, even though change was a hallmark of the period. I would like to shift the emphasis away from the debate over subversion, however, and put it on the assumptions Greenblatt makes about himself and about the culture of early modern England as he undertakes his task of analysis. Such a shift is appropriate, because New Historicism emphasizes the mediated quality of criticism – the ideological commitments that construct what critics write, as well as what they write about.

Greenblatt approaches Shakespeare's plays about Henry V as prince and king by way of marginal and little-known texts, one by Thomas Harriot, the chronicler of Sir Walter Raleigh's joint stock venture to create an English colony in Virginia in the 1580s, the other by Thomas Harman, who wrote a pamphlet called *A Caveat for Common Cursitors* exposing the confidence tricks of street criminals. Greenblatt conducts his argument by analogy. In Harriot's case, he analyses an idealist but cynical use of Christian providentialism to defend colonial exploitation and compares it with Shakespeare's searching analysis of Christian monarchy. The argument is powerful, and it illuminates the history plays in a way that is strikingly different from Tillyard's argument. Greenblatt's marginal texts are not 'background' in Tillyard's sense; Greenblatt never suggests that Shakespeare was 'influenced' by them or that they are part of a shaping tradition that led to Shakespeare's history plays. Rather, they contribute to 'the circulation of social energy' to which Shakespeare and the new commercial theatre of London also belonged and of which they are analogous manifestations. Moreover, Greenblatt does not take the plays as tributes to a supposed national consensus in favour of divine-right monarchy; rather, he shows how the plays subversively interrogate providentially sustained monarchy, even as they celebrate it.

In the process of making this argument, Greenblatt tells us a good deal about himself, both implicitly and explicitly. Implicitly he tells us that he is widely read, keenly perceptive, both about archaic texts and human nature, and a witty and accomplished stylist as well as an original thinker. Twice he interrupts the flow of the third-person argument to refer to himself explicitly, once in an engaging story about a bawdy solecism he committed unintentionally in Italy,[26] and once in the following remark about Elizabethan hostility to atheism: 'The stance that seemed to come naturally to me as a green college freshman in mid-twentieth-century America seems to have been almost unthinkable to the most daring philosophical mind of late sixteenth-century England'.[27] Greenblatt informs us of more in this suave aside than his own atheism; he tells us that atheism came to him 'naturally' (that is, presumably with little or no opposition on his part) when he first encountered serious ideas as a naïve first-year college student. In other words, atheism is obvious even to relatively simple modern minds, and 'the most daring philosophical mind of late sixteenth-century England' must therefore have been simple indeed.

Two points ought to concern any reader who comes across this passage in Greenblatt's essay. First, his easily assumed atheism makes him, on the face of it, an unsympathetic reader of texts from a traditional culture that was deeply religious; and second, his easy dismissal of 'the most daring philosophical mind of late sixteenth-century England' as inferior because of its denseness to a 'green college freshman in mid-twentieth-century America' is breathtakingly arrogant. Greenblatt dismissively describes Harriot's and Spenser's attitude toward the religious excesses of primitive peoples in the New World: 'They are viewed with a touch of amusement'.[28] But Greenblatt's dismissiveness means that his description applies equally to his own view of Harriot and Spenser: he views *their* religious excesses with a touch of amusement.

This lapse in 'Invisible Bullets' is small but revealing. Even if the personal aside about atheism were removed, the problems it raises would remain in this essay and in virtually all Greenblatt's work. His keen perception of hypocrisy and the religious misuse of power is real, but he exercises that perception to the exclusion of any positive moral contributions that religion may have made in the sixteenth century. Not all Christians were cunning confidence tricksters – not even all Christians in positions of wealth and power, as Greenblatt well knows from his reading in Bartolomé de las Casas. Moreover, Greenblatt has no perception whatever of the difficulty of maintaining Christian virtue in one's own life and in the community one is responsible for, if one is in a position of power in a Christian community, particularly when the community is fatally divided against itself on points of doctrine and practice, as Tudor England was. Few people negotiate such difficulties very successfully – successfully, that is, in light of their own moral affirmation. Stories about King David suggest that the problem is not exclusively Christian, for David is 'a man after God's own heart' though he commits horrendous moral lapses and abuses of power. God loves David *in spite of* his moral failures, not *because* of them. The few who negotiated the pitfalls of power with a high degree of moral success in Tudor England tend to have had unhappy stories, like Thomas More's. Nothing more clearly shows Greenblatt's insensitivity to the culture he writes most about than his treatment of More in *Renaissance Self-Fashioning* as little more than a politically successful Thomas Harriot.

My point is not to reject Greenblatt's argument but to emphasize its limitations. Like other criticism among the best produced by those who have recently returned to history, Greenblatt's writing needs to be approached with both gratitude and wariness. It deserves gratitude for its wit, grace, insight, learning, and – yes – for its moral wisdom. But that wisdom is reduced by its debt to the materialist metanarrative – a story that is not the Christian story and is, in fact, antithetical in many respects to it. One way to tell Stephen Greenblatt's story might be to position his moral wisdom more accurately against his Jewish cultural background than against historical materialism – in other words, to show what his moral wisdom owes to the ongoing narrative of God's faithfulness to Israel, including God's faithfulness to Stephen Greenblatt. But this is not the place to attempt such an account. More important for Christian readers is to remember their own story and always to endeavour to assess other stories in light of it, rather than the other way around.

6

The woman's place

Elisabeth Jay

1. *Caveat lector!*

Feminist literary criticism is the handmaiden, or tool, of readers
and writers with a prior commitment to a wider agenda of
political theories and causes.

This opening remark will probably have raised some hackles.
Those who disliked the choice of the word 'handmaiden', trailing
in its wake a world of female servitude, will further have wished
to repudiate its casual apposition with the notion of a 'tool' or
instrument of exploitation. Other readers may feel irritated by the
strident politicization of an activity that, confined to the world of
academic discourse, might seem to allow for the sympathetic
exploration of woman's predicament, without suffering the taint
of 'bra-burning radicalism'.

My crude opening gambit has behind it, however, the serious
purpose of alerting readers to the fact that feminist literary
criticism is only one academic wing of a broad-based political
movement, concerned to expose the way in which women have
been marginalized and oppressed by the structures and institutions of a patriarchally centred society.[1] For American readers,
now habituated to the presence of multi-disciplined Women's
Studies departments, this is easier to perceive than it is for their
British counterparts who have witnessed no such widespread
flow of funds into providing an institutional base for feminist
activities. Recognizing feminism as a broad-based political movement carries several implications for Christian students of
literature. 'Feminism', and by association 'feminist literary criticism', are broad umbrella words incorporating a wide range of
positions and internal disagreements. The virtue of feminist
criticism is an eclecticism that, because it felt itself to be operating

at the margins or frontiers of the academic world, felt free, in its early stages, to seize whatever weapons and literary techniques came to hand and shape them to the purpose of creating a new discourse. Soon, however, dissenting voices were to be heard within the female compound, asking whether it was legitimate or profitable to use the master's tools to deconstruct the master's house,[2] and consequently repudiating the use of anything, from male colleagues to techniques, developed in patriarchal institutions. Attempts to specify the part that feminist literary criticism could play in revealing and righting the injustices done to womankind soon raised potentially schismatic questions about the functions of literature and the complex relations between text, author and reader. Feminism speaks with many tongues; so, before enlisting under the 'feminist' banner, it is worth investigating which of its competing voices seem compatible with a commitment to Christian belief and practice.

Recognizing feminist criticism as part of a broad-based political movement carries two further implications for Christian students. First, to seek the apparent safety of the 'don't know' or 'don't care' apolitical contingent is in effect an irresponsible concession of power to those, of whatever persuasion, who care more passionately. In practice neutrality has probably become increasingly difficult as feminist notions have become disseminated to a wider public. Nowadays even the most conservative Bible study group finds that taking Pauline writings seriously tends to set it at odds with the dominant culture, and often reveals sharp divisions within its own membership. Secondly, there is a problem that Christian activists through the centuries confronted when they threw in their lot with political campaigns: enthusiasm has a habit of rigidifying into intolerance when it encounters opposition. Christians are regularly reminded 'that all have sinned and come short of the glory of God' (Rom. 3:23), and this might translate practically into resisting critical positions that merely substitute a matriarchy for patriarchy, or even entertaining, as an exercise in humility, the notion that those who oppose feminist interests might also see themselves as serving God.[3]

2. Can anyone become a feminist reader?

In the early stages of feminism, some women's groups excluded men from their proceedings, partly because they felt that women could develop the self-confidence to attend to their own voices only in the absence of male voices, who had no difficulty in assuming their traditional right to a hearing. In America this feeling was exacerbated by bitter memories of the way in which women's voices had been suppressed, even when they were apparently collaborating with politically radical males to fight for equality and freedom from oppression for all black Americans.[4] It will always be easier for women who have in some sense 'found their voices' to look back and dismiss the politics of difference as a form of sexual apartheid necessitated by a particular historical situation, but it may be the case that both individuals and groups will continue to need this stage of self-definition and self-affirmation.[5] Such exclusiveness, however, taken as a final resting-place, might also be thought to develop the politics of the ghetto.[6] If the main goal is seen as improving women's position, this cannot be done without reference to the other half of the population. Moreover, defensive ghetto politics have a tendency to lay all ills at the door of the absent, unindividuated enemy, that sits ill at ease with a Christian belief that women and men were both banished from Eden and are equally entitled to be the recipients of the grace and revelation of God.

There is, of course, the further problem that men by definition cannot have full experiential access to the process of reading 'as a woman'. Even if one takes the view that gender is a social construct, rather than a biological given, most men will have to make a greater imaginative leap than most women to imagine what it might mean to live life on the margins. Nevertheless, just as the early pioneers of feminist criticism, who often owed their own academic training to patriarchal institutions, had to learn to question the validity for women of each critical manoeuvre they executed, so men can be sensitized to feminist issues. As one feminist philosopher expresses it, the process of educating men to become feminist readers is like teaching heavy smokers to detect the smell of smoke on their own clothing: a hard task, but not impossible.[7] In our currently anti-smoking culture, this analogy may seem heavily loaded, but it may also serve as a reminder that 'convert' males are sometimes in danger of being unequally rewarded for their sympathetic stance or having their regenerate views regarded as offering an academic imprimatur to a previously suspect approach.[8]

You will perhaps have noticed the implication in the previous paragraph that being a woman is not of itself a sufficient qualification for becoming a feminist reader and that some women may find it harder than others to achieve this position. Indeed some Marxist-feminist women's groups in the early 1970s were actively hostile to the notion of recruiting 'successful women', who must, they thought, have internalized male ethics to succeed within a patriarchal society. They may have been right, but Christian teaching would surely suggest that although the rich and successful find it harder to pass through the eye of the needle, salvation should be freely offered to all.

Conversely, as feminist criticism has developed more complex theoretical strands, it may also be in danger of alienating or excluding the very marginalized and oppressed it was first designed to serve. Specialist jargon necessarily privileges those with the training to deploy it, and can contrive to make the untrained woman feel just as 'stupid' and disregarded, just as much an 'object for discussion' as she ever felt in the patriarchally dominated intellectual environments. This tension in feminist discourses – between the emphasis upon personal response and the desire to plunder the philosophical, political and psychological language and methodology currently in use in the world of critical theory – is particularly marked in the academic world and merits a little further exploration.

A number of factors lay behind the importance attached to articulating the personal position from which criticism was being voiced. Such a practice offered resistance to the totalizing use of the impersonal, 'objective' view that often masked the obliteration of different views and perspectives. Moreover, women began to feel that it was important to assert that they were reading and writing *as women*: that is to say that they were writing out of a female experience which seemed in many ways to be different from that of male readers. They wished to free themselves from the guilt, leading to disguise, or anonymity, that had frequently characterized previous generations of female writers. Moreover they wished to assert that female experience carried an authority as valid as that previously reserved for critical discourses predicated upon traditional hermeneutics and supported by male institutions, such as the church or the university. These convictions and desires were not, of course, new: Chaucer's wife of Bath flaunted her credentials from 'the school of life' in the face of her church-trained audience:

> Experience, though noon auctoritee
> Were in this world, is right ynogh for me
> To speke of wo that is in mariage.
> For, lordynges, sith I twelve yeer was of age,
> Thonked be God that is eterne on lyve,
> Housbondes at chirche dore I have had fyve . . .

Yet Chaucer's character is, after all, a drag act, whose subsequent flamboyant sophistry in wrenching traditional texts to her own advantage, combined with a militant defence of biological essentialism (the notion that women are inherently and therefore fatalistically defined by physical difference), blind her to the logical implications of her own tale, and so invalidate her reading. The new generation of feminist scholars were bent upon drawing attention to their gender as readers, as part of a larger enterprise of asking the institutions (primarily the universities and the publishing world)[9] responsible for nourishing and promoting critical thinking, to take women's experience seriously as providing themes, sources and an audience for art. This part of the enterprise was able to draw upon the fashion for reader response theories which saw in the 'death of the author' an opportunity for 'the birth of readers' who brought along their baggage of cultural and personal experiences to the work of interpreting the text. Exploited in tandem, reader-response theory and feminist conviction offered support for questioning whether reactions previously labelled 'emotional' might not be as important to take into account as those validated as 'logical' or 'intellectually respectable', particularly in explaining changes in literary fashion or in determining entry to the literary canon. This critical duo was also in a good position to alert readers to any totalitarian tendencies which might be thought to attach to other contemporary critical discourses, offering repeated reminders that the reading community needed to take account of the variety of gender, ethnic and class positions contributing to the potential workforce engaged in the hermeneutic enterprise.

Nevertheless, the notion of 'personal response', even as it evolved within feminist reading communities, had run into a series of problems. In the 1960s there had been much investment in collective women's projects, which were seen as offering an alternative to the typically competitive, individualist structures favoured in male institutions. Academically speaking, this led not only to feminist workshops, but to the slightly bizarre delivery of lectures in alternate paragraphs by the joint authors, Gilbert and Gubar. Though doubtless conceived in a spirit of cooperation, in practice it seemed to seek to evade individual responsibility. Again, collective enterprise was envisaged as a sharing of different kinds of gifts, but working in 'the same Spirit' (1 Cor. 12:4).

Once again the particular political background against which feminism was developing in the United States raised pertinent questions for feminist writers and readers. In her 1983 essay 'Blood, Bread and Poetry: The Location of the Poet', Adrienne Rich had written,

> I write for the still-fragmented parts in me, trying to bring them together. Whoever can read and use any of this, I write for them as well. I write in full knowledge that the majority of the world's illiterates are women, that I live in a technologically advanced country where forty per cent of the people can barely read and twenty per cent are functionally illiterate. I believe that these facts are directly connected to the fragmentations I suffer in myself, that we are all in this together.

This apologia seems to mark an interesting transitional phase between earlier female involvement in fighting racial discrimination, where cooperation had seemed all-important in the pursuit of the 'melting pot philosophy' of American citizenship, and the more recent ethnocentric 'patchwork quilt' philosophy of a nation. Although Rich claims 'full knowledge' of the divisive forces still at work there is a shade of ethnic patronage in the notion that her writing cannot only speak to, but speak for or figure the fragmentation and sufferings of other women whose experiences are so vastly dissimilar. The problem of patronage by the articulate of the inarticulate is particularly clear here because of the ease with which it can be identified against its political backdrop, but the temptation to turn 'speaking up for' into silencing other dissimilar voices, so often the subject of the feminist attack upon patriarchalism, is a particular danger of varieties of the academic feminist critical enterprise. Toril Moi has been forceful in her attack upon Julia Kristeva's theoretical position because of its tendency to obscure the particularities of disadvantage by lumping them together 'on the margins'. Christianity's global perspective might be of help here as a reminder that marginality is only the product of one group or position's perspective. Worldwide religious orders might also offer models of 'sisterhood' more fully responsive to varieties of difference than has been true of the utopian ideal of sisterhood which was sometimes 'coercive in its unacknowledged universalism, its unrecognized exclusions'.[10] Christianity also has a long tradition of being able to hold in synthesis the notion of the universality of the human experience, and the significance of the individual, by appealing to the doctrine of an 'original sin', in which we all share, alongside the absolute need for personal salvation.

3. Is there anyone left to become a feminist reader?

It would of course be unfair to suggest that the problematic nature of feminism's appeal to the authority of 'women's experience' has not occurred to feminist theorists, working from a number of different positions. From the first, the notion of 'women' as possessing an identity beyond time and place has been both the irritant that brought the movement into being and the object of much internal debate.

Adrienne Rich's statement of mission, cited in the last paragraph, perfectly encapsulates the notion that, mutilated and scattered as womanhood has been by centuries of suffering, there is a process of personal healing and reassembly that bears direct relation to the corporate body of 'women'. Deconstructionist theory has directly challenged such thinking by dissolving the responsible individual consciousness, with access to 'truth' and 'reality' upon which to ground decisions, into a site upon which various larger cultural, historical and other unrecognizable forces have constructed an illusion of selfhood. This 'disappearance of the subject' calls into question the high value early feminism ascribed to identifying the personal position of the woman as critic. Indeed post-structuralism's view, that personal identity is not a given, but only brought into existence and defined as that which can be perceived as different by and from others, contrives to suggest that feminists who continue to work within the confines of liberal humanist assumptions are guilty of unthinking complicity with 'traditional bourgeois' unproblematized 'phallic' ideology. By clinging to the 'autobiographical fallacy', Anglo-American feminist criticism has been fatally compromised, claim such critics as Mary Jacobus, Julia Kristeva, Hélène Cixous and Toril Moi. In such hands as Elaine Showalter's, they complain, texts become transparent, passive (feminine) mediums, through which to catch sight of male-defined 'reality'. The unregenerate, old-fashioned nature of such an enterprise is further proved by its tendency to work with 'nineteenth-century realist texts', and steer clear of, or find fault with, the teasing strategies of modernist or postmodernist texts.[11] 'Gynocriticism', a word invented by Elaine Showalter to describe the study of women's writing, conducted without benefit of the critical tools of male aesthetics, and against a freshly revealed history of women's culture, is, of course, seen as part of the retrograde ghetto mentality of this school's work.

As the vocabulary of the attack upon the unproblematized 'authority' of women's experience suggests, the attack upon the liberal humanist culture, within which Ellen Moers, Sandra Gilbert and Susan Gubar, Myra Jehlen and others have been perceived as working, was not confined to the artilleries of postmodernism. Marxist feminists feel that the attempt of such leading female academics to mark out a separate sphere for their studies within the prevailing institutions, combined with their naïve belief in the representational, mimetic status of literature, necessarily confines them to the old 'bourgeois' politics of oppression. For Marxist critics, placing emphasis upon the individual consciousness and its powers of self-determination is a delusive carrot waved by a bourgeois, capitalist society, to distract from the need for a radical socialist overhaul of this very system.

The challenge of deconstruction and Marxism to the notion of selfhood poses a problem for Christians. Reduce man or woman to an Aeolian wind-harp, played upon by various cultural cross-currents, and concepts such as responsible decision-making, blame or guilt lose much of their ethical potency, though it is surely worth remarking that the influence of human personalities is itself a constituent part of these cultural forces, just as texts are not merely shaped by the culture, but contribute to its re-shaping. In practice, feminism's overriding commitment to the work of revealing and redressing oppression may provide the Christian's way out of the philosophical impasse. Postmodernism's revelations of a multiplicity of possible subject positions, and Marxism's resistance to the impotence generated by an obsessive concern with the individual, can usefully be harnessed to provoke a practical and compassionate awareness of other's needs, and a stringent examination of the institutions and ideologies within which we each work. Just as no feminist literary critic would allow herself to become becalmed upon a sea of theoretical introspection, so for Christians spiritual and intellectual effort have always been most safely judged by the practical fruits they bear. A religion which elevates love and fellowship may find these central values jeopardized if its intellectual energy is wholly focused upon locating the centres of power either in society at large or in its own institutions. Conversely, the speed at which feminism has developed might also provide a counsel of caution: enthusiasm to embrace new ideologies requires the balance provided by time in which to examine whether they can be harnessed to the central enterprise, or whether they will prove to be at least incompatible and at worst a dangerously subversive force.

4. Can readers be damaged by anti-feminist texts?

One of the earliest forms of feminist criticism was a concern to examine how women had been presented in literary texts through the ages. Certain stereotypes quickly emerged: women had often been polarized into victims or aggressors: Snow Whites or wicked stepmothers; silent sufferers or malicious gossips; hectoring viragos or 'patient Griseldas'. Literature, it was argued, had been used as a weapon by which phallocentric thought could characterize women as the 'other', always relying for their definition upon the degree of their compliance with or militant opposition to a male norm. Furthermore, many male texts seemed to weaken women's self-image, not only by leaving female readers no female spaces outside the stereotypical to inhabit, but by encouraging them to an identification with the male position that seemed to approximate to the text's desiderated norm for human achievement.

More recently, attempts have been made to explain why, discounting their importance in the patriarchally defined canon and 'academic system', demonstrably sexist texts should continue to appeal to good feminist readers. One response has been to suggest that 'the male text draws its power over the female reader from authentic desires, which it rouses and then harnesses to the process of immasculation'.[12] Well-tried feminist reading techniques such as role and voice reversal can play their part in winnowing 'authentic desires' from the ideologically inscribed chaff. Rendering conscious the androcentricity of so many of our reading habits has its uses, but when we start to apply these to the Bible, a patriarchal text by most definitions, the dangers of such critical tricks also become clear. While writing this I turned on the radio and caught a report of protests directed to the Dean and Chapter of Coventry Cathedral for allowing a service to take place in which an effigy of a female crucified Christ had been paraded. The device was defended on the grounds that this image had been used as a reminder of the suffering of women everywhere. Yet here the 'trick' is revealed as dangerously simplistic because it fails to take account of both historical context and theological implication.

Given the patriarchal culture from which biblical texts emerged, it is unsurprising that God is gendered as a male. Daphne Hampsen, who describes herself as a post-Christian feminist theologian, argues that by choosing to reveal himself at a precise historical moment in such a culture, the Christian God renders himself unacceptable to feminists. Her answer is to abandon all attempts to re-read texts for more acceptable interpretations and 'start afresh'.[13] Laying aside the impossibility of 'discarding' all patriarchal texts as part of our hermeneutic tradition, her proposal for a fresh start seems conveniently to ignore the fact that the new religion in which she hopes to encode future 'hopes and aspirations' will also have a historical entry point, possibly equally suspect to a genderless thirtieth century, and seems unlikely to escape the ideological baggage in which 'our hope and aspirations' come wrapped once we resort to any religious mythology.[14]

The image of the female Christ also seems fraught with theological misunderstanding, because it fails to distinguish between the idea of Christ identifying with the suffering of the oppressed and a romanticized notion that suffering renders victims spiritually superior and therefore better able to mediate Christian salvation. In effect it confuses the notion of Christ identifying with humanity by becoming man, with humans, male and female, becoming identical with Christ.

Gynocriticism has been seen as another way out of the impasse of discovering male strategies in every text and every aesthetic judgment. By recovering a woman's literary heritage, not only were lost voices to be restored, but the economic, social and political conditions contributing to the experiences validated in the male canon were to be challenged. Such an enterprise tends to place a high value upon 'strong women' who have in their day offered resistance, or at least employed their voices in subverting male conventions. The tendency to conflate author and text, 'voice' and construct, is instantly apparent. The pleasure taken by late twentieth-century feminist readers in the powers of a Toni Morrison to transform the story of black female oppression into tales of female resourcefulness all too easily reads backwards into disapproval of female authors who resisted a utopian vision.[15] The rallying cry most often associated with this form of criticism: 'listening to our mothers' voices' also gives me pause for thought. Those of us who are mothers may feel that the precise point at which we hear our mothers' voices echoing in the things we say to our children is the point at which we have become trapped within a culturally defined image of motherhood: over-protective nurturers who can only voice concern in nagging tones as we stand on the doorstep, half-resenting children's ventures into an outside world of non-domestic concerns.

The problem of retreating into a woman's world, without prior discussion of what exactly constitutes 'the female', begs very important questions and can lead to contradictory positions. It is thus possible to condemn all images of women as carer, nurse or mother as an attempt by the patriarchy to marginalize women into positions always supportive of or subordinate to male needs; this in turn can lead to being unconsciously patronizing of people of either gender, but particularly women, who choose to take on these roles. Alternatively, these roles are sometimes arrogated as images to be valorized in support of a notion that sees them as biologically encoded qualities of women, contra-defined against such qualities as 'male' ambition, competitiveness or aggression. By analogy it may also seem that feminism is prepared to embrace almost any marginal group within its sympathies, simply because it has been defined as a deviant 'other': it therefore finds it easier to explore lesbianism or homosexuality than to open up the roles valued by 'mainstream' morality. Once again these confusions are particularly apparent when transferred to the theological arena. Daphne Hampsen, for instance, manages both to object to mariolatry as implying an inferior position for women and to take exception to the fatherhood or male image of God. It would seem that what may need attention here are the concepts of fathering and mothering as biologically defined attributes. The recent preponderance of single parent families, where mothers have become breadwinners by default and fathers have been notable only as absences, might suggest that it would be better to describe God not as 'our Father' but as one who displays fatherly qualities. It may be that some recent attempts to image God and the Christian life in terms more acceptable to feminists will also run aground because of their biological exclusivity: rethinking the sacrificial ideal of Christianity offered to women by turning from the Madonna Pietà to the more positive image of childbirth may make childless women feel doubly underprivileged and excluded.

5. Do French feminist theories have anything to say to Anglo-American Christian readers?

The distinguishing feature of French feminist theory has been its attention to this very question of sexual difference, what it consists in and whether it should be thought of as coterminous with biological difference. For some feminists, working out of the Anglo-American tradition, the philosophical and psychoanalytical traditions within which the French debate was conducted automatically deprived it of the true feminist imprimatur: its theoretical manoeuvrings were perceived as neglecting the actual oppression of real women both in history and in the contemporary world, privileging textual 'play' over political engagement. Julia Kristeva is a Bulgarian-born, French psychoanalytical linguistician. She has come to suspect the assumption of collective responsibility by 'sectarian female groups' of potential totalitarianism, and claims that 'the time has perhaps come for each and every woman, in whatever way we can, to confront the controversial values once held to be universal truths by our culture, and to subject them to an interminable analysis. In a sense this may be a theoretical task; it is above all a matter of ethics'.[16] The French debate's allegedly apolitical nature, taking place at the heart of a traditionally anti clerical, intellectual arena, has tended to make it less accessible both to Christian appropriation and Christian criticism. Possibly we are also seeing the difference between the Catholic heritage of authority invested within the church's teaching, against which French intellectual life defined itself, and Protestantism's vested interest in the individual and the particularities of individual texts within which Anglo-American academic traditions developed.

Paradoxically, the event that gave rise to 'Protestant' feminism's distrust of French theory was a political statement that precisely expressed their differences of approach. Members of the influential French feminist groups known as 'Psych et Po' (Psychanalyse et Politique) demonstrated under the banner 'Down with feminism' on International Women's Day because they felt that, by demanding political acknowledgment from the present political systems, women were colluding in the patriarchal process that transformed genderless desires into culturally constructed binary oppositions always aligned along sexual frontiers. The enterprise was either profoundly revolutionary, or unpractically utopian, according to your point of view. They turned from woman-centred activities, such as the study of female authors and texts interpreted, in however sophisticated a manner, as predicated upon the experiences of 'real life', to considering the 'feminine' as it is inscribed and decoded in writing.

Two further, and apparently contradictory, feminist anxieties were triggered by the French approach.[17] By taking the whole debate back to pre-linguistic origins in 'the voice of the mother', which exists as a 'voiceless' form of communication inscribed in the body, needing no entry into a male world of abstract logical discourse, their work seemed at first to offer as much of a threat to such treasured projects as recovering the female tradition in writing as ever the patriarchy had done. Yet the intention of French feminists operating within the psycho-analytical tradition was to recuperate 'the voice of the mother', experienced as a voiceless form of communication inscribed in the body, from the evolutionary primitive associations that Lacan's reading of this as a 'pre-Symbolic' or 'Imaginary' order had given it. Lacan's notion of entry into the Symbolic order as a gain consequent upon the Law of the Father, segregating male from female and thus imposing an awareness of gender difference, became, under French feminist reading, as much a loss of the freedom which existed prior to the appearance of a male world of abstract logical discourse.[18] Secondly, however, by working with the endless play of language by which Derrida sought to free the multiple nature of language from the constricting formula of binary difference, these French feminist theorists, it was feared, were diverting attention to language rather than the lived experience of oppression as the root of the feminist crusade.

It might at first seem that French theory potentially poses just as much of an implicit threat to our reading of certain kinds of text as certain 'purist' Anglo-American positions ever did. Searching always for evidences of 'feminine' writing that destabilizes (Kristeva's preferred position), or offers a revolutionary challenge (the position Cixous adopts) from within the text to the stable, symbolic order of logically constructed discourse, their procedures work best with and make most use of modernist texts, which encourage a post-Freudian awareness of the challenge to stable meaning and identity offered by the unconscious. While it is true that Cixous in particular emphasizes the importance of using 'texts' that 'touch' her, by which she seems to mean the texts, whether written by men or women, in which she can most clearly recognize the element of 'feminine' rebellion, she has nevertheless repeatedly been drawn to biblical texts. If, as Kristeva would suggest, 'feminine' writing has to do with that which cannot be represented, that which is not spoken and resists naming, and can only ever become visible in the gaps, margins or disjunctures of patriarchal discourse, where better than the Bible to examine the ways in which cultural constraints and logical codes have endeavoured to suppress and bury the disturbing, revolutionary and Unnameable? It is only fair to say that Kristeva herself would reject this identification of 'otherness' with the absolute other of Godhead.[19]

Another facet of French feminist theory is the frequent attention to the 'maternal' or 'motherhood' as providing a route to the understanding of the human predicament. Motherhood is seen as occupying the borderline between the pre-Oedipal stage of pre-linguistic chaos and involvement in experiencing the process of loss, or acknowledgment of 'otherness', that leads to the need for language. For Kristeva, that recognition, once embodied for western society in the figure of the grieving Virgin Mary beside the cross, must now be relocated, since the crumbling away of the religious edifice, in the 'corporeal and psychological suffering of childbirth'.[20] Theoretically, this position is safeguarded from the claim to a universality that in fact excludes many women by the assertion that the 'feminine' is not coterminous with the biological fact of being a woman. Nevertheless, the dangers of trying to turn language more normally associated with clinical sexual differentiation into a philosophical trope can be seen at their clearest in Hélène Cixous' lecture, 'Difficult Joys'. Although she starts from the premise, 'I don't believe in rigid positions or categories, or oppositions. I don't think that women are sheerly women and men, men', the abstract concept of androgyny is far harder to hold on to when the collective noun slides into the singular: 'Sometimes it has to do with the difficulty for a woman to affirm her powerlessness in front of those for whom she feels responsible, that is, somehow a woman is always bound to be a mother.'[21] The conclusion of this lecture contrives to suggest that 'femininity' is defined by motherhood. Men can thus gain metaphoric access to this quality or position, but 'women', as a result of their cultural construction, are more likely than men to occupy this position. Whatever the philosophical distinction, the language employed when speaking from notes demonstrates a tendency to collapse back into an everyday understanding of these words: 'mothering' all too quickly elides with the biological motherhood that is likely to have forced women into ethical consciousness.

> When you start thinking in terms of the ethics of writing and reading, then you may become a mother whether you are a man or a woman. (But in our time it's mostly women who are driven by experience to think ethically.) And then you know that you are going to give birth to all kinds of persons and effects of identification.[22]

A more orthodox Christian critique might see this not so much as a question of slippage but as a consequence of an endemic materialism that wholly neglects the possibilities inherent in the spirit/body matrix of Christian theology.

This attempt to harness the vocabulary of sexual differentiation to a non-gender specific programme is but one of the linguistic strategies employed by French feminist theorists and others for effecting the escape from the prison-house of patriarchal discourse.[23] One of Luce Irigaray's most significant contributions in the field was her attempt to recover the role of 'hysteric', traditionally used to denigrate women's supposed affinity with the mysterious, primitive and uncivilized forces of irrationality, as a 'privileged place' where woman display the symptoms of their forbidden speech. Hysteria, which can take the form either of silence or of an unintelligible mimicry of the learnt patriarchal discourse, is ascribed a positive value because it both caricatures and subverts the dominant discourse.[24] Once again, opponents within the feminist movement claim that this is another verbal sleight of hand that does not in fact recuperate women from the designated roles of mutes or babblers to which the discourse of oppression first condemned them. Between silence and a scream, how are women to find an effective voice in the current political debate?[25] The irritation with which the fruits of the psychoanalyst's couch are greeted by American women professors striving to challenge such stereotypes in their daily encounters with academe is easily intelligible. Nevertheless, Christian history would support the view that women have repeatedly managed to transform the various, apparently pejorative, descriptions of 'ranting hysteric', '*silent* witness', or '*vessel* of Divine Grace' into *creative* ways of interpreting the evangelical imperative.

6. *Speaking personally*

I should be loath to suggest that Christian feminists should simply rest content with subterfuge and tactful subversion as the means through which to fulfil their Christian duty to preach the word. Nevertheless, it is easier to accept such strategies as milestones on the route to a universal recognition that '*male and female* he created them' (Gn. 1:27), if we recall that it is 'the same Spirit' working in all (1 Cor. 12:4), and that the human purpose is to recall the divine image, not to dispute degrees of relationship. If we refuse to allow as full a scope for the idea of the feminine as historically we have done for the masculine, we are in effect propping up the barriers preventing us from recovering the Edenic vision and so ignoring the redemptive purpose of Christ's incarnation.

In my opinion, feminist critical theory cannot be neglected, if only because it provides a battlefield where the discerning reader is forced into thinking out the cross-implications of many another contemporary hermeneutical ideology in a context which refuses to allow neat packaging in mutually independent theoretical boxes. Like other essayists in this book, I am in favour of turning this critical school's strategies back upon itself and plundering its diverse coffers for ideas that seem not only compatible with, but illuminatory of, Christian purposes. There are moments when feminism's originating vision of oppression, marginality and difference can seem very easily to translate into the Christian desire to work ceaselessly for 'heaven on earth' if (and this 'if' is still the stumbling block for many feminists) we are prepared also to embrace the notion of 'goodwill toward men'. Perhaps the radical equality of opportunity afforded by Christian redemption really can provide the route envisaged by French feminist theory for escaping from simple binary oppositions. If so, the exciting position in which this might leave Christian feminists to exercise their 'diversities of gifts' is suggested in one of the more positive articulations of recent feminist speculation:

> Perhaps because we do not, as women, feel we have everything to lose, but in fact have everything to gain, it is easier for us to be more radical, more daring in envisioning change, more 'feminine' than it is possible for men to be.[26]

Some practical points for discussion

As women's studies courses make their way on to the academic syllabus in institutions, forced by the numbers game to the increasing use of lectures over colloquia, what practical means can teachers and students invent to resist the authoritarian positions often implicit in conventional teaching methods and structures? Is it (or should it be) possible to grade, and therefore fail, readings of texts that are based upon particular individuals' explorations of the self they bring to their understanding of a text? If we refuse such a possibility are we thereby once again excluding feminists from access to the posts which might allow them to change an institution's thinking? Is such thinking itself bedevilled by a liberal humanism no longer adequate to the demands of a postmodernist culture? Can Christianity, which lays claim to an existence *in* without becoming *of* this world provide a way out of a secular feminist impasse?

7

Words and presences: the spiritual imperative

Kevin Mills

Introductory

In his General Editor's Preface to the *New Accents* series, Terence Hawkes writes of the radical changes apparent in the field of literary studies:

> The erosion of the assumptions and presuppositions that support the literary disciplines in their conventional form has proved fundamental. Modes and categories inherited from the past no longer seem to fit the reality experienced by a new generation.[1]

Profound social and cultural upheavals have been augmented, in the field of the human sciences, by equally profound shifts in linguistic and hermeneutic (interpretation) theory, to produce a ferment of critical ideas and arguments, and a bewildering array of theories, schools and subdisciplines. Whereas structuralism seemed, for a while, to offer a new explanatory system which would unify and renew those disciplines (particularly literary and anthropological studies), deconstruction served to undermine that confidence, lodging its disturbing questions against the fundamental presuppositions of the structuralist enterprise.

Many of these shifts and upheavals have involved the rejection of *Christian* values, the erosion of *Christian* assumptions and presuppositions. For example, deconstruction and postmodernism have often been characterized as atheistic discourses which pull the rug out from under the feet of those who claim access to truth, and who entertain ideas of an ultimate reality. In this chapter I want to examine, as closely as space will allow, the claims of deconstruction and of certain forms of postmodernism, from a Christian perspective, and then go on to offer a possible line of resistance. Given the complexity of contemporary theory, and the brevity of this essay, all that I can do is try to indicate what seem to me to be the main lines of thought in these approaches. This is necessarily an exercise in over-simplification. It is intended to prompt interest and further study, and not to provide an easily grasped handle on contemporary theoretical issues.

I will not make any attempt to deal with deconstruction or postmodernism as specifically literary phenomena, for three reasons. Firstly, taking account of the difficulty of much contemporary criticism, I believe that the background of ideas needs to be given as much space as possible. Secondly, other chapters (such as John Schad's reading of Thomas Pynchon's *The Crying of Lot 49*) offer a much better insight into that literature than I could provide. Thirdly, even though deconstruction and postmodernism have each had an impact on literary studies, they are not exclusively, or even primarily, literary phenomena, and are not really explicable within the framework of literary disciplines.

1. Derrida's deconstruction

There are many difficulties associated with attempting to give an adequate account of deconstruction. The very process of definition which such an account seems to involve is a target of the deconstructive approach to language. This difficulty is compounded by the fact that, despite its use by literary critics, it is not a critical methodolgy which can be described, learned and then applied to literary texts. The critic is not able to identify and appropriate a set of analytical procedures which together make up a pre-formed deconstructive technique. Perhaps the least reductive way to present it, without wading through a large amount of complex technical detail, is by means of some brief quotations from Jacques Derrida's *Of Grammatology*, one of the definitive texts of deconstruction (although the notion of a 'definitive text' is very much in question in deconstruction). Derrida characterizes his approach as an immanentist one – it does not import a set of standards (either literary or moral), does not appeal to external details (biographical, historical, and the like), and does not employ predetermined interpretative devices (such as genre distinctions, intention, allegory and irony). He writes: 'The movements of deconstruction do not destroy structures from the outside. They are not possible . . . except by inhabiting those structures . . .'[2]

What makes deconstruction possible, as an immanentist approach to texts, is an alarmingly simple opposition which Derrida evokes: 'no practice is ever totally faithful to its principle'.[3] Deconstructing a text involves locating the points at which principles are betrayed, problematized or even invalidated by practice. If textual practices were faithful to their principles then deconstruction would have no room to work, no conceptual-metaphoric 'play' to exploit. This distinction between practice and principle requires that both are recoverable from, or discernible within, the text. How can we know that any given practice is not faithful to its principle unless we are also able to learn that principle from that practice? Here, the whole project of deconstruction can be seen to depend upon this opposition (at which point it is untrue to its own principle of showing the instability of meaning produced by binary oppositions of this kind!). Of course, the deconstructionist would point out here, as Derrida says, 'deconstruction always in a certain way falls prey to its own work'.[4] So, deconstruction works within the text like Samson in the temple of Dagon.

2. *Signifier and signified*

Developing an approach to the structural linguistics of Ferdinand de Saussure (and so to the whole structuralist enterprise which derived from it), Derrida deconstructs the binary opposition between the components of the linguistic sign – the 'signifier' and the 'signified'. Saussure insisted that the signified is a 'psychic imprint', an image in the mind (such as the picture that is conjured in my mind when I hear the word 'cat'). Language, then, does not unite words and 'things', but sounds and images. The mental images evoked by language are, however, also signifiers: they represent the world of objects. Language can never make contact with that world; all that it can do is *represent a representation* of it. Derrida argues that if this is the case then 'the signified always already functions as a signifier', so 'the difference between signified and signifier *is nothing*'.[5] He sees the insistence on the opposition between signifier and signified as 'theological' because it depends upon the positing of a 'transcendental signified', an absolute term which anchors meaning beyond the play of signs and the multiplicity of interpretations. Without recourse to such an Origin the 'play of signification' is endless, like the chain of reflections between two mirrors.

This 'transcendental signified' derives, in western metaphysics, from the Greek *logos*, a term familiar to Christians from John's gospel, where it is identified with Christ. Derrida's strategy involves replacing the *logos* with the *trace*: '*The trace is in fact the absolute origin of sense in general. Which amounts to saying . . . that there is no absolute origin of sense in general.*'[6] This raises some difficult and challenging questions for Christian readers. Does this view of language demand that we rethink our understanding of Jesus as the Word made flesh? Or, is it the case that language simply looks different when we start from a position of faith? Should we perhaps mistrust (deconstruct) the opposition *logos* versus trace? If so, how are we to think about language in a way that provides an adequate response to the power of deconstruction? Before engaging further with these problems, I want to offer a brief account of postmodernism.

3. Postmodern conditions: Lyotard

Postmodernism is not a single monolithic set of ideas or beliefs that can be neatly summarized and assessed. In fact, it could be seen as the intellectual acknowledgment that knowledge is reduced and falsified by the kind of categorization applied to it by philosophers, historians of ideas, or builders of explanatory systems. Postmodern thought stresses the plurality of political opinion, the diversity of human interests, and the challenge of cultural difference to any belief in universal truths or values. Drawing on the philosophy of Frederich Nietzsche, it asserts that truth is a product of the 'will to power', and that 'knowledge is power'. On this account, the Christian claim to know God through Jesus Christ should be seen as an attempt to assert hermeneutic mastery over the biblical text and religious experience, and to claim an advantage over those who do not know God. The church, by the same token, is an instrument of political power which helps to maintain the *status quo* with threats of eternal punishment and promises of eternal bliss.

Jean-François Lyotard defines the postmodern as 'incredulity toward metanarratives'.[7] The term 'metanarratives' (or 'grand narratives') refers to the old explanatory discourses such as philosophical systems, religious beliefs and political theories, emerging out of the Enlightenment elevation of Reason, and in which Reason is the ultimate test of truth. These 'grand narratives', used to underpin and validate the production of knowledge within the limits of learned disciplines (such as the sciences, politics and economics), have broken down under the strain of cultural and linguistic change and scientific progress. These have broken down to the point where it is now necessary, Lyotard claims, to have done with any appeal to such *passé* notions as 'reason' or 'truth', and to look for more localized replacements for those now defunct universal values.

In *The Postmodern Condition*, Lyotard proceeds by setting up a number of oppositions, establishing networks of positive and negative terms. This can give rise to a familiar kind of criticism, one which has produced large numbers of 'deconstructive' readings of all manner of texts. But it has a peculiar force here, since the notion of the 'postmodern' involves thinking the radical non-correspondence (heterogeneity) of modes of knowledge or ways of thinking which cannot be brought into meaningful contact. Adapting the notion of mutually unintelligible 'language games' from the work of Ludwig Wittgenstein, Lyotard writes of hermetically sealed 'phrase regimens' between which there can be no interaction. He offers no explanation as to how such a situation can be reconciled with the setting up of the oppositions which he wants to establish (or takes for granted) between 'science' and 'narrative', 'homology' and 'paralogy', 'expert' and 'philosopher', 'modern' and 'postmodern', 'consensus' and 'dissensus'. The terms in each pair cannot be commensurable if they really belong to radically different, mutually unintelligible language games. They could not, in that case, engage one another in opposition.

Lyotard refers to the small-scale replacements for the 'grand narratives' as 'little narratives'. They do not need to be capable of explaining or validating large systems of knowledge, since knowledge is now broken down into 'phrase regimens' or 'language games'. Such limited discourses are no longer necessarily judged by reason. 'Paralogical' explanations (explanations which transgress the dictates of reason) are deemed to be just as effective. This raises the question: Is it possible to ground meaning in non-meaning, or reason in un-reason? Paralogy is the seizure of reason, the negation of the only faculty that could possibly define paralogy. If reason is no longer able to serve as a ground for some 'grand narrative', how is 'paralogy' to be recognized? From what 'little narrative', what non-reasonable point of view, is Lyotard able to observe the break-up of knowledge into these phrase regimens? Does not the diagnosis of this postmodern condition become another grand narrative, surveying the entire field of human knowledge?

4. Postmodern realities: Baudrillard

Jean Baudrillard, following Nietzsche's genealogical tracing of the emergence of truth out of metaphors (mistaken for concepts), offers a different account of postmodernity. Simulation replaces the 'real' and the 'true', for Baudrillard, so that there is no getting beyond appearance to any underlying reality, and any attempt to do so falls prey to the delusion that 'truth' was ever more than a convenient fiction. The postmodern age, then, is characterized by the 'hyperreal': the mass-media production of 'public opinion'; the rhetoric of political campaigns; the 'reality' of Disneyland (which is there, Baudrillard says, 'to conceal the fact that it is the "real" country').[8] Watergate, he claims, played a similar role, in that it served as a palliative against the unmasking of the 'incomprehensible ferocity' and 'fundamental immorality' of the capitalist system. The episode was characterized as 'scandalous' in order to reinforce belief in the system that could expose and purge such aberrations.[9]

Despite Baudrillard's strenuous disavowals, a reality which underlies appearance has to be smuggled into his rhetoric. In the above quotation about Disneyland, he refers to *concealed fact*. This suggests a deceptive appearance, covering over an accessible truth. What status can possibly be attributed to 'facts' as distinct from appearance, if, as Baudrillard claims, 'only simulacra exists'?[10] A similar rhetorical gesture occurs later in the essay when he discusses Watergate. Claiming that the scandal was a dissimulation, he adds: 'Today, the task is to conceal the fact that there is none.'[11] That there was no scandal, that the underlying system is corrupt, is a 'fact' to be concealed under dissimulating appearance. But, if fact and appearance are equated in the 'hyperreal', then 'concealed fact' is an oxymoron: fact is precisely that which cannot be concealed. The truth is that it is impossible to make any claims at all, even that there is a 'postmodern condition', or a 'hyperreality', without some notion of *fact* as opposed to *appearance*. The very idea of a 'condition' demands a recognition that certain defining characteristics correspond with what is really the case.

The very process of describing the 'hyperreal' is self-defeating, since it involves interpreting the effects of our media-saturated society. Interpretation involves arranging the evidence according to certain strategies, or towards a certain end: every act of interpretation involves an exchange of the apparent for the discernible. If 'hyperreality' had any validity, then it would be utterly beyond diagnosis from within the 'hyperreal', just as the postmodern condition requires that we suspend its characteristic epistemology in order to recognize the inevitability of that very epistemology.

5. Christian postmodernism?

Christian approaches to literary criticism have often had a partially obscurantist tendency, whether this has involved a determination that Christian thinking should work to its own agenda, rather than to that of secular thought, or just the well-known (ecclesiastical) failing of arriving late for everything. When, for example, C. S. Lewis wrote of the contrast between New Testament imitative practice and the language of 'creative', 'original' and 'spontaneous' art, the target seems to have been Romantic aesthetics rather than contemporaneous ideas about tradition and the 'escape from personality' propounded by T. S. Eliot.[12] More recently T. R. Wright has elected not to engage with the challenge of deconstruction, opting instead summarily to distance it from Christian thought. He writes: 'The belief that language does point to a "real" referent, however indirectly, seems to me to be crucial to Christian faith.'[13] Whatever sympathy I have with this claim is tempered by the need to argue that it cannot be asserted effectively unless the linguistic difficulties raised against such a position by deconstruction are addressed and overcome.

Some attempts (Thomas Altizer, Mark Taylor, for example), have been made to reconstruct theology in line with the anti-metaphysical thrust of deconstruction and the postmodern rejection of universal values. Kevin Hart's *The Trespass of the Sign* (1990) effectively exposes the weakness of some such adaptations, and goes on to argue that, despite its characteristic use, deconstruction is not necessarily atheistic. Hart's counter-claim is that negative theology (which proceeds by asserting the inade-quacy of language to describe God, and is often associated with mystical experience) is a deconstructive discourse which resists the 'illusions' of metaphysics. I have written elsewhere about the problems associated with Hart's concentration on negative theology.[14] Here, it can be observed that deconstruction and postmodernism need to be engaged critically from a Christian perspective, rather than accommodated and accepted as a challenge to rethink theology in a post-theistical era. I want to resist the belief that postmodernism confronts Christian thought with a *fait accompli* to which we simply have to adjust as well as we can, and to suggest that deconstruction can be a useful strategy in that resistance. I am not suggesting that a deconstructive approach can simply be adopted by the Christian reader without any qualms, but that engaging critically with it can yield important insights.

6. Logos *and trace*

I return now to the problems raised by my earlier assessment of deconstruction and language, in order to reconsider it alongside Paul's distinction between the letter and the spirit. That distinction is crucial here, not only because it suggests a Christian view of language and interpretation, but also because Paul's assertion that 'the letter kills, but the Spirit [or spirit] gives life' (2 Cor. 3:6) is often cited as a classic statement of what Derrida calls 'logocentrism' – the desire for a 'transcendental signified', without which language becomes a freeplay of unattached signifiers. The problematic of the letter and the spirit is, for Derrida, carried in the 'presence-absence of the trace'. The history of metaphysics, his argument goes, is the history of the reduction of the trace in favour of a positive, active *logos*.

The trace (re)appears when the notion of a 'transcendental signified' is made problematical by the deconstruction of the linguistic sign (see above). Language, however, can be characterized in other ways; it is not necessarily best understood as a system of signs. Paul Ricoeur, in his book *The Rule of Metaphor*, shows that important aspects of linguistic meaning arise at the level of the sentence, and at that of discourse.[15] So, the sign cannot totalize language, and its deconstruction is limited in scope by the explanatory power of the hermeneutics of discourse. That is to say, a critique of the sign may uncover the metaphysical implications of semiotic theory, but it does not finally overthrow the *logos* in favour of the trace.

Quite apart from these technical, linguistic reservations, there is another, specifically Christian problem associated with the *logos*: does the centrality of Jesus Christ, the Word (*logos*) made flesh, make the Christian faith a 'logocentric' metaphysics? Answering that question requires a closer look at the way in which the distinction between the letter and the spirit works. Before moving on to that consideration, I think that it is important to remember two things. In the first place, as I have already pointed out, the *logos* (as a philosophico-linguistic principle) cannot be conjured away by means of a critique of the sign. Also, the role of faith in the production of linguistic meaning, in Christian experience and interpretation (which cannot, for reasons of space, be examined here), is crucial to our understanding of what is meant by *logos*, and will determine our starting point in engaging with these questions.

7. Letter and spirit

The commitment to a distinction between appearance and reality which underlies that between the 'spirit' and the 'letter', is usually regarded with suspicion by deconstructionist critics, and, as I have already shown, by postmodernist thinkers. It has come to be seen as a version of the metaphysical conceit that presence, speech and the intelligible are good, positive terms, while absence, writing and the sensible are bad or negative. Thus, aligning the 'letter' with writing and absence, and the 'spirit' with self-present speech, Christianity is characterized as profoundly Platonic and 'logo-centric'. In *Of Grammatology*, Derrida offers impressive evidence, from a wide range of sources, that these and related binary oppositions persist in the western metaphysical tradition, from Plato to Ferdinand de Saussure. On this account, Christianity, with its privileging of the 'spirit' over the 'letter', simply inherits and perpetuates a 'metaphysics of presence' which is rendered untenable by the deconstruction of the network of oppositions in which it is constituted. In line with this assessment, deconstruction could be characterized as a form of (broadly) anti-Christian polemic, very much akin to other postmodern discourses. I believe this to be mistaken, not simply because to label Christianity as a species of Platonism is profoundly misguided, but also because deconstruction can be useful in arguing precisely this contention. A closer look at Paul's text should help show that his letter/spirit distinction is not reducible to a Platonic metaphysical gesture.

The spirit/letter dichotomy, in Paul's writings, works alongside other oppositional pairs such as 'spiritual' *versus* 'worldly' or 'carnal' (1 Cor. 3:1–4), and 'inward' (or 'hidden', *kryptos*) *versus* 'outward' (or 'apparent', *phaneros*) (Rom. 2:28–29). His use of allegory is often seen as a means of liberating the spiritual meaning and discerning the literal, of making the 'inward' nullify the 'outward', and of decrying the flesh in order to advocate spirituality, in a way that seems to confirm the Platonic influence. In fact, Paul's use of allegory is very limited. He expressly describes his method as allegorical on only one occasion: he interprets the story of Hagar and Sarah (Gn. 21) allegorically in Galatians 4:21–31. The key term, *allēgoroumena* (verse 24), has been translated variously as 'which things *are* an allegory' (Authorized Version, 1611); 'which things *contain* an allegory' (Revised Version, 1881); 'These things *may be taken* figuratively' (New International Version, 1973) (my emphasis). The historical reference of the originary text (that is, the portrayal of actual past events in the Genesis narrative) is progressively accepted, as a shift is evidenced from an understanding of Paul's hermeneutic as calling for the text to be treated as an allegory, through calling for a recognition of the *possibility* of treating it as an allegory, to a position where its status is historical, but it is being interpreted allegorically in this context. The Greek term allows these possibilities, and sustains a tension between levels of meaning which resists the reading of Pauline allegory as a nullifying of the letter by the spirit.[16]

This tension can be discerned in a number of key points in Paul's text, disrupting the Platonic categories and oppositions. In 1 Corinthians 3:1–3a, he writes:

> And I, brethren, could not speak to you as unto spiritual, but as unto carnal, even as unto babes in Christ. I have fed you with milk, and not with meat: for hitherto ye were not able to bear it, neither yet now are ye able. For ye are yet carnal . . .   (Authorized Version)

Carnality, here, is that condition which cannot be fed with 'meat' (the extrapolation of flesh). Meat is for the mature, for the 'spiritual'. This chiasmus, which places the cognate of the body ('meat') alongside the spirit, and in opposition to a carnality that is unable to come to terms with its own cognate, closely resembles the relationship between spirit and letter implied by the tension associated with allegory: the relation of the spirit with its 'opposites' is in question in both cases. This occurs again in 2 Corinthians 3, the most important passage on the letter and the spirit in the Pauline canon.

> . . . ye are manifestly declared to be the epistle of Christ ministered by us, written not with ink, but with the Spirit of the living God; not in tables of stone, but in fleshy tables of the heart.   (2 Cor. 3:3, Authorized Version)

That which is 'hidden' or 'inward' in Romans 2 (the inscription in the heart) is manifest (*phaneroumenoi*) here, and the letter of the

Spirit is no less material than that written in ink. It is written 'in *fleshy* tables of the heart'. Once again the spiritual is not discrete from the physical, but can only be described in terms of an interrelation. The realm of the intelligible is accessible only through that of the sensible.

I do not mean to suggest that Paul does not conceive of a clear demarcation between the 'spiritual' and the 'carnal'. He often seems to be at pains to make just such a distinction, but close attention to the rhetorical construction of his argument reveals the investment of the 'spiritual' in the material: they may be distinguishable, but they are not wholly separable. In other words the *ontological* difference is subordinated to an *epistemological* moment: we may insist on the reality of spiritual experience, but are constrained to do so in terms of its phenomenal occurrence. The very language that we have to employ in order to speak or to write of spirituality, and in which our spiritual experience is often constituted, returns us to the social relations, conventions and conditions which inhere in that language. We come to terms with spirituality not by denying our physical, material and phenomenal existence, but by reading the material signs in which the meaning of our existence is embodied. This is the significance of the incarnation. There is no unmediated access to an undifferentiated spiritual realm from within our material, sensible, mundane and linguistic milieu. 'God is spirit', John's gospel tells us (4:24), but only after insisting that 'the Word was God' (1:1) and that 'the Word became *flesh* and made his dwelling among us' (1:14).

8. Letter and spirit since Paul

The letter and the spirit could be said to name two moments in the life of language. The letter kills, not because it masks an undifferentiated spirit which is available as an alternative to language-mediated communication, but because, as Sollace Mitchell observes, 'no sense can be made of writing except as the mark of an intentional activity'.[17] In other words, the life of language is produced by a sense that it does not appear accidentally or without motivation. Sounds, or marks which strike the senses as deliberate, drive us on to interpret them as acts of communication. Without that sense of a motive or intent, language would be dead. This is necessarily true of any and every form of linguistic utterance, and each use of language thus demands interpretation. Linguistic intentionality witnesses to the validity of the 'spiritual' sense, but does not make it available as anything but a kind of postulate which orients interpretation. The history of the interpretation of the Scriptures, and of literary criticism, illustrates that the hermeneutic venture drives on toward the 'spiritual' meaning because the very idea of literality is wraith-like, elusive and undependable.

The literal sense has never been able to abide alone without some version of its spiritual counterpart. Not content with the spiritual and literal senses, Origen (*c.* 185–254), adding a third (intermediate) meaning to Scripture, began a process of multiplying senses which continued throughout the Middle Ages. Beryl Smalley documents the continued project of attempting to keep the senses of Scripture apart in medieval interpretations. John the Scot, for example, re-divided them into mystery or allegory on the one hand, and symbol on the other. This dichotomy transgressed the letter/spirit distinction by making symbol include metaphor, parable, doctrinal discourse and history, while allegory maintained the interplay of history and its 'meaning'. Paschasius reasserted a primary historical sense as the basis for interpretation to discover a spiritual sense.[18]

The spirit/letter distinction was thus repeatedly reworked and renewed. This continued through the Reformation splitting of the literal sense between 'literal' and 'figurative' meanings; Romantic notions of the sublime shining through the 'translucent' text; Victorian preoccupation with extracting the moral sense from the supernatural *Aberglaube*; Higher Critical concern with the original production of the text as a means of establishing the validity of its continuing authority; Rudolf Bultmann's distinction between 'myth' and '*kerygma*'; and so on.

It is difficult to imagine an absolute literality. So difficult, in fact, that the history of interpretation offers no final definition for it. It does not reside comfortably in the 'historical' sense, because the meaning of history changes in terms of what counts as historical, what socio-cultural norms prevail in its interpretation, and what relation holds between history and historiography. What is taken as 'literal' by one age and culture may be read as 'figural' by another. The developing sense of the historicity of Scripture, evidenced by the changing interpretations of Paul's *allēgoroumena* (described above), attests to this.

This story interweaves with that of literary criticism. When the so-called 'New Criticism' reacted against the positivism and historicism of the nineteenth century, it came to see in poetry what another age had discerned in the Bible – a self-transcending language that would not be totalized by interpretation. The important New Critical notion of 'tension' became a kind of cryptic sublime which poetry expressed, but which the critic could not reproduce in prose. When formalism and structuralism took over, the distinction remained in oppositions such as story and discourse, speech and writing, and surface structure and deep structure. The consideration here was less aesthetic than technical, as it was the signifier or signified structure of the sign which gave rise to such oppositions, rather than any commitment to the consideration of literary value. Although meaning came to be seen as the product of difference, the notion of the linguistic 'signified' still required a presence which privileged self-present speech over writing. The latter is the mark of the author's absence and, consequently, of a lack of control over meaning. I have already indicated what effect deconstruction, in the form of Derrida's critique of the linguistic sign, had on structuralism, the central pillar of which was thus demolished. Post-structuralist criticism developed out of this deconstructive turn.

Deconstruction, then, questions this historical attachment to the spiritual meaning in all its manifestations, yet this very questioning helps to refocus critical attention on Paul's text. If, as I have suggested, that text yields a surprising resistance to logocentric metaphysics, in its disruption of Platonic categories, then the historical development of its interpretative insights may actually represent a reduction of its potential. When reactivated in engagement with deconstruction, that disruptive power is recognizable as a spiritual imperative which orients all interpretation, even that which stresses anti-spiritual, anti-truth (anti)values.

9. Christian engagement

The deconstruction of what appear to be oppositions, showing that they are not *opposed* but are in a reciprocal relationship, in the Pauline text, enables a reading that keeps faith with the text itself, but also helps in the application of this crucial, contested part of Scripture to the issues of representation and interpretation which surround the study of literature today. What is already clear from this Christian engagement with deconstruction is that the confrontation yields a strong paradox: even though deconstruction (in part) proceeds from a disruption of apparently Christian categories, that very disruption allows Christian thought to question deconstruction's approach to the letter and the spirit. From this dialectical entanglement it is possible to produce a

Christian commitment to the critical eloquence of deconstruction as a rigorous mode of textual enquiry, which can be brought to bear on the postmodern questioning of values, whether in its literary or its (anti)philosophical texts. I hope that I have already indicated, in my approach to Lyotard and Baudrillard, that such texts often yield to the pressures of their own rhetoric without the reader having to import any religious or moral arguments. Deconstruction can be useful in alerting the reader to just these rhetorical *aporias* which confront principles with practices, making room for alternative principles and practices.

If the Christian commitment to a spiritual imperative is not negated by deconstruction, but is (paradoxically) strengthened by it, then there is good reason for the latter to be employed by Christian readers to reject the anti-values of the postmodern discourses. I do not mean that we should indulge in a blanket dismissal of all cultural products with a postmodernist label, but that we should learn to probe each textual practice with a critical faculty which has been sharpened by our encounters with the difficult rhetorics of deconstruction and the post-structuralist approaches which have developed from it.

It may be that deconstruction has now begun to pass into literary history, yet another entry in the catalogue of twentieth-century critical fads. Even if this is so, the current debates surrounding literature and interpretation have been shaped by its imperatives, and by the unrelenting rigour of its approach to the problems of language and the text. It is not difficult to believe that reading texts in terms of their blindness to their own insights, or locating unsustainable binary oppositions in their rhetorical make-up, as deconstructionist criticism does, should have palled after more than two decades. It is much more difficult to believe that deconstruction as an approach to philosophy and to the problems of language and representation, crucial to any literary endeavour, has been superseded.

The current 'alternatives' to engaging critically with deconstruction seem to be an uneasy alliance with the deeply problematical and potentially anti-Christian discourses of generic post-structuralism and postmodernism, or an increasingly marginalized naïveté. I do not want to suggest that the endless round of word games and rhetorical sophistry that has passed for literary criticism under the aegis of deconstruction is anything worth preserving, or that its philosophical content is altogether compatible with Christianity. What I *do* wish to claim is that deconstruction can provide a broadening of our hermeneutic competence which is vital in resisting the excesses and pitfalls of postmodernism, and that it is enabling when it comes to reading in a way which is not hedged around with archaeology, philology or theology.

Finally

The relation that holds between deconstruction and the increasingly comprehensive postmodern is not at all clear. There is a continuing debate between those (such as Christopher Norris) who see deconstruction as a philosophical necessity, the rigours of which are in conflict with an anti-rational, post-Enlightenment ideology of linguistic and cultural freeplay, and those who adopt the more common stance of appropriating a broadly deconstructive approach to texts which enshrine precisely those Enlightenment values. These latter postmodernists seem to be ignoring the fact that deconstruction jeopardizes not only the texts to which it is deliberately applied, but also those that thus apply it. There is a telling analogy between deconstruction and nuclear power: the former split the linguistic sign, releasing a potentially devastating force, the full impact of which is yet to be determined, and which, even when 'harnessed' for constructive purposes, is not easily contained. Such a force takes its toll on all who come into contact with it. Linguistic 'radiation sickness' may be one way of describing the postmodern condition, in which the elements of language 'melt with (the) fervent heat' of polemic and counterblast.

In conclusion, it is perhaps needful to point out that, despite its anti-theological origins and deployment, deconstruction represents the kind of rigorous approach to the text which should characterize committed readers. If Christian approaches to interpretation are to avoid charges of obscurantism, and if Christian readers are to develop a critical approach to the postmodern malaise, then we could do worse than allow deconstructionist models to inform our work. This is a daunting prospect. The arguments and the rhetoric involved are extremely difficult to understand, let alone to evaluate, counter and re-deploy according to Christian requirements and criteria. Any such attempts at appropriation, of course, call for cautious assessment of the losses and gains (which I have briefly attempted to outline) and for a keen awareness of what is at stake in our reading. Whether of biblical, 'religious' or 'secular' texts, the task of interpretation is a spiritual imperative, not only because we continually reassert the importance of the letter/spirit distinction whenever we interpret, but also because discerning between them is, in Paul's terms, a matter of life and death.

Suggestions for further reading

Structuralism, deconstruction, post-structuralism
T. Hawkes, *Structuralism and Semiotics* (London: Methuen, 1977).
C. Norris, *Derrida* (London: Fontana, 1987).
J. Sturrock (ed.), *Structuralism and Since* (Oxford: Oxford University Press, 1979).

Postmodernism
H. Lawson, *Reflexivity: The Post-modern Predicament* (London: Hutchinson, 1985).
C. Norris, *What's Wrong With Postmodernism: Critical Theory and the Ends of Philosophy* (New York and Hemel Hempstead: Harvester Wheatsheaf, 1990).

The Bible and contemporary theory
D. Jasper, *The Study of Literature and Religion: An Introduction* (Basingstoke: Macmillan, 2nd ed., 1992).
S. Prickett (ed.), *Reading the Text: Biblical Criticism and Literary Theory* (Cambridge, MA. and Oxford: Blackwell, 1991): a historical survey of how biblical and literary scholarship has been hermeneutically interwoven.
R. Schwartz, (ed.), *The Book and the Text: The Bible and Literary Theory* (Cambridge, MA. and Oxford: Blackwell, 1990).
M. Warner (ed.), *The Bible as Rhetoric: Studies in Biblical Persuasion and Credibility* (New York and London: Routledge, 1990).

Part 2

Texts

8

The Bible and literary study

Leland Ryken

Kevin Mills closed the last chapter by analysing several passages from the biblical text, and recommending several books on the literary study of the Bible. We now need to turn to the biblical text, since the Bible is central not only to the life of a Christian but also to literature and its study. Yet Christian students of literature have found it difficult to maintain this dual allegiance. More often than not, they have regarded the Bible as a sacred book rather than a literary book, and it has seemed more natural to read the Bible for religious purposes than as part of their literary experience.

In previous eras, relegating the Bible to specifically religious uses was easy. But today it is not an option. The Bible is now prominent in literary circles as both a text to be studied and a perceived influence on literature. Meanwhile, literary methods of analysis have invaded religious scholarship and even the pulpit. What sense is a discerning Christian reader to make of all this? Should Christians allow the wedding between literature and the Bible to occur? Or should they declare just impediment why these two should not be joined together?

My claim is that the wedding can be a legitimate one, depending on how we define the terms of the relationship. The context in which the Bible is joined with literature in the academy is largely a secular one, with the Bible regarded as a literary anthology much like *The Norton Anthology of English Literature*. But Christian readers add a second allegiance to the Bible, viewing it as a revealed book that nourishes their souls and enlightens their minds and awakens godly affections as well as a literary book that possesses the qualities of a drama by Shakespeare or an epic by Milton. In the discussion that follows I will suggest that discerning Christian readers need abandon neither of their loyalties, or their willingness to enter into dialogue with literary people who do not share their religious allegiance to the Bible.

1. The popularity of literary interest in the Bible

There can be no mistaking the popularity of the Bible-as-literature movement on the current scene. Book titles tell part of the story: *A Complete Literary Guide to the Bible; Matthew as Story; The Art of Biblical Narrative; Literary Criticism and the Gospel; Reading the Text: The Bible and Literary Theory*. Publishers are falling over themselves to claim that their approach to the Bible is literary, even when the actual content of the books employs traditional (non-literary) methods.

The new movement encompasses both literary and biblical scholarship. Literary approaches have increasingly attracted the allegiance of biblical scholars; in fact, academic biblical scholarship has undergone a paradigm shift to literary approaches during the past two decades. For literary critics, the revolution has not been methodological but canonical: the Bible is now part of the canon of works that literary scholars teach in their courses and about which they publish critical essays and books. Both literary and religious presses have recently unveiled series that take a literary approach to the Bible.

While no one person or event produced the current popularity of interpreting the Bible with literary methods, an influential figure in the movement was literary scholar Northrop Frye. In the early 1960s Frye claimed that 'the Bible forms the lowest stratum in the teaching of literature. It should be taught so early and so thoroughly that it sinks straight to the bottom of the mind, where everything that comes along later can settle on it . . . The Bible . . . should be the basis of literary training.'[1]

While Frye's vision has never been completely realized, in a modified sense it has. Several years ago the president of the Modern Language Association said at a national convention that all the needs of a core curriculum in literature can be accomplished through the teaching of one text – the Bible. Literary critics Robert Alter and Frank Kermode chronicle how the literary establishment, which was in the past interested in the Bible simply as 'the most important single source of all our literature', has recently witnessed 'a more striking development: the Bible, once thought of as a source of secular literature yet somehow apart from it, now bids fair to become part of the literary canon'.[2]

In the current flurry of literary interest in the Bible, it would be easy to be misled into thinking that the twentieth century invented the idea. But the idea that the Bible is literary is as old as the Bible itself. Consider, for example, the self-portrait of the writer of the Old Testament book of Ecclesiastes: 'Besides being wise, the Preacher also taught the people knowledge, weighing and studying and arranging proverbs with great care. The Preacher sought to find pleasing words, and uprightly he wrote words of truth' (Ec. 12:9–10, Revised Standard Version). Here is a portrait of the biblical writer as self-conscious composer, carefully selecting and arranging his material. Here, too, is the biblical writer as stylist, searching for 'pleasing words', valuing beauty of expression as well as truthfulness of content. The writer also signals his awareness of literary genres, in this case the collection of proverbs.

There is additional explicit and implicit evidence that the writers of the Bible had literary intentions. For one thing, they frequently use technical generic labels such as chronicle, song, complaint, parable, epistle and prophecy. Furthermore, biblical texts sometimes bear unmistakable resemblance to similar literary texts from surrounding ancient near-eastern cultures. For example, the Song of Solomon is similar to Egyptian love poetry, and the book of Deuteronomy and the Ten Commandments resemble the suzerainty treaties of ancient Hittite kings.

Most convincing of all, though, are the literary qualities of the Bible itself. Biblical narrative, for example, displays such time-honoured principles of storytelling as beginning-middle-end construction, plot conflict, dramatic irony, foreshadowing, echo and climax. Biblical poets knew that a lament psalm had five main ingredients and a praise psalm three main parts. They knew how to discover apt metaphors and arrange their material into the verse form of parallelism. In sum, biblical writers were as aware as modern scholars that the collection of books now known as the Bible is a thoroughly (though not totally) literary book.

2. Obstacles to a literary approach to the Bible

Despite all the current enthusiasm over literary approaches to the Bible, Christians in our century have often been resistant to the idea. This resistance begins with a reverence for the Bible as a sacred book that claims to be a revelation from God to people. However unwarranted the reaction turns out to be, there is an initial feeling that it takes something away from the Bible to read and interpret it as we do Shakespeare's *Macbeth* or a poem by Wordsworth. C. S. Lewis gave impetus to this reservation in the oft-quoted statement that the Bible 'is not merely a sacred book but a book so remorselessly and continuously sacred that it does not invite, it excludes or repels, the merely aesthetic approach'.[3] The key word here is the word 'merely', which evokes the picture of someone who reads the Bible devoid of the special religious belief and authority that Christians ascribe to the Bible, a practice that Lewis elsewhere described as reading the Bible 'without attending to the main thing it is about'.[4]

But this instinctual resistance to approaching the Bible as literature is mild when compared to the resistance that is likely to arise when a discerning reader starts reading around in current literary commentary on the Bible. The main features of this commentary, which I have space only to summarize here, are frequently hostile to an evangelical Christian view of the Bible.[5]

To begin, there is no consensus on what constitutes a literary approach to the Bible. Virtually anything that a critic claims to be literary – studying the ideas in a passage, establishing a cultural context, delineating the history of interpretation of a text, exploring the generic properties of a text – is allowed to sail under the literary banner. The current climate is extraordinarily chaotic, threatening to undermine the credibility of the Bible-as-literature movement on scholarly as well as religious grounds.

Other trends are also prominent. Scholars who take a literary approach are endlessly fascinated by what is problematical in a biblical text. They love to see complexity, contradiction and indeterminacy of meaning in biblical stories and poems. Equally popular is the practice of producing original 'counter-readings' to traditional religious interpretations of texts in the Bible, accompanied by the assumption that pious readers through the centuries have misread the Bible. Freudian readings (in the form of finding sexual overtones wherever possible) and a preoccupation with violence are currently in vogue, as are claims that the high degree of literary artifice in the Bible means that it is fictional and cannot be historically or factually accurate.

Overall, the literary approach to the Bible in the larger world of scholarship is a movement toward the desacralizing of the Bible, or of reading it outside the context of a community of religious faith. Critics regard themselves not as helpful travel guides through the Bible, revisiting familiar sights informed by the received wisdom of the religious past, but as liberators from the prison-house of conventional readings of the Bible.

We should also be aware of the concealed ideological agenda of current literary criticism of the Bible that may claim to be viewing the Bible just like other literary documents. In addition to the desire to undermine traditional interpretations of the Bible, secular scholars begin from a stance of disbelief of what Christian readers generally attribute to the Bible, including its inspiration, reliability, historical and theological accuracy and authority for life. While Christian readers need not object to a literary approach to the Bible in principle, neither should they abandon their religious convictions in assessing the validity for them of a given piece of literary criticism of the Bible.

We should be aware, of course, that literary approaches are not the only ones to raise suspicions. The methods and conclusions of liberal biblical scholarship have been inimical to an evangelical approach for years. More people lose their faith in the pew and religion courses than in literature courses. Biblical scholars and preachers desacralized the Bible before literary critics did. Furthermore, many of the features I have ascribed to current literary criticism of the Bible are equally characteristic of literary criticism in general, so that if we were to use this as an excuse not to read the Bible literarily we should by the same logic cease to read literature this way.

The obstacles to reading the Bible as literature are formidable, but not insurmountable. We need not reject literary analysis of the Bible simply because much of it is suspect on both literary and religious grounds. What we need is standards or norms by which to differentiate good from bad literary criticism, whether of the Bible or Shakespeare.

3. A discerning reading of the Bible as literature

A good starting point is to go back to what can be called traditional literary criticism. One of its central convictions is that literature is incarnational – that it enacts rather than states. Instead of giving abstract propositions about virtue or vice, for example, literature presents stories of good or evil characters in action. Literature gives the example instead of the precept, or combines the example with the precept. The knowledge that literature imparts consists of our living through an experience or (in the case of poetry) picturing a series of images. The language of literature is prevailingly concrete rather than abstract. The fifth commandment states propositionally, 'You shall not murder' (Ex. 20:13). The story of Cain and Abel incarnates that same truth, without, however, using the abstraction 'murder' or commanding people to refrain from it.

Several corollaries follow from the incarnational nature of the Bible. Because the aim of a literary text is to re-create an experience, the first item on the agenda for the reader or interpreter is to relive the text as vividly and concretely as possible. Furthermore, the fact that a literary text embodies an experience means that the whole story or whole poem is the meaning. There is something irreducible about a literary text. The generalizations that we make about such a text never convey its full meaning.

All of this has big implications for how we view the truthfulness of the Bible. For most people, truth is synonymous with ideas that are true rather than false. But the truthfulness that literature imparts is largely in another category. It consists of truthfulness to reality and to human experience. The story of the fall in Genesis 3, for example, is a truthful portrayal of such human experiences as temptation, guilt, rationalization of sin, fear of discovery, shame, alienation, and irremedial loss.

Our ability to see this kind of truth in the Bible is rendered easy because of a further trait of literature – the fact that it embodies *universal* human experience. History tells what *happened*, while literature tells what *happens* – what is true for all people at all times.

At the level of content, the Bible is more than a work of literature, but it is not less. It combines three impulses in a way that partly accounts for its uniqueness. These impulses are the theological, historical and literary. Usually one of these dominates a given passage, but not necessarily to the exclusion of the others. Thus the claim that Genesis 3 tells how the fall into sin *happens* need not bring into question the fact that it also tells how the original fall *happened*. Yet a touchstone that allows us to gauge whether a text is literary is the degree to which we can see universal human experience in it.

How much of the Bible is literary when judged by the criterion of concrete embodiment of human experience as distinct from abstract argument? If we acknowledge the mixed nature of biblical writing, 80% is not an exaggeration. Already, therefore, we can begin to see that the Bible does not simply allow for a literary approach but that it requires it. Everywhere we turn in this book we find characters, events and settings, not primarily ideas. To view the Bible as a theological outline with proof-texts attached is to distort the kind of book it is.

If literature is definable partly by its experiential content, it is also characterized by its technique and forms. Through the centuries, people have agreed that certain genres (such as story, poetry and drama) are literary in nature. Other genres, such as historical chronicles, theological treatises and genealogies, are expository in nature. Still others fall into one category or the other, depending on how the writer handles them. Letters, sermons and orations, for example, can move in the direction of literature if they display the ordinary elements of literature.

Every literary genre has its distinctive features and conventions. These should affect how a person reads and interprets a biblical text. Readers and interpreters need to come to a given text with the right expectations. If they do, they will see more than they would otherwise see, and they will avoid misreadings. Literary genre is nothing less than a 'norm or expectation to guide the reader in his encounter with the text'.[6] An awareness of genre can programme one's reading of a biblical passage, giving it a familiar shape and arranging the details into an identifiable pattern.

The Bible is an anthology of genres that partly correspond to those that we find in an anthology of English or American literature. The dominant genre is narrative or story, which provides the organizing framework for the Bible as a whole and which makes up approximately half of the individual parts as well (in the Bible, history tends to be cast in narrative form). Poetry is likewise prevalent, not only in the poetic books but the prophetic ones as well. Beyond this, we find such familiar genres as satire, pastoral, tragedy, comedy, proverb and epistle. And even when the genres are distinctive to the Bible, as in the case of prophecy and apocalypse, the need to read the Bible in terms of its genres – to be aware not only of what the Bible says but how it says it – is itself a literary approach, as distinct from traditional preoccupations with historicity and theological content. Again, therefore, we find that Christian readers can assent in principle to the notion of the Bible as literature.

Regardless of the genre in which a given work is written, literature is identifiable by its special resources of language. Literature exploits such devices of language as metaphor, simile, allusion, pun, paradox, irony and word-play. The prevalence of these throughout the Bible explains why a literary approach is necessary for reading the entire Bible, not just the obviously literary parts. C. S. Lewis, who sounded a caution about reading the Bible *only* as literature, also asserted that 'there is a . . . sense in which the Bible, since it is after all literature, cannot properly be read except as literature; and the different parts of it as the different sorts of literature they are'.[7]

In any utterance, meaning is communicated through form, beginning with language itself. The concept of form should be construed very broadly here. It includes anything that touches on *how* a writer has expressed the content of an utterance. While this is true for all forms of writing or discourse, it is especially crucial for literature. Literature has its own forms and techniques, and these tend to be more complex, subtle and indirect than those of ordinary discourse. Stories, for example, communicate their meaning through character, setting and action. To understand a story, we must first interact with the form, that is, the characters, settings and events. Poetry conveys its meanings through figurative language and concrete images.

The literary critic's preoccupation with the *how* of biblical writing is not frivolous. It is evidence of an artistic delight in verbal beauty and craftsmanship, but it is also part of an attempt to understand *what* the Bible says. In a literary text, it is impossible to separate what is said from how it is said, content from form. Of course the aesthetic dimension of a biblical text is also important. Literary criticism is capable of showing that the Bible is an interesting rather than dull book, and a book that is beautiful as well as truthful. There is as much artistry and craftsmanship in the Bible as in any other anthology of literature. A notorious non-Christian of our century called the King James Bible 'unquestionably the most beautiful book in the world'.[8] It should be more than this, but not less, for Christians. Aesthetic considerations were important for the writers of the Bible and should be for readers and expositors as well.

To sum up, the Bible does more than sanction a literary approach – its literary nature *compels* a literary approach if we are to read it in keeping with the kind of book it really is. The Bible more often than not presents human experience instead of abstract ideas, and it does so in the form of discernible genres and by means of literary resources of language.

It is obvious that the literary approach I have described is traditional literary criticism, not the more specialized recent 'schools' of criticism. This is the safest foundation on which to build any literary criticism of the Bible. Notwithstanding Kevin Mills' analyses, I believe that literary critic John Sider has correctly stated that 'what biblical scholars need to hear most from literary critics is that old-fashioned critical concepts of plot, character, setting, point of view and diction may be more useful than more glamorous and sophisticated theories'.[9] The deep structure of literary criticism that undergirds any genuinely literary analysis of the Bible includes an awareness of how stories and poems work, how metaphor and other figurative language communicate, and an appreciation for the artistry of an utterance.

It would be a mistake to set up the religious or devotional reading of the Bible as a rival to a literary approach. A literary approach enhances any devout reading of the Bible by showing us more dimensions of the text, and by opening up the affective imaginative and aesthetic powers of the Bible. As for the objectionable conclusions that appear in much literary criticism of the Bible, these are not a necessary part of reading the Bible as literature, as a history of literary criticism of the Bible will show.

4. The Bible as literature: a brief history

Because the Bible-as-literature movement has been championed in our day by the secular academy, it comes as a surprise to learn that this is a relatively recent development that came on the scene only two centuries ago. For more than fifteen centuries, literary appreciation of the Bible was largely the domain of believing Christian scholars and poets.[10]

The first chapter in the story was the attempt of the church fathers of the Middle Ages to reconcile the Bible with their love of classical rhetoric and literature. Although Augustine originally found the Bible unliterary when compared with classical writings, his final opinion regarding the biblical writings was that not only can nothing 'be wiser, but also that nothing can be more eloquent,' and that all the 'powers and beauties of eloquence' found in classical writing 'are to be found in the sacred writings which God in His goodness has provided to mould our characters and to guide us from this world of wickedness to the blessed world above'.[11] In such an utterance we catch no hint of tension between literary and religious views of the Bible.

In the era of the Reformation and Renaissance, biblical scholars such as Luther and Calvin and literary figures such as Sidney and Milton viewed the Bible as a book possessing literary qualities. In a definitive survey of this tradition, Barbara Lewalski has shown that exegetes interpreted the Bible in terms of literary qualities and that poets used the Bible as a literary model to imitate in such matters as genre, language and symbolism.[12] Milton can be taken as representative of this synthesis between Christian belief and poetic practice when he claimed that the poems of the Bible are incomparable 'over all the kinds of lyric poesy', not in 'their divine argument alone, but in the very critical art of composition'.[13]

The Romantic movement of the nineteenth century began what might be called a secularized literary interest in the Bible – an appreciation for the literary qualities of the Bible devoid of religious belief in it as an inspired authority. Even here, though, the literary qualities of the Bible that chiefly interested the Romantics – its primitive simplicity, its sublimity and its mythic or visionary qualities – are not inherently antithetical to a Christian's view of the Bible as a sacred book.

Even in the twentieth century, much of the literary commentary on the Bible is congruent with Christian attitudes toward it. Erich Auerbach's classic comparison of storytelling technique in Homer and the book of Genesis is a case in point.[14] The contrast that Auerbach draws between the embellished narrative style of Homer and the spare, unembellished style of biblical narrative not only enhances a reader's understanding and enjoyment of the stories of the Bible but also implicitly affirms the special qualities of the Bible.

The history of literary interest in the Bible shows that reading the Bible as literature is not inherently hostile to a Christian reading. In fact, it is easy to identify an evangelical 'school' of literary criticism of the Bible within the current landscape (see 'Further Reading' at the end of this chapter).

5. The Bible as literary influence

The Bible is important to the study of literature in ways beyond the literary analysis of the Bible itself. One reason the Bible keeps coming up in literature courses is that it is western literature's 'greatest source' and 'the major influence on literary symbolism'.[15] When critics utter such statements, they do not mean the general Christian element in literature but a direct indebtedness of literature to the Bible. C. S. Lewis bequeathed to scholarship a helpful distinction between the Bible as a literary source and as a literary influence. In Lewis' words, 'A source gives us things to write about; an influence prompts us to write in a certain way.'[16] The Bible is a continuous presence in western literature in both ways.

Writers have used the Bible as a source in a wide range of ways. They have raided the Bible (which is, we should note, a very aphoristic book) for titles of works (and nowhere oftener than in the twentieth century): *Go Down Moses; Absalom, Absalom; The Sun*

Also Rises; Go Tell It on the Mountain; The Power and the Glory. The Bible has also been a frequent source for characters' names in stories. Thus Charles Dickens names a martyred victim of the judicial system Abel Magwitch, and Nathaniel Hawthorne names his courageous heroine Hester (a variant of Esther) and her illegitimate child Pearl (echoing the 'pearl of great price' of Jesus' parable).

Mainly, though, the Bible has provided the subject matter of poems, stories and plays. At the simplest level, writers present a biblical character or event in an attempt to make it come alive. Usually writers go beyond this and provide an interpretation of the biblical character or event as well. With even more interpretive latitude, writers use biblical material as the vehicle for presenting their own view of life. Milton's closet drama *Samson Agonistes*, for example, goes well beyond the story of the Old Testament hero to embody Milton's worldview, including such Christian experiences as patient suffering, repentance and salvation. Modern writers are likely to move even farther afield and to offer reinterpretations of biblical characters and events (for instance, Archibald MacLeish's rewriting of the ending of the book of Job in his play *J.B.*, where the moment of epiphany is not an encounter with a transcendent God but an affirmation of human love).

The Bible is also a source for allusions at every stage of English and American literature, and again the range of usages is immense. In simple or straightforward allusion, writers refer to the Bible in such a way that our knowledge of the biblical source is necessary to the bare construing of a passage. In complex allusion, a reader must go beyond simply making a connection and must interpret *how* a detail in the text relates to a biblical precedent. At the far end of the continuum is the phenomenon of intertextuality, where the important thing is not what a literary work says in itself but rather in the interaction *between* the biblical source and the literary work that reinterprets or inverts it (see, for example, David Barratt's essay on Thomas Hardy later in this book).

Closely akin to biblical allusions are biblical archetypes. An archetype is a recurrent plot motif, character type or image. The Bible is the most familiar and definitive version of the archetypes of literature. Northrop Frye calls it 'a grammar of archetypes – the place where we can find them in their most systematic and complete form'.[17] It is therefore possible to travel a very fruitful two-way street between the Bible and literary texts. On the one hand, an awareness of archetypes in the Bible can supply a context that enriches our experience of archetypal patterns in the literature that we read (for example, much in Dickens' *Great Expectations* falls into place when we realize that the shape of Pip's moral journey follows the pattern of the prodigal son). On the other hand, our growing experience of archetypes in literature opens doors and windows into the Bible itself.

We should note in passing that the same type of two-way street between the Bible and literature can be set up at the level of genres. On the one hand, there is something prototypical about the Bible, so that if we want to see how stories and poems and metaphors work, we can usually do no better than to look at examples in the Bible. Working the other way, as readers of literature we will see more in the Bible if we apply what we know about comedy and tragedy and satire and lyric when we read the Bible.

In addition to serving writers as a source, the Bible has been a major *influence* on western literature. Its Authorized (King James) Version has influenced the style of poetry and prose – the language, syntax, imagery, even the rhythm and cadences that writers choose. The Bible has also influenced how writers handle genres, even when the genres themselves come from extrabiblical sources (for example, Milton got his epic genre from the classical tradition, but he was influenced by the book of Genesis in creating a pastoral and domestic epic, and by the book of Revelation in spiritualizing many of the old epic motifs).

To sum up, there is a close connection between the Bible *as* literature and the Bible *in* literature. Northrop Frye correctly notes that 'no book could have had [the Bible's] influence on literature without itself having literary qualities'.[18]

From the foregoing analysis of how storytellers and poets use the Bible in the *composition* of literature, it is easy to determine how the Bible enters the *study* of literature. In addition to reading the Bible as literature, students of literature must refer to the Bible as they identify and interpret allusions. Since the Bible is the definitive source of doctrinal belief for Christians, readers need an acquaintance with the Bible as they assess the degree of Christian allegiance in works of literature. The archetypes of the Bible can help us see the master images and motifs of literature more clearly, just as a knowledge of biblical genres can often show us exactly what is happening in the works of writers who have used the Bible as a source or influence for their genres. Finally, a sensitivity to stylistic features of the Bible not only enhances our aesthetic enjoyment of Bible reading but also alerts us to effects in works of literature whose authors have been influenced by the Bible's stylistic techniques.

6. *The Bible and a Christian aesthetic*

Something remains to be said about the implications of the literary nature of the Bible for a Christian's theory and practice of literature itself. The literary nature of the Bible itself strongly affirms the legitimacy of the literary enterprise. If God did not wish us to have literature in our lives, he would not have given us a literary Bible. The incarnational bent of the Bible – its tendency to embody its vision in story and poetry, in character, action and image – implicitly asserts that we assimilate the truth with our imagination (our image-making and image-perceiving capacity) as well as our intellect. Literature itself is based on the same premise.

As a work of literature, moreover, the Bible shows that literary form and technique have value in themselves and are therefore self-rewarding. The craftsmanship evident in the stories of the Bible, the aptness of the images and metaphors of biblical poets, the skill that the writers of the Bible show in their handling of language and syntax all suggest that biblical writers did not have something better to do than to be artistic to the glory of God. Can we justify the time spent in polishing a poem or reading a novel? The literary nature of the Bible implies that we can.

A consideration of the literary dimension of the Bible also suggests something about the liberating range that Christian writers and readers are free to pursue in their literary interests. Although the Bible is a predominantly religious book, it includes literature that is not specifically religious – a collection of love lyrics that does not explicitly bring God and spiritual values into the picture, a patriotic elegy about national heroes that does not mention God (2 Sa. 1:17–27), historical narratives devoid of obvious religious meaning. Based on evidence like this, Francis Schaeffer rightly concluded that 'Christian art is by no means always religious art . . . Man as man – with his emotions, his feelings, his body, his life – this is important subject matter for poetry and novels . . . What a Christian portrays in his art is the totality of life.'[19]

The Bible shows a similar gusto in embracing the two great literary poles of realism and fantasy. On the one hand, the Bible shows the impulse to copy or 'imitate' real life characters, events and settings. Like literary realism more generally, it gives us the proverbial 'slice of life', firmly rooted in history. But the writers of the Bible are equally at ease with fantasy – literature that takes us to an alternative world remote from lifelike reality. In a single short chapter of Zechariah, for example, we read about a flying scroll that destroys the wood and stones of houses, a woman named Wickedness sitting inside a cereal container, and two women with wings like those of a stork who lift the container 'between earth and heaven' (Zc. 5). In the visionary parts of the Bible we read about a ram's horn that grew to the sky and knocked stars to the ground (Dn. 8:9–10), and about a dragon sweeping down a third of the stars of heaven with its tail (Rev. 12:3–4).

The Bible, then, can answer some of our questions about literary theory simply by being literary itself. Are realism and fantasy legitimate media? Can the imagination express truth? Do literary craftsmanship and beauty have value in themselves? Must literature be explicitly religious to justify itself in the eyes of a Christian? Are tragedy, comedy and satire compatible with the Christian faith? By being literary, the Bible provides helpful answers to some perennial questions of literary theory.

Summary

The discerning reader need not apologize for regarding the Bible as central to literary experience as well as the religious life. The Bible itself is a work of unsurpassed literary power and beauty. In it we find an anthology of the main genres and techniques of literature, used in the service of religious and moral truth of the greatest possible consequence. It is a book whose beauty and truth not only invite but require a literary approach.

At the same time, the study of literature itself requires an awareness of the Bible. Literature alludes to the Bible, takes biblical material as a source, and shows the influence of the Bible on its style and genres. In the words of Frye, 'Without some knowledge of the Bible one simply does not know what is going on in English literature.'[20] In arguing for the inter-relatedness of literature and the Bible, Michael Edwards writes that 'the Bible calls for a literary understanding; literature homes to the Bible'.[21]

Further reading and activities

A good introduction to what a literary approach to the Bible means to evangelical Christian scholars is Leland Ryken and Tremper Longman III (eds.), *A Complete Literary Guide to the Bible* (Grand Rapids: Zondervan, 1993). In the same vein are Ryken's books *How to Read the Bible as Literature* (Grand Rapids:

Zondervan, 1984) and *Words of Delight: A Literary Introduction to the Bible* (Grand Rapids: Baker, 1992).

A towering figure in the larger academic world is Robert Alter; his books include *The Art of Biblical Narrative* (New York: Basic Books, 1981), *The Art of Biblical Poetry* (New York: Basic Books, 1985), and *The World of Biblical Literature* (New York: Basic Books, 1992).

The definitive source on the Bible as a presence in English and American literature is David L. Jeffrey (ed.), *A Dictionary of Biblical Tradition in English Literature* (Grand Rapids: Eerdmans, 1992).

The best way to convince yourself of the validity of a literary approach to the Bible is to take a specimen text, beginning with a psalm or a story, and apply the usual literary tools of analysis to the passage.

9

Shakespeare and Christianity

Rowland Cotterill

The previous chapter stands as a bridge between the theoretically based and the textually based approaches. While Leland Ryken raised a number of theoretical issues, it must clearly be seen that the Bible is a specific, though unique, text, capable of literary analysis. We turn now to other texts commonly met with in lecture halls and seminar rooms, and seek to show how Christian insights must be brought to bear on them.

No-one supposes it is easy to ask about Shakespeare's relations to Christianity. His religious practices, as a member of the English church of his time, can be known; the many echoes of biblical and liturgical language in the plays are no surprise, given compulsory frequent attendance at services in which extensive passages from the Bible were read. His opinions on the turbulent history of his church, and on the other churches of his lifetime, are unavailable. Since 'Christian belief' was, then as never before, self-divided, between and within churches, this must seem a major limitation.

In any case, talk of 'Shakespeare's opinions' is deeply unfashionable. It is widely held to be a critical fallacy to seek an author's intentions, presumably also 'opinions', in any work of literary art; especially a dramatic work where speakers lack any frame of authorial commentary. Shakespeare's plays, moreover, are (frequently) also poetry, committed to the rhetorics of metre, symbol and formal architecture rather than plain statements of truth. Even when it is argued that scriptural doctrine, or the symbolism of Christian sacramental practice, undergirds the structure of a play or the texture of its language, that play's meanings would still be substantially determined by the extent to which particular performances realize such texture and structure, and the power or will of particular audiences to receive them and be received, or taken in, by them. All these commonplaces of modern criticism have made it plausible to see Shakespeare's plays as offering not 'meaning', still less 'truth', but the dispersal of meanings, some asserted but subverted, some proclaimed from the margins, of the stage and of the text.

On this view, it seems to me, we are in fact claiming to know important things; if not directly about Shakespeare's beliefs, then about his place in relation to belief. If his audiences were, in Christian terms, at odds with themselves, then so was he. He, and his audiences, I suggest, experienced, and suffered, the 'dispersals' of truth, from and across Bible and church, which were, and remain, common and even defining experiences of a discerning Christianity – a Christianity, that is, committed to faith, and to its difficulties.

So I shall begin by discussing some features of Shakespeare's presentation of biblical texts, and of the problems of reading them, and of the church's exposition of them and of itself. I shall suggest that he can be seen to be concerned with the difficulties of applying texts to cases; the questionable value of 'wisdom'; the relations between the 'sacred' and the 'secular'; and the interpretative problems arising when texts are at odds. I shall also suggest that there is a marked absence, from the plays, of 'Christian practical wisdom'.

Pursuing more detailed interpretation of three specific plays, I shall then argue for a Shakespeare particularly interested in the risks to which people expose themselves when interpreting God's Word, or God's purposes, in isolation, or with self-confidence, or to their own advantage. Such temptations, amounting to the pride which plays at being God, can be seen as giving rise, in more than one of these plays, to a vision of a world at war with itself and a nightmare of a God at odds with himself. Against such 'terrors of the earth'[1] there may be remedies – patience, mutual recognition, mutual forgiveness; I will not suggest that these are shown to be of any more than limited value. But then that may be all we are being led to expect – the dangers of treating theatre as in itself offering 'knowledge' or 'salvation' are, I think, apparent in Shakespeare's work. Instead, I'll say, his theatre should be seen as involving an audience participation which recognizes itself and its self-difference; it is thus valuably guarded against closing off the endlessness of interpretative contexts in its own interests. It follows, finally, that we should not expect too much, even, or especially, of these plays. It is more to the point to discover what they expect of us. The differences in God's world, and Shakespeare's worlds, can be received as a challenge not to appropriation or assimilation, but to wonder, love and praise. Here, too, is 'God's plenty'.

1. Features of Shakespeare's presentation of biblical texts

Within Shakespeare's use of the Bible, we can find a strongly thematic citation, in the title *Measure for Measure*, and the powerful near-quotation by the Duke:

> The very mercy of the law cries out
> 'An Angelo for Claudio, death for death'.
> Haste still pays haste, and leisure answers leisure;
> Like doth quit like, and measure still for measure.
> (*Measure for Measure*, V. i.404–408)[2]

And yet there will be no deaths, but rather 'an apt remission', and 'the law' is neither enforced nor reformed but, on the whole, surpassed: and perhaps this was Jesus' idea too, his words about 'measure' being a warning, not a recommendation; the very space of Shakespeare's play, we may feel, lies in the opening between Matthew 5:18: 'not a letter, not a stroke, will disappear from the Law',[3] and Matthew 5:20: 'unless you show yourselves far better men than . . . the doctors of the law . . .'

A different case is the paradox involved in Bottom's dishevelled half-memory of Paul:

> I have had a most rare vision. I have had a dream past
> the wit of man to say what dream it was . . . The eye of
> man hath not heard, the ear of man hath not seen, man's
> hand is not able to taste, his tongue to conceive, nor his
> heart to report what my dream was. I will get Peter
> Quince to write a ballad of this dream. It shall be called
> 'Bottom's Dream' because it hath no bottom . . .
> (*A Midsummer Night's Dream*, IV. i.202–213; *cf.* 1 Cor. 2:9)

Bottom's synaesthetic mistakes and 'misquotations' here achieve, through comedy, a noble humility. 'Translated', like and unlike Paul, to 'Heaven', Bottom has seen (and has been) the unutterable, and a certain incommensurability hangs around all the expressions he devises for it. Was Shakespeare's mind working in, here, an awareness of another 'Corinthian' passage?

> Divine folly is wiser than the wisdom of man . . . to shame the wise, God has chosen what the world counts folly . . . He has chosen things low and contemptible, mere nothings, to overthrow the existing order.
>
> (1. Cor. 1:25, 27–28)

On such a view, Shakespeare would be seen as not 'quoting' or even 'using', but as 'interpreting' a rather extensive tract of biblical text.

The case of Antony and Cleopatra seems to have provoked a still larger leap of creative appropriation: Charmian's fantasy,

> Let me be married to three kings in a forenoon and widow them all. Let me have a child at fifty to whom Herod of Jewry may do homage. Find me to marry with Octavius Caesar, and companion me with my mistress . . .
>
> (*Antony and Cleopatra*, I. ii.22–26)

promiscuously fuses Luke with Matthew and both with legend (and, perhaps, Old Testament miracle stories). But history, Rome's Empire, is itself already in the business of preparing the way for a 'new testament'; the lovers exchange the challenge to 'find out new heaven, new earth';[4] Cleopatra's death images the nurturing of divine child by (divine?) mother,[5] just as her part in Antony's death scene can be seen in terms of a curiously reversed *pietà*, with the raising (instead of lowering) of the stricken body of a martyr of love and forgiveness.[6] Well may Charmian (again) murmur, 'O eastern star!' – the parody (is all this parody?) is, like the lass, unparalleled.[7] Clearly more than the Bible is involved here: I am claiming not that the play is 'about' the Bible, or the narratives of Jesus' birth, or the book of Revelation, but that it is about what these are about – the possibilities of love and the possible resistances to it; and that for us to reflect on these parallels, parodies and possibilities involves us in asking whether the resistance we may feel to the closeness of these lovers' love, and God's love, to each other, in this play, amounts to a defence of love, or a resistance to it; a defence of, or a resistance to (say), such a challenging promise as 'Behold! I am making all things new!' (Rev. 21:5).

These cases have offered, on the whole, rather euphoric appropriations of biblical texts. One remarkable speech finds a Shakespearian character more critically, explicitly and gloomily considering the bases of such appropriation – 'Richard II on biblical interpretation':

> For no thought is contented. The better sort,
> As thoughts of things divine, are intermixed
> With scruples, and do set the faith itself
> Against the faith, as thus: 'Come, little ones,'
> And then again,
> 'It is as hard to come as for a camel
> To thread the postern of a small needles's eye.'
>
> (*Richard II*, V. v.11–17)

The more familiar reading here, 'set the word itself against the word', is perhaps a false memory from the previous scene, where the ('accidental') contradiction between the English 'pardon' and the French *'pardonnez-moi'* provokes the Duchess of York to condemn such misapplied verbal play and to plead for (unambiguous) 'pity'. But the two scenes are in any case similar enough to set us thinking of Richard's hopes of God's pity, and of what support his thoughts may claim from the faith, the word, of God. And so the hermeneutic problem is also a problem about salvation.

And of course it has to be our problem too (at least I can find, in my own faith, no 'assurance' entitling me to forget the warnings to which those with 'great riches' are exposed).[8] Perhaps the Shakespearian context is rather specific – Richard has always oscillated between extremes, in mood, in plans, in intercepting other's plans and moods. He is obsessed with his likeness, and unlikeness, to Christ:

> He in twelve
> Found truth in all but one; I, in twelve thousand, none –
>
> (*Richard II*, IV. i.161–162)

No wonder it is he who shows us a Jesus, a Bible, like and unlike themselves . . . But then the thought of specificity, and of context, can quickly be seen as another way in which Shakespeare's text, and his stage, have to be felt not as making use of the Bible, but as being like it; context always explains context, and 'God', like Shakespeare, 'is his own interpreter'.[9]

2. Shakespeare and the church

As for my second question: if Shakespeare found the Bible confusing, how did he find the church? *Richard II* offers a Bishop of Carlisle staunchly defending the divine right of a legitimate king and the glory of the crusading call.[10] Other English histories present active self-interested priests and cardinals – Winchester and Pandulph, Southwell and Hume; and ('we are all diseased') the Archbishop of York, nobly gloomy in rebellion, in the *Henry IV* plays.[11] These share a general ecclesiastical stake in politics, expressed by the Archbishop of Canterbury in *Henry V*:

> For all the temporal lands which men devout
> By testament have given to the Church
> Would they strip from us . . .
> > (*Henry V*, I. i.9–11)

This was an unfulfilled fear, in the context of the play, but an accomplished fact for Shakespeare's audience. But Shakespeare's plays are very short on *Protestant* clergy. (Cranmer, in *Henry VIII*, is the clearest case, and of course a telling exception, though his lines may not be Shakespearian.) The plays also lack priests with any credible claim to discernment or authority that is spiritual.

Theatrical censorship, and self-censorship, no doubt explain in large measure why that should be so. The effects are important. Control of events and governance of human relationships may be entrusted to representatives of human skill (such as Prospero), or of human authority and justice (Theseus in *A Midsummer Night's Dream*, the Duke in *Measure for Measure*). Or the operations of chance, or the collisions of divergent human wills and manipulations, may dominate for better (*The Winter's Tale*) or worse (*King Lear*). Such trains of events may inspire far-reaching secular reflections ('The readiness is all';[12] 'Ripeness is all';[13] 'We are such stuff as dreams are made on'.[14]) But Shakespeare's plays offer no distinctive Christian practical wisdom. If Christian truth is to be seen as drawing support from events or characters in these and other plays of Shakespeare, the truth will have to be brought to the plays; it will not convincingly or distinctively be derived from them.

3. Richard III

But characters in the plays do themselves from time to time claim the power, right or gift to make such derivations, and to shape or impose specifically Christian interpretations of the course of events. The clearest cases are in *Richard III*. In many ways this play is the closest approach to 'religious drama' in Shakespeare's work. Schiller spoke of it as 'one of the noblest tragedies I know' and compared it to Greek tragedy. Anthony Hammond, developing this judgment, speaks of its 'highly organized and formal' structure, and of conventions which reinforce the sense of a ritual expiation of collective guilt.[15] Elsewhere he contrasts the 'brutal, un-Christian, Old Testament concepts of retributive justice', embodied for him in the figure of Margaret, with Richmond's 'New Testament of forgiveness and reconciliation'.[16]

This view develops the influential claims of Tillyard that Shakespeare's English histories embody a coherent theology of history, whose appeal to Shakespeare's contemporaries lay at once in its Christianity and in the strong support it gave to the legitimacy and providential underwriting of the Tudor dynasty. On the basic form of this argument, divine retributive justice punished those guilty of the murder of Richard II by visiting upon them the ills of a troubled conscience (Bolingbroke), a short though glorious life (Henry V), and, climactically, a realm torn apart by civil war (Henry VI); the house of York, and its final member Richard of Gloucester, thus act as God's scourge, while at the same time, in Richard's machinations against his brothers Clarence and Edward, providing a final symbolic instance of a whole kingdom given over, by divine permission, to the primal woes of fratricidal strife.[17]

Christian readers of Shakespeare and Tillyard may find it natural to see such arguments as meriting defence rather than critique. Hammond's uneasiness is therefore notable. He suggests, first, that given the needs both for visible providential intervention in human history (so that we may not lose faith) and for the deferring of many merited rewards and punishments until a last judgment (for this has been promised), instances of divine intervention in history may be believed and claimed, but not proved, even retrospectively.[18] A conception such as Tillyard claims to identify in Elizabethan authors would then imply improper human confidence in the power to detect God's purposes. In the world of the play, such improper confidence is typical of Margaret:

> O, but remember this another day . . .
> And say, poor Margaret was a prophetess.
> Live, each of you, the subject to his hate.
> And he to yours, and all of you to God's.
> (*Richard III*, I. iii.299, 301–303)

Secondly, 'all the characters in the play (except for the Princes and Richmond) are at least partly guilty'.[19] Shakespeare's treatment of the plot moves us from fascinated acceptance of Richard's claim for sole responsibility to an increasing sense of how his efforts intersect with the aims and characters of others. Edward has displayed his own animus against Clarence. Clarence's murderers are given room to set their own responsibility for murder alongside the excuse of 'the Duke of Gloucester's purse'. Edward's death gives Richard grounds for self-congratulation but cannot seriously be attributed to him. Hastings and Buckingham ensnare themselves, naïvely and with naïve wiliness, by their personal and familial alliances with Richard. And many characters become increasingly cautious. Richard never persuades any fellow nobles that the claim of Prince Edward to the monarchy can be justly set aside – even Buckingham, eager in meta-theatrical intrigue, is cautious in voicing any opinion of his own. Derby, the play's great survivor, is an emblem of such political caution; he could equally, I think, be taken as representing (in the short sub-scene immediately before King Edward's death) a general human guilt and, more, a general human need of forgiveness and duty to forgive.[20]

Another important point, in Hammond's reinterpretation, concerns Richard. 'It is Richard who elects to become an anti-Christ, whose free choice of evil is also (by the familiar Christian paradox) the means by which God brings about good.'[21] One might link this to his previous point; Richard is unable to forgive himself:

> What do I fear? Myself? there's none else by;
> Richard loves Richard, that is, I and I . . .
> Alack, I love myself. Wherefore? For any good
> That I myself have done unto myself?
> O no, alas, I rather hate myself
> For hateful deeds committed by myself . . .
> I shall despair. There is no creature loves me,
> And if I die, no soul will pity me –
> And wherefore should they, since that I myself
> Find in myself no pity to myself?
> (*Richard III*, V. iii.183–184, 188–191, 201–204)

A refusal of forgiveness is manifest here, beyond individual words, through the intense will towards absolute clarity in the language, the syntax and the logical form of the whole speech. For

Richard there is nothing outside – outside his tent, his wound, himself. He is his own fellow – 'I and I'; at once actor and audience. And outside him there is no other God – 'I am I'. The 'anti-Christ', appropriately, is both enemy of and substitute for God.

There is a potential collision of thoughts here in which I see the dramatic focus of the play as a whole. On the one hand, God brings good out of evil by the work of Jesus. On the other hand *Richard III* shows the Anti-christ-like Richard, bringing evil out of good. The play can itself then seem a dramatized Anti-christ. Or, that in Richard's behaviour, and in his conception of himself which is 'theatrical' can seem anti-Christian. My point is that these two thoughts co-exist in our experience of the play. Consider these lines of Catesby:

> He is within, with two right reverend fathers,
> Divinely bent to meditation;
> And in no worldly suits would he be moved
> To draw him from his holy exercise.
> *(Richard III*, III. vii.60–63

We immediately decipher one level of irony here – Richard hopes for nothing better than to be addressed by 'wordly suitors'; and perhaps another joke (common in the play's verbal texture), concerned with being 'bent', and with the predetermination of this by God or by something else. There remains a greater uncertainty, 'ironic' in a subversive sense; what if Richard's ambition is indeed a 'holy exercise'? A more worldly Richard might have bided his time, content to await Edward's death, to be Protector and 'King-maker' to his nephew, to be an ironic observer of others' affairs or of his own. Richard, in these senses, is not 'worldly'. Instead he seeks to include the world in himself, to punish it and to punish himself, to make its evil his good.

To see his relation to the rest of the play in these terms is to associate Richard with God. Both develop their purposes through the wills and purposes of others. Both are emotional absolutists. And, if Richard is self-divided, a virtuoso actor, unable to live with himself, so, it may appear to a thoroughly theatrical imagination (Richard's or Shakespeare's) is God: between a 'brutal . . . Old Testament' and a 'New Testament of forgiveness and reconciliation'.

Christian readers will be swift to question such an open profession of what remains a very common sense – that the

Christian Bible offers not one God but (at least) two. They should of course be just as swift to question the particular terms of the division; as though the Old Testament were not the story of God's forgiving and restorative acts; as if Jesus did not speak of judgment; as if the relationship between Christians and Jews, and their respective Scriptures, were possible to contemplate, today, in any merely academic spirit. But if reading and viewing Shakespeare are to be informed by God's Word, they will necessarily be informed by the salutary difficulties expressed within that Word. And these difficulties – the difficulties of Christianity, the reason Christianity is difficult – are present in any human claim to possess knowledge of God's will, or (which may be the same thing) of the way in which eternity and time, Father and Son, judgment and mercy, belong together.

4. King Lear

These questions, which beset the theological controversies of the sixteenth and seventeenth centuries, affected playwrights with special force in this period. Generations of dramas staging biblical narrative, and presenting on stage an incarnate God, had left among their legacies an unlimited scale of theatrical ambition, and a fascination with identity and differences between actor and role, character and situation. The immense limitations placed, by censorship, upon any direct representation of church practice or biblical narrative forced such fascination and ambition into narratives neither divinely inspired nor susceptible of any single or simple Christian interpretation. Such are the narratives appropriated by Shakespeare for *King Lear*. It is not surprising that the play has provoked debate on the religious issues at stake in its interpretation; it has indeed to some extent focused already existing differences, among its critics and among audiences at large, to the point of being seen as a central text within the tradition of religious debate in world literature.[22]

For many, the heart of the play's scheme of values lies in its assertions of one or more of the following priorities; human mutuality, forgiveness and patience. The first can be found in lines such as Lear's:

> If thou wilt weep my fortunes, take my eyes.
> I know thee well enough; thy name is Gloucester . . .
> *(King Lear,* IV. v.168–169)

The second is normally understood to shape our awareness of the scene next after this, in which Lear and Cordelia at last meet once again, and in which the king's last lines are:

> You must bear with me. Pray you now, forget
> And forgive. I am old and foolish.
> *(King Lear*, IV. vi.81–82)

The third, named by Lear,

> Thou must be patient. We came crying hither . . .
> *(King Lear*, IV. v.170)

is more ambiguously claimed by Gloucester earlier in the same scene:

> O you mighty gods.
> This world I do renounce, and in your sights
> Shake patiently my great affliction off . . .
> *(King Lear*, IV. v.34–36)

This may be connected with the words, whether deeply meditated or evoked by sheer urgent contingency, of his son Edgar:

> What, in ill thoughts again? Men must endure
> Their going hence even as their coming hither:
> Ripeness is all. Come on.
> *(King Lear*, V. ii.9–11)

And that is true, too. But – as 'too' implies – Edgar's conclusion, even the terms of his argument, are not the only ones available. And our power to elicit these values out of the other passages quoted will depend on many factors, including our discernment of their immediate and often confusing contexts.

Addressing Gloucester, Lear may be tender (as Jay Halio, the New Cambridge editor, sees it)[23] in offering his eyes. He may, not 'instead' but 'also', be malign in unnecessarily re-emphasizing Gloucester's blindness. Also – uncomfortably for the value of 'mutual recognition' – he seems to be saying that Lear's fortunes can properly be bewailed only by one who sees, or has learnt to see, as Lear himself now sees. The 'double plot' of the play is sometimes seen as affirming, by a repetition of emphasis, the value of the 'learning process' that Lear and Gloucester have in common; but this scene, and Lear's words here, might suggest rather the difference between their paths through the play, and suggest that no-one can learn anyone else's lessons.

'The necessity of mutual forgiveness' might be the most important of such lessons. How well does Lear learn it? The pathos of his second encounter with Cordelia may make the question impertinent. A way of registering this sense of impertinence would be to say that no-one, outside a specific relationship, can know whether there is forgiveness there, or whether that forgiveness has been achieved, enacted, accomplished.[24] Certainly it seems naïve to claim that the delay before Lear's plea for forgiveness, in this scene, makes the plea false; it could more sympathetically be read as showing Lear's sense, and his awareness of Cordelia's knowledge, that the forgiveness has already been granted, long since. But can it be granted before it is begged? By God: and, as so often, we are left to ask where God's forgiveness, in this scene and this play, manages to get itself on to the stage. In Cordelia's very presence? Her speech can at times command Christian resonance:

> And wast thou fain, poor father,
> To hovel thee with swine and rogues forlorn
> In short and musty straw?
> *(King Lear*, IV. vi.35–37)

Halio here hears allusion to the parable of the prodigal Son, and I also would hear echoes of the post-scriptural imagery of the nativity.[25] But this co-exists, in her too, with other and less emblematic, more human, qualities – stubbornness, bitchiness, divided loyalties (between father and putative husband). Such an awareness of context, in character, plot and language, makes the presence of Christian themes in the play more questionable.

And Edgar's words to Gloucester certainly raise questions. Halio's gloss suggests:

> Providence or the gods control our lives; hence, we must endure the time of our death even as, perforce, we endure the time of our birth. Providence, or the gods, not man, determines when the time is 'ripe', an idea which has little to do with modern theories of maturation or development.[26]

What does Edgar think Gloucester (or any of us) has to

contribute to the gods' 'control' or 'determination'? Perhaps we have to achieve some kind of 'development' in order, precisely, to recognize that they are in control? Perhaps divine control assumes different characters in proportion to the extent, or the different forms, of human 'development'? Perhaps Edgar's failure to be specific about any of this is because it is the result that matters more than the particular process of development – and because, to be able to say this, or to say it by not quite saying it, one must avoid identifying one's own state with such a general claim. Edgar's next words are, 'Come on'.

This could explain something of the difficulty about Gloucester's 'patience'. Halio, in his Introduction, remarks on this as an 'incongruity': 'Were he truly patient, Gloucester would not try to shake off his "great affliction", and if he really believes the gods' wills are "opposeless", would he attempt suicide?'[27] And of Lear's later remark, Empson writes: 'It is a comic impudence for the entirely impatient Lear to preach patience to Gloucester, but the idea is that his impatience and his clowning are what have taught him to understand the nature of the world.'[28] Take these comments together, and one could speculate that, for Gloucester, 'patience' involves the refusal to become angry with 'the gods' – a refusal which, were he to go on living, he would be unable to sustain – while the 'impatience' that Empson attributes to Lear involves a fruitfully perceptive anger, or at least rebellion, against 'the gods', which is in tune with 'the nature of the world'.

On this Empson offers more help.

> I do not see that we can regard the blasphemies against the gods as pious ejaculations in favour of Christianity. Not indeed that they are specific attacks on it; they are not more shocking than the Book of Job. The point surely is that the world is a place in which good intentions get painfully and farcically twisted by one's own character and by unexpected events. A record-breaking display of evil is let loose by the process.[29]

Shakespeare has taken care to equip his play with 'unexpected events'. The death of Cordelia – absent in this form, from any of the sources Shakespeare used – is the most obvious example. How does Shakespeare achieve his effect here? The 'record-breaking display of evil' has also set records for the speed of its escalation. And, as the plots of the wicked are directed against themselves with a spiralling intensity, so the good, or the redeemable, increasingly achieve mutual recognition, casting off the disguises in which prudence or madness or luck has enabled them to survive. Lear's recognition of Gloucester, and his reconciliation with Cordelia, are landmarks in this process, as is the death of Oswald and the warning Edgar delivers to Albany. All these complex and powerful 'machinations' (Edgar's word) form the basis of an audience's expectation that Cordelia will not die. But, in thinking this, we may be victims of a typical imbalance in our categories of interpretation; more plainly, we may have succumbed to wishful thinking, against both the claims of political probability and the implications of Christian discernment.

On political probability Empson can again be quoted (and I do this, also, because it is common to read surveys of criticism of the play which leave his essay unmentioned; it can be recommended to Christians for both its militant secularism and its scarifying intelligence): 'That the execution was carried through after the change of government is just the kind of thing that happens in the confusion of a liberation, and indeed is almost typical of the forces that Lear had set loose.'[30] I do not see that Christian discernment need object to this view. Walter Stein, in another excellent, little-read and discerning essay, would go further: 'Cordelia's life and death fall within a significatory pattern – incomplete at the point where the play ends (the point where common sense ends) – defined by the Gospels – and whose completion lies beyond common sense.'[31] This pattern involves the evocation of an 'allegory' of 'Christian redemption'. And for the allegory to be recognizable, it is requisite that Cordelia die; without death, no resurrection and no redemption. I think there is a danger here that Christians may be found arguing that she was too good to live. I have suggested that her goodness is, whatever else, humanly definable – achieved, we may say, against the odds. Beyond this point, we may check ourselves with the observation that at least one character in the play is shown capable of the more 'complete' awareness to which Stein seems to refer.

Edgar presides over the situation in which his father attempts suicide and can (probably) be saved from it; saved, moreover, from the impulse which could otherwise lead him to renewed attempts. His wonderful speeches, before and after the 'fortunate fall', imply Edgar's awareness of the Christian dimensions of the symbolic (as it successfully proves to be) action here, as he urgently says, 'Do but look up'.[32] But Gloucester's reply seems to me crucial here in its savage bitterness:

> Alack, I have no eyes.
> Is wretchedness deprived that benefit
> To end itself by death? 'Twas yet some comfort
> When misery could beguile the tyrant's rage
> And frustrate his proud will.
> > (*King Lear*, IV. v.60–64)

The conditions and limits of human survival speak eloquently here; no less are we reminded of the limited power of 'allegories' or 'symbolic actions'. It is a fair rule of thumb, in relation to this most capacious of plays, that the tendency of any critical position adopted towards it by academic interpretation can be identified with the attitudes of one of its characters. Edgar is Stein's man – the protagonist of 'symbolic' criticism. The ending of *King Lear* finds him, like us, exhausted rather than triumphant. He may well feel that it is time to

> Speak what we feel, not what we ought to say.
> > (*King Lear*, V. iii.298)

To follow this injunction is to accept, among other things, that a play is a play, a symbolic action is a symbolic action – and that neither is a sacred history. I am arguing for the acceptability of a secular reading of *King Lear* – for the sake of identifying its compatibility with Christian truth. To seek more would, I think, involve the desire that the play prove or exemplify – and thus tend to displace, or at least replace – Christian truth. Instead,

> It is required
> You do awake your faith.
> (*The Winter's Tale*, V. iii. 94–95)

5. The Winter's Tale

The line is spoken by Paulina, in the final scene of *The Winter's Tale*. Shakespeare's choice of name for the character has seemed to some critics appropriate by its implied connection with Paul, the theologian of justification by faith. Paulina is a character of considerable moral courage and rhetorical force, displayed in her defiance of Leontes in the extremity of his jealous madness and, later, in her psychological dominance over him in his repentance. She is also a manipulator of him, and of all those whom she sustains in the belief that Leontes' wife, struck by her husband's unjust charges, has died:

> I say she's dead. I'll swear't. If word nor oath
> Prevail not, go and see.
> *(The Winter's Tale*, III. ii.202–203)

In the final scene Hermione's appearance naturally provokes demands – as this from Camillo:

> If she pertain to life, let her speak too.

Paulina replies:

> That she is living,
> Were it but told to you, should be hooted at
> Like an old tale. But it appears she lives . . .
> *(The Winter's Tale*, V. iii.114, 116–118)

The play's title declares it a 'tale'. Its nature allows it what Paulina suggests to be the superior reality of 'appearance'. For Brecht[33] (and for Dorothy L. Sayers),[34] theatre tested beliefs and ideologies with a thoroughness superior to that of rational argument or archival research; it displayed behaviour in a form where the reasons for it and the aims informing it had to be clear to its performers. If Hermione's survival – or resurrection – is to become credible, on this view, to those who watch and hear her and Paulina, it should be possible to give an account of them, and of the play to which they form a climax and conclusion, that will explain how they can be performed.

How might this be done? To get at the case of Paulina, one might begin with the case of Camillo. Leontes is swift to marry them off to each other; as if those who know most should share with each other what each other does not quite know – and, perhaps, as if such 'knowing' no longer matters to Leontes himself: as if the questions of 'credibility', and of Camillo's past treachery or fidelity or both, to himself and to Polixenes, are precisely, in their obvious interestingness, what he now wishes to leave to others.[35] Camillo's situation, in Act 1, Scene 2, requires that, to save his position and perhaps his life, he promise to Leontes to bring about Polixenes' death; and, next, that – to preserve his own self-respect, his sense of what is plausible in particular and in general, his whole sense that there can be criteria of credibility – he should, instead of killing Polixenes, tell him of his instructions, betray his own master and enable the escape of Polixenes – who duly becomes his new master.

> I must be the poisoner
> Of good Polixenes, and my ground to do't
> Is the obedience to a master – one
> Who in rebellion with himself, will have
> All that are his so too. To do this deed,
> Promotion follows. If I could find example
> Of thousands that had struck anointed kings
> And flourish'd after, I'd not do't . . .
>   (*The Winter's Tale*, I. ii.353–360)

The words 'ground' and 'example' are doing a lot of work in this passage. And the logic of Camillo's argument with himself links such words with the case of one who, like Leontes, is 'in rebellion with himself'. The effect of Camillo's attempt to avoid the case of Leontes, the attitude of Leontes to evidence and example, is that he becomes in rebellion with his master rather than himself. It is a feat he imitates, with nice variations, in Act 4, Scene 4, where he undertakes to secure the welfare and the love of Florizel and Perdita only to arrange for their immediate betrayal to Polixenes – the consequence of which will be that he, Camillo (and in some sense all the rest of them too) gets back where he, where they, started: to Leontes, to Sicilia, and, as Camillo cannot guess, to Hermione. Camillo's case indicates how falsehood leads from the will to preserve integrity – or, in the terms I used earlier, how intelligible motives and aims lead to, and subsequently operate in, a world which they have made to some extent unintelligible.

Camillo's conventionally polite words to Archidamus in the play's first scene can be heard as pregnant with a similar sense:

> Sicilia cannot show himself over kind to Bohemia. They were trained together in their childhoods, and there rooted between them then such an affection which cannot choose but branch now.
>   (*The Winter's Tale*, I. i.21–23)

The fruitfulness of 'nature', on which Camillo's metaphors play, is heavy with the more threatening implications of the word 'branch' (the two kings and their countries will part, as branches on a tree when they come to full growth) and of the formulation 'cannot show himself over-kind' (Leontes cannot afford to be more than conventionally kind – he cannot very much insist on their kinship – he cannot afford such natural kindness). Nature's growth, nature's divisions, are, at this early stage in the play, shown to proceed, in some sense, against nature. And I hear another intimation behind Camillo's words here: that none of this sense of nature's problems with its own nature can be shown; the roots of privacy, of the special awareness and self-awareness which Leontes will claim ('I have drunk, and seen the spider'), lie in a fear of growing, of growing apart, which is at the same time a fear of showing, of showing a part.

> Go play, boy, play. Thy mother plays, and I
> Play too, but so disgraced a part, whose issue
> Will hiss me to my grave . . .
>   (*The Winter's Tale*, I. ii.188–190)

This intense embarrassment of Leontes has to be kept in relation to the force of his earlier, great, obscure speech;

> Affection, thy intention stabs the centre,
> Thou dost make possible things not so held . . .
> With what's unreal thou co-active art,
> And fellow'st nothing. Then 'tis very credent
> Thou may'st co-join with something, and thou dost
> And that beyond commission; and I find it –
> And that to the infection of my brains
> And hard'ning of my brows.
>   (*The Winter's Tale*, I. ii.140–148)

At one level his problem lies in the difficulty of distinguishing between 'something' and 'nothing' (If Lear's claim, that 'Nothing will come of nothing',[36] were valid, then 'something' must have been there, from which *The Winter's Tale*, and all its attendant 'somethings', are to be seen to have come; a gesture, a performance, a trick of rhetoric, a woman's womb – a lost origin). At another level, the problem lies in 'joining', in what it is to be 'co-active'. Leontes cannot bear the refusal by his courtiers, of his own certainties. He seeks the further assurance of an oracle: when it speaks against him, he rejects that too. Much as he talks, he would (I take it) most love it for people simply to stop talking about it all (he was grateful for Camillo's plea that, Polixenes once dead, Hermione's public honour be left unblemished).[37] If

Camillo's is a part whose aims and motivations outrun its own control, Leontes' is a part which seeks not to appear, not to be played at all.

Two wonderful passages from Stanley Cavell's essay on the play are guiding me here:

> The failure of knowledge is the failure of acknowledgement . . . the result of the failure is not an ignorance but an ignoring, not an opposable doubt but an unappeasable denial, a wilful uncertainty that consitutes an annihilation. These formulations suggest that *The Winter's Tale* may be taken as painting the portrait of the sceptic as a fanatic . . .

> We are bound, it seems to me, at some point to feel that this theatre is contesting the distinction between saying and showing . . . If the concluding scene of this theatre is telling something, it is not something antecedently known; it is rather instituting knowledge, reconceiving, reconstituting knowledge, along with the world.[38]

From these I take the following very limited and impoverished train of thoughts. Scepticism seeks certainty, and annihilates what it seeks and that world in which it seeks it. The sceptic in some way knows this too. To see might be to be certain – but Leontes sees that it is not so. To perform, to act, to play one's part, might be what proceeds from certainty – how then could the sceptic ever be found to be doing such things? But then, performance always outruns its intentions anyway. To say this another way, the performer must know what, before her performance, does not exist, and cannot therefore be known. (The performer knows her part; but to play her part is to show that it has not previously been known; she makes it before she knows it.) The cure for scepticism is then not knowledge but performance. Are works the proof of faith? Is faith the substance of things hoped for, the evidence of things not seen? In all this, which comes first? How can we ever be sure? Who then may be saved? Well – 'God was in Christ', and this plays its part.[39]

Hermione, then, as Leontes rightly intuits, 'plays' (as, more obviously, do Polixenes , and Florizel, and Autolycus, and in other ways the shepherds old and young – 'Whatever is begotten, born and dies').[40] Is it clear that Paulina plays? (Does her name, on this argument, imply not so much faith as justification, therefore certainty beyond the need of play?) One is tempted to see her as surrogate author-producer, obscure and transparent as Shakespeare. It is perhaps more helpful to see her as a human analogue for the figures of Time and the bear; that is, for the nature that preserves and also consumes.[41] She preserves, that is, Hermione, while devouring, in her reticence, Leontes' hopes and regrets and embarrassments concerning Hermione's fecundity, her doubleness, her power to 'branch'. The Hermione whom Paulina represents, and who, by Paulina's preservation is also empowered to re-present, to perform, herself, and with herself her marriage, their marriage, to her husband – this Hermione is no longer solely due to 'great creating Nature'.[42] My argument leads me to say, then, that Hermione's re-presentation is due to art, and to theatre. But I am saying this not with a view to stressing the 'magical', or abysmal, or domineering, or even the ineluctable in what we call theatre; but rather the many ways we have of re-presenting to ourselves theatre's power to re-present. Theatre, which evokes the sceptic and the fanatic, always for its evocations, posits credibility of some kind. Shakespeare's theatre is invariably, and perhaps increasingly over the length of his career, concerned with the nuances, the limits, the conditions of this credibility. Is this to say that theatre is about religion? About Christianity? About the Christian claim to credibility? About Christ's claim on our faith?

It is to say these things, and I have tried to say them. But it is also to say that Shakespearian theatre is about what all these things are also about. 'Religion is Shakespeare's pervasive, hence invisible, business. The resurrection of the woman is, theatrically, a claim that the composer of this play is in command of an art that brings words to life, or vice versa, and since the condition of this life is that her spectators awake their faith, we, as well as Leontes, awake, as it were, with her.'[43] Or we awake her, as we awake ourselves.

We may well feel that, if Shakespeare asks this, he asks more than we are prepared to grant, or, as Christians, should grant. I think this resistance is proper. We have to stand back – as Brecht argued – from such theatre if we are to 'awaken' it, and awake with it. But then it was the publican who stood back, where the Pharisee stood within the temple (Lk. 18:9–14). Christian discernment is a good approach to or distance from Shakespeare's theatre. And Shakespeare's theatre in turn shows us how we branch from God, as a condition of being rooted in him.[44] If the cure for scepticism – and the other annihilations practised by

Shakespeare's unhappy ambitious rulers, manipulators, Stoics – is acceptance, the road to acceptance is to be accepted.

Some questions for discussion

1. Do you consider Shakespeare to have been a Christian? Did he believe the Bible? What do you think he believed about the church? What church allegiances did he have, if any?
2. In what ways does the Bible appear textually in Shakespeare's plays? With what intentions do the plays use it? Obviously, you will need to think about the plays you are familiar with.
3. In what ways does Shakespeare depict the church? 'Professional' Christians, especially clergy? Committed Christian believers? What do we make of their portrayals?
4. Do any plays *require* a Christian reading? Make a distinction between plays where we might expect a Christian outline but in which Christianity actually appears to be absent (such as *The Tempest, As You Like It*), and plays which depict an apparently pagan society, but in which Christian values or concepts appear to be present (such as *The Winter's Tale, Coriolanus*). Consider particularly *The Merchant of Venice, Measure for Measure, Richard II, Hamlet, King Lear, Antony and Cleopatra, Richard III* and *Macbeth*.

10

Reading *Paradise Lost*

U. Milo Kaufmann

The critic Frederick Crews once referred facetiously to an imagined freshman text with the title *All Previous Knowledge*. The novice reader of *Paradise Lost* is apt to suspect that Milton presupposed just such an encyclopaedic background as a prerequisite for enjoying his poem, and this is only one of the challenges posed. On at least one occasion, at the opening of an undergraduate course in Milton, I have urged students to close their eyes and imagine themselves totally at ease on a balmy tropical beach. 'Soak it up,' I have encouraged. 'Now, take a deep breath, for you are going to be leaving that behind for an encounter with some of the most demanding literature you will ever read.' Such a stratagem is meant to be disarming, of course. Milton *is* difficult. But he is also uniquely rewarding. No other poet has attempted in English the full range of the impossible as he has, offering the reader, if the poet's own hopes have been fully realized, nothing less than a sequel to inspired Scripture.

A few more words about the difficulties, and then many more words about the rewards. An undergraduate told me that she found Milton's language to be very difficult, and she was referring not to the wealth of allusion but rather to a diction with all the challenges of late Renaissance English as well as the poet's Latinate idioms and syntax. Add to these the intricate structure of a poem which offers to frame both universe and the whole of history, and the sum is indeed daunting. But I believe that most students are neither cowards nor fools. In life, complexity is often inescapable, and while we need not take up with those who find it virtuous for its own sake, we can certainly acknowledge that grappling with it is often the only way into especially rich experience. I recall a *Scientific American* article of several years back which sketched out the inner workings of a pocket calculator. I was made to see that while the device is one you can hold in your hand, it is roughly as complex as the total mechanism of an automobile. In something of the same vein the poet Richard Wilbur refers to Milton as 'the greatest verse architect in history'.[1] Wilbur witnesses to devoting days in class teasing the structure out of relatively simple poems like 'L'Allegro' and 'Il Penseroso'. What must *Paradise Lost* then deserve?

I am conceding, you see, the challenges posed by Milton's range of allusions, by his language, and also by his form. Yet what I choose to dwell upon here is the great benefit to all those who will grant him his due. And granting that due means, first off, that one is obliged to read the *whole* of *Paradise Lost*. My own first encounter with the poem, apart from the illustrated version I had looked at as a child, was in a course which presented only excerpts. I do not recommend this. We do not expect to view the Mona Lisa with her neck and left eye covered, nor do we expect to attend to only the high points of Beethoven's ninth symphony, omitting, perhaps, that noisy chorus at the close. I do not encourage abridgments of *Paradise Lost*, not even of the last two books, which are, after all, a summary of God's mighty acts in history.

An attentive reading of the poem admits one to a universe utterly charged with meaning. All coheres, everything points beyond itself. While along the way the reader may find a thousand doors and windows opened upon the source materials of western culture, the real pay-off is the invincibly hopeful Christian vision which informs the work. Milton believes utterly that the promised end of all things is a marriage of earth and heaven in which the human is transfigured.

In the following pages I shall comment upon six dimensions of the reward for the faithful reader of this masterwork of Christian art and hope. These are:

1. *Paradise Lost* as the supreme demonstration in English poetry of the positive way, or the way to God and the heavenly by way of the imagery of created things;

2. *Paradise Lost* as uniquely inclusive story, covering the whole of time from beginning to end;

3. *Paradise Lost* as an epic achieving a balance between public and private or psychological action;

4. *Paradise Lost* as a courageous theodicy offering two related solutions to the perennial problem of evil;

5. *Paradise Lost* as a frame for the earthly paradise, asserting the

biblical conviction that creation and fall are not identical, and that the material world is not to be eschewed but rather restored and perfected;

6. *Paradise Lost* as both a critique of Promethean freedom and a celebration of a human freedom which collaborates with God in making what is to be for ever the case.

1. Paradise Lost *and the positive way*

While Theravada Buddhism and certain other mystical traditions have been the main exponents of the negative way, insisting that the transcendent is best approached by mistrusting and denying the concepts and images which the natural order offers, biblical religion incorporates at its core certain convictions which make the positive way the preferred approach to God and the heavenly. The positive way is that which makes use of the creatures in a regimen of devotional ascent, and the central doctrines honoured in this ascent are those of the good creation, the God active in providential history, the incarnation (God takes on human flesh), the resurrection both of Christ and of the believer, the church which (as Hebrews 12 has it) even now joins the living and the dead, angels and humans, in enduring community, and finally the marriage of earth and heaven implied in the images of the new Jerusalem and the exalted Christ. Before Milton's poem the greatest poetic example of the positive way was of course Dante's *Divine Comedy*, and indeed there are significant likenesses between these two magisterial poems. Dante and Milton both work with a notion of figure or symbol which moves from the familiar to the accommodated transcendent realm. There are differences between the two poets, to be sure. *Paradise Lost* involves a much more dynamic universe, with significant action initiated in many quarters. And in a variety of ways Milton, drawing upon ideas made popular by Giordano Bruno, Thomas Digges and others, affirms a cosmos and history which are open. Everything in *Paradise Lost* converges upon the quite remarkable confidence that new things happen in eternity; they always have and always will.

Now the immediate matrix for Milton's conviction in this matter was a tradition in Reformed thought which we can call the discipline of heavenly-mindedness. Calvin in his *Institutes* devotes a chapter to meditation upon the future life (III.ix), and in Milton's England a host of splendid souls gave themselves energetically to working out all the details. One can point to works such as

Richard Baxter's *The Saint's Everlasting Rest*, *The Life of Faith* and *Dying Thoughts*; to Jeremiah Burroughs' *Moses His Choice* (which gives something like a hundred pages to discussing the positive way); to John Owen's seven-volume commentary on Hebrews, to the sermons of Richard Sibbes, to Bunyan's *The Pilgrim's Progress*, and so on. The most consequential conviction endlessly spelled out in these works is that for the believer the heavenly life is a continuum of earth and heaven and that there is no better way to improve this earthly life than to set it in the context of its heavenly continuation. A related confidence is that heavenly devotion admits one here and now into the heavenly places. We should not wonder that in Book III of *Paradise Lost* Milton dares to move into the very throne room of heaven, something which even Dante does not venture to do. The whole of Book III with its eavesdropping upon conversation between Father and Son, and its detailed imagery of the heavenly landscape, is the supreme embodiment of the devotional boldness worked out at length and by many hands in Reformed heavenly-mindedness.

Milton's commitment to the positive way is implicit in three of the most remarkable features of *Paradise Lost*. Access to the heaven of heavens we have already noted. A second is the richly diverse *bonhomie* which holds in the poem between humans and angels. The conversations between Adam and the 'affable' Raphael are wide-ranging and animated, with a rich play of feeling on both sides. The transactions with Michael in the closing books are more solemn, since Michael comes to announce the details of the divine sentence, but it is plain that in the variety of angel-human relationships Milton intends just that commerce among rational kinds which Baxter and others had insisted should be a natural and continuing element in the Christian life.

A third manifestation of Milton's commitment to the positive way is the ultimate reach of the myth of *Paradise Lost*. This most resounding of Milton's affirmations about last things is the destined marriage of earth and heaven, 'One Kingdom, Joy and Union without end' (VII.161).[2] Such a consummation Milton finds to be implicit in the biblical promise of new heavens and a new earth, set forth by Isaiah and John. One of the more controversial details of this consummation is the suggestion that while ordinary time will cease a heavenly time will take its place. The marriage of time and eternity of course allows for change in the heavenly reality, and it is this which gives one pause. Yet the Almighty in Book VII of the poem speaks of the creation which will follow upon the war in heaven as diffusing good to 'Worlds and *Ages* infinite' (VII.191, italics mine). Certainly Milton's contemporaries were convinced that resurrected bodies were vital and lively, and it is difficult to imagine active bodies functioning in anything other than some version of time which, after all, is the measure of motion. Milton pointedly allows for spiritual bodies even for his angels, and we conclude that for him the heavenly reality accommodates in a transfigured form much of what we would consider temporal and material. This creation will be redeemed.

2. Paradise Lost *as inclusive story*

Professor Marjorie Nicholson once suggested that if Shakespeare was the poet of time, then Milton was the poet of space. There is some point in the epigram, for Shakespeare is assuredly the poet of lived time with its intense moments and pregnant hours, while no-one can miss the spatial scope of a poem such as *Paradise Lost*. Where the epigram is less apropos, even misleading, is in pointing attention away from Milton's very real obsession with time in all its kinds. He composes an early lyric on the subject ('On Time') and his Nativity Ode distinguishes among mythic time, ordinary time, *chairos* (or fullness of time) and eternity. More relevant to our concerns here is how in *Paradise Lost* Milton is concerned with nothing less than the entire career of time as ordinarily understood. C. S. Lewis has remarked that one virtue of Milton's work is that he has the big story, and it goes somewhere. I want to look at some of the details of this strength.

In the *Poetics* Aristotle speaks with disarming simplicity of the action of a tragedy as having a beginning, middle and end. The genius of the remark becomes evident when one considers the skill required in giving a plot an adequate point of departure. Behind the beginning of an action are its causes and the causes of those causes. To persuade us of a true beginning is at least so to veil the framing background of action that we can suspend disbelief. The challenge Milton confronted in his poem is unusually difficult: how do you plausibly make an action begin in the supposedly timeless order of eternity? I pause to make a related point of some consequence. Often, to a degree quite beyond any conscious acknowledgment, modern readers in the West have in fact grown up inside Milton's story of all things. Our culture, with the Bible still in the near background, has as one of its artifacts the myth that behind the fall of Adam and Eve was the fall of the angels. The details from the Bible on this point are quite sketchy and inconclusive. Genesis, at least, makes no connection between wise serpent and Lucifer, and John's Revelation would appear to make the war in heaven late in the total story, rather than early. It is Milton who takes these scattered nuances and makes a masterly and coherent single action of it, borrowing, to be sure, from centuries of tradition, but crafting it into as nearly a seamless whole as the material seems to permit.

But back to the matter of the beginning of action in *Paradise Lost*. Milton's brilliant invention is to make the absolutely first action God's exaltation of the Son, drawing upon the details of coronation psalms, such as Psalm 2, for an incident which mysteriously provokes the jealousy and anger of Lucifer. From this departure, in a sequence which Milton has made the common cultural inheritance, there follows the war in heaven, terminated after three days in such a way as to suggest that God's epic champion, the Son, can wrap up summarily what no numerical superiority in mere angels would ever be able to achieve. The rebels are banished to hell and, in a dazzling stroke, Milton has God announce the impending creation as his superabounding and generous response to the diminution of the angelic ranks. In Milton's logic, then, the universe exists because there was a heavenly rebellion. This is not the only or the last example in Milton's works of a remarkable link made between evil and a greater good which otherwise would not have obtained.

The details of the war in heaven and the creation are narrated to Adam in Paradise by Raphael, constituting the bulk of Books V to VIII. This material is something like a third of the entire poem, and it is apparent that Milton assumes that Adam can have no understanding of his present situation in Paradise without an extraordinary history lesson. Though the lesson does not prevent mankind's fall, it serves to make that fall more plausible, for we are asked to believe that while Lucifer was not tempted, and so is unforgivable, Adam and Eve both were, and are therefore more deserving of mercy. In this prominence given to the wisdom of the past, Milton is consistent with the whole of the rest of his writing about true education. Central to this Christian outlook is the resounding conviction that the knowledge needed for the fulfilled human life does not wait to be discovered for the first time, but lies behind, waiting recovery.

The point is an important one and I can underline its current relevance with two anecdotes. Several years ago a young woman who was part of a student group visiting our home figured out that I was a Christian believer. I shall never forget the exquisite caution with which she put a question to me. The gist of it was that she wanted to know if I actually believed that the events of the passion week in fact made a lasting difference in human history, reaching right into the present. But to her it was so plainly unthinkable that such a link could exist between a singular event in the remote past and the living present – and she so much wanted to save me the embarrassment of attributing to me a silly and incredible notion which I did not believe – that she began about four different times to phrase the question. 'Do you actually believe that . . . No, let me try again. Do you think it is impossible that something that long ago could change everything . . . No, no, you don't believe that, you surely couldn't.' I saved her from her own awkward uncertainty by cutting her short. Yes, I most certainly did believe such a link was possible. More encouraging than this young woman's incredulity was an informal survey I have taken a time or two in a large fantasy-literature course which typically enrolls 175–200 students. This literary genre often presents imagined or idealized pasts, and the question I put is not inappropriate. Do they believe that 'saving truth' – that is, truth essential for living a fulfilled human life – is still remaining to be discovered out ahead, or does it lie behind us, already present in the records of human culture? The vote invariably goes to the latter.

The term indispensable for developing the thought implied here is *wisdom*. I grant that this is not a term often conspicuous in the college curriculum, but it is always implied, or had better be. It sums up the hope of education in so far as it is more than information and job-training. Mysteriously, it is hoped and expected that knowledge will be alchemized into this nobler metal. Yet the idea of wisdom is incoherent and incomprehensible without a cherishing of the past, and Milton is a worthy example of the transformation. If in his tract on education he seems to argue that the student should learn everything, if he insists that the proper end of education is regeneration (!), if he asks from the reader of his poems a familiarity with the gamut of traditional lore, it is all of a piece with his conviction that things do add up. Knowledge is pointed. Under God the whole of history is plotted, proceeding to a resolution devoutly to be wished but also firmly promised. In connections like this I often think of the logo of my university's centre for advanced study. It represents an empty box, with rays or spokes going out in many directions from the perimeter of the box. What to my mind is most striking about this is that the box is empty. Surely those rays, suggesting individual scholars out on their private projects, *surely* they must intersect at the box's centre if projected inward. But this would be to make explicit what in the secular university is ordinarily left as an unexamined hope: knowledge does converge upon a centre, a point of greatest value, the point of it all: wisdom.

Milton honours the past in his inclusive story. Without it there can be no purchase upon true wisdom. How ironic the results of a survey taken of graduate students in my department a while ago! Those polled were asked to suggest graduate seminars they would like to see offered, and something like 90% of the suggestions prescribed twentieth-century literature. This is what we might fairly call temporal provincialism, the sort of position for which Milton's work and life are a telling refutation. We dare not spend our lives in the village of our own century alone.

3. Paradise Lost *as epic*

As an epic, *Paradise Lost* is an extended narrative which develops the heroic traditions of the Christian people. In English we read it alongside *Beowulf* and *The Faerie Queene*, Wordsworth's fragmentary *Excursion* and perhaps Joyce's *Ulysses* and Tolkien's *The Lord of the Rings*. The category encompasses an enormous amount of excellent literature, but there are just two features of epic and its history that I want to give a moment to here. The first concerns the density of value in the epic poem, and the other concerns the place held by *Pardise Lost* in the historical development of the kind.

It is customary to say that the two related revolutions in literature, those of Romanticism and Realism, immensely increased the range of material engaged by literature. We would want to say that, on balance, this has been a positive development, but it is not without its down side. Arthur Miller's protagonist Willie Loman (*i.e.*, Low-Man) is, like other tragic protagonists, a failure, but he is definitely not a glorious failure. Criminals, whores, vagrants, sociopaths, crazies and fools can be presented artfully, and often have been, but they seem to be the obsessing subjects of modern times, whereas in ancient times both tragedy and epic featured the noble and elevated. It is obvious that much recent literature has brought to centre stage the least admirable of society, along with contexts of meanness, ugliness and brutishness. What is less obvious, perhaps, is that for such to be included other matters must be omitted, and this is where the tradition of epic is instructive. The epic milieu is a heightened one, charged by the presence of the most precious, honourable, noteworthy, desirable and sacred. Noble persons, memorable places, pedigreed artifacts – all this is the stuff of the epic. The plain rationale for Milton's opulent inventories of exotic places redolent of myth and exalted history, his devotion to the proper noun and the received title, is all part and parcel of the epic. In all this there is an assumption not so axiomatic to the modern reader as it was to the reader of the Renaissance: some things are more important than other things, and you should spend your time with the former. The modern homogenization (a term I prefer to democratization) of values means, in so many cases, that relevant ideals are quite lost sight of. But Milton keeps us focused, in epic fashion, on matters deserving our attention.

Another consideration about Miltonic epic concerns how *Paradise Lost* fits into an interesting historical sequence. In the West we can trace epic from the nearly anonymous works of Homer, through Virgil, the later Italians, Spenser, and on to the contemporary epic romance. In this history a curious pattern emerges. Whereas earliest epic offered vast public action with the artist-maker all but invisible, the historical development is towards inward action, with the poet more and more apparent as the real hero. Romantic epic as we find it in Wordsworth (who knew his Milton well) and twentieth-century epic as we see it in Joyce's *Ulysses* offer us psychological action as dominant.[3] In the long move towards internalization of action and the featuring of the artist-hero, Milton's epic occupies an interesting middle position with a notable balancing of the public and the personal. The external action of *Paradise Lost* is, as we have seen, all-inclusive. Yet we miss much if we ignore the substance of the invocations which open Books I, III, VII and IX. In these invocations not only does the poet make plain his continuing reliance upon the Holy Spirit, but he also provides much illuminating insight into the creative process which is the framing action of the poem. We learn that he proposes a kind of sequel to Scripture, for he invokes the muse of Moses who set down the opening books of the Bible; he testifies to his need to have what is low in him elevated; he refers to his physical blindness; he refers to his Muse dictating to him each night his 'unpremeditated verse'. Yes, we are abundantly aware of the Miltonic consciousness which holds all the public action of the poem in solution. Yet the artist-hero is a chastened one, dependent and limited, whatever his pretensions *vis-à-vis* the secular epic poets of the past. I would add that his lines about taking dictation from his Muse (IX.23–24) are easily misread. He chooses to give the preponderance of credit to inspiration, but all the evidence indicates that rarely has a poetry been so totally premeditated. The young Milton insisted that his poems came only with sustained effort. All we know adds up to a picture of a poet who from his early twenties understands that to write of noble things the poet's own life must be disciplined, above reproach, with a memory as thoroughly furnished as time and the available texts permit. In short, Milton is the normative example of how spiritual vision follows upon spiritual discipline. Aquinas once observed that the loss of spiritual vision is the first consequence of an unchaste thought life, and in one of his prose tracts Milton points up the absurdity of his adversary's suggesting that he haunted bordellos, just as in another prose work he insists that the epic poet must fashion a life that is itself a true poem. In Milton's career there is a clear *modus operandi* for the creative life: vision depends on that hearing which is hearkening, hearing with a heart to obey. His own life is a spiritual epic in which *Paradise Lost* emerges as the fruit of a life-long discipline and devotion, along with a responsible involvement in public life.

4. Paradise Lost *as theodicy*

In the opening lines of his poem Milton announces that he intends to 'justify the ways of God to men' (I.26). Such an effort is called a theodicy, that is, a defence of God in the face of evil. Admittedly, theodicy blinks at or downplays the scriptural insistence that God's ways are not man's ways and are undoubtedly resistant of justification on human terms, but it engages a longstanding perplexity of those faith-positions which honour a good God behind nature and history. It should be noted at once that the Bible does not venture to offer anything like a complete theodicy. Jewish tradition, indeed, long denied any clear connection between Genesis 3 and the generality of evil in the world, and we have noticed above that the Scriptures are less than transparent on how and when a war in heaven may have occurred. Significantly, on those occasions when Jesus was most directly asked about the problem of ·evil he side-stepped any explanation in terms of origins (for instance, the sins of the parents, or the particular nastiness of those on whom the tower of Siloam fell), but declared instead that however it came about, each and every evil could be an occasion for the response which glorifies God. In recent years a useful typology has been proposed by John Hick[4] and insightfully applied to Milton by Dennis Danielson.[5] This typology distinguishes between Augustinian and Irenaean theodicy. The former, more popular by far in Christian tradition, was advanced and made normative by St Augustine. It offered to explain evil in terms of origins particularly in terms of primordial free creaturely choices, whether angelic or human. The latter theodicy, which takes its name from a second-century bishop of Lyons, looks more to the future than to the past for explanation. However evil arose, it is being wrought by God into a greater good than otherwise would have existed. God will be seen, finally, to have wrought all things well, as Julian of Norwich famously acknowledged.

One can argue for the presence of both lines of thought in *Paradise Lost*. Of course the explicit theodicy traces evil back to Lucifer's choice of rebellion, and later to the unfortunate choices of Eve and Adam. Yet in putting Lucifer's primordial choice under high magnification, as it were, Milton manages (surely without intending it) to highlight the difficulties that inhere in this argument. Readers have difficulty grasping what antecedent deficiency in Lucifer predisposed him to entertain God's gracious act in exalting the Son as an impairment of his own person and position. If there was none, the response seems capricious. If there was, the question of evil's origin becomes caught up in an infinite regress. I repeat that this sequence in the poem is largely Milton's invention and whatever its merits as art it does not suffice as theodicy.

There is, however, another line of thought developed which we may call the implicit theodicy of *Paradise Lost*. In this implicit theodicy evil again and again evokes extraordinary providence. The best example would be creation as the divine response to the rebellion in heaven; another example, perhaps equally good, is the promised incarnation as the response to the fall in the Garden. Earth and heaven are both the richer for God's creative response to evil. I cite the most germane lines:

> Who seeks
> To lessen thee, against his purpose serves
> To manifest the more thy might: his evil
> Thou usest, and from thence creat'st more good.
> Witness this new-made World, another Heav'n
> From Heaven Gate not far . . .
>
> (VII.613–618)

The implicit theodicy is one of firm hope rather than rigorous logic, and is a needed complement to the explicit theodicy.

5. Paradise Lost *as frame for the earthly Paradise*

At the close of God's week of work in Genesis 1, he pronounces the whole very good. In the entire account there is no hint of resistance to the divine purpose in the creation. It is in root-texts like this that the Hebraic and Christian celebration of the world is grounded. The natural issue of this confidence is the picture of the paradisial garden which we are given in Genesis 2. In a capsule, we might say that finiteness can be, and was, and will be, a mode of perfection.

This is to forswear the practice of identifying creation and fall which seems natural to a variety of mystical and neo-Platonic systems. In such schemes to be finite (limited) is to be estranged from the divine or absolute. One version of this is to affirm the evil of matter, since anything material has all the limitations implied in the qualifications of matter such as location and size.

Paradise Lost Book IV is a sublime pastoral, ravishing the senses in describing what the world was meant to be in God's original design. Many authors have observed that a primary theme of western literature is the paradise once enjoyed but now lost. I think of M. H. Abrams' discussion in *Natural Supernaturalism* and to Tolkien's observation in a letter that the loss of Paradise is the central plot in literature. Omar Khayyam's wish to grasp the entire world and remake it closer to the heart's desire is a common one, and it implies a mysterious human awareness of a standard from outside the sum of things as they are.

It is Milton's genius to present us, despite the difficulties of imaginatively unworking the fall in all its consequences, the prelapsarian world, and what a splendour it is. Golden fruit in pristine groves, a garden which crowns a wilderness peak of verdant growth, plumbed by a subterranean river which rises as a fountain of living water. True, the close reader of the account will understand that Milton has not achieved the impossible. Even the regenerate artist cannot wholly penetrate behind the fall, and the inconsistencies of Eden when spun out at length in narrative must be acknowledged. The language and skills with which the newly created Adam acts are incorrigibly mysterious. The dynamic balance of a green world with its veritable ark of charmed beasts is equally mysterious, so long as one assumes no predation. But we allow these concerns to remain recessive, for the artifice of Milton's earthly paradise is indeed exquisite. I cite one brief passage:

> Thus was this place,
> A happy rural seat of various view:
> Groves whose rich Trees wept odorous Gums and Balm,
> Others, whose fruit burnished with Golden Rind
> Hung amiable, *Hesperian* Fables true,
> If true, here only, and of delicious taste;
> Betwixt them Lawns, or level Downs, and Flocks
> Grazing the tender herb, were interpos'd,
> Or palmy hillock, or the flow'ry lap
> Of some irriguous Valley spread her store,
> Flow'rs of all hue, and without Thorn the Rose ... .
>
> (IV.246–256)

With the exception of a word or two like 'irriguous' – whose meaning we can guess – the passage builds upon a host of charged and apt monosyllables: 'Gums and Balm', 'Rind', 'Lawns', 'Downs, and Flocks', on to the memorable 'without Thorn the Rose'. Here, plainly, the primal splendour of the things themselves, the Edenic simples, requires no remarkable diction. Herb and beast and tree and fruit are all perfect in their kinds. No-one has been more artful than Milton in canvassing the earthly paradise, and where he fails we forgive him for attempting the impossible.

6. Paradise Lost *as critique and defence of freedom*

Milton is one of the several greatest apologists for freedom to write in English. His *Areopagitica* remains the classic defence of the freedom of the press. His *Tenure of Kings and Magistrates* argues the inalienable right of the people to remove any ruler whose acts are not the clear expression of the popular good, his four tracts on divorce argue (controversially, to be sure) for the freedom to dissolve a marriage in which minds have not been truly joined; he will even argue, in his defence of the English parliamentarians, that the populace has the right to execute a king.

Many have supposed there to be some tension between his prose and *Paradise Lost*, for in the latter the rebels are uniformly in the wrong – Lucifer and his angelic party, Adam and Eve in the Garden. But the matter is by no means adjudicated that readily. The attentive reader will find in *Paradise Lost* not only a resounding condemnation of those abuses of freedom we might call Promethean, but an equally resounding affirmation of a creaturely freedom, which holds measureless promise for the human future. Milton's position, encapsulated, is the Christian view that human freedom is both boundless and constrained, with the constraints embodied in those prescriptions which grow out of the divine character.

Professor Zwi Werblowsky makes the definitive case for the Promethean dimensions of Milton's archfoe.[6] The essential line of thought runs something like the following: Prometheus and Lucifer are both arch-rebels, both are integrally involved in events which launch humankind into culture and history, and both are implicated in the alienation of the divine and the natural orders. It is plain enough that Prometheus, in giving fire, language and craft to mankind, provides those resources which separate people from nature, and for this and other reasons the Titan is himself alienated from Zeus. I stress that the classical stories of Prometheus should be required reading for every college student, for they develop what has become the dominant myth of the modern West. William Lynch has argued, as his subtitle implies, that Prometheus has proved to be the image of modern autonomous man, man come of age.[7] Prometheus is titanic man, saying, 'I can do it on my own; I don't need any divine help, thank you.' Prometheus has his counterpart in Faust, whose name means 'fist'. The irony is that the modern Six Six Prometheans forget or ignore the fact that Prometheus was anything but free, and his rebellion against the divine forever defined him.

Nowadays Promethean freedom tends to be synonymous with cultural activity, all that human enterprise which changes nature or the 'givens' and is not obliged to fit into some larger plan. Here the human race remakes the world and designs the future. Yet, while Milton's Lucifer is quintessentially Promethean when he says that he prefers reigning in hell to serving in heaven, he at least never forgets that there is a grand scheme outside of which he stands. More recent Prometheans slight that possibility.

In a notable exchange between Adam and Raphael just prior to the archangel's telling Adam of how the war in heaven came about, Milton is careful to advise the reader, through Raphael, of certain bedrock principles. Man and angel alike are free, but within the bounds of divine ordaining. All creatures, Adam is told, proceed from and return to the Almighty, 'Each in their several active Spheres assign'd, / Till body up to spirit work, in bounds / Proportion'd to each kind' (V.477–479). Here is the magnificent promise held out for the sublimation of all things material, but the 'bounds' are essential, for all works according to the Almighty's overall design. Raphael elaborates on the possibilities:

> . . . time may come when men
> With Angels may participate, and find
> No inconvenient Diet, nor too light Fare:
> And from these corporal nutriments perhaps
> Your bodies may at last turn all to spirit,
> Improv'd by tract of time, and wing'd ascend
> Ethereal, as wee, or may at choice
> Here or in Heav'nly Paradises dwell;
> If ye be found obedient, and retain
> Unalterably firm his love entire
> Whose progeny you are.
>
> (V.493–503)

Adam's response is fitting:

> O favourable Spirit, propitious guest,
> Well hast thou taught the way that might direct
> Our knowledge . . .
>
> (V.507–509)

There follows Adam's stated understanding of the 'contemplation of created things – the positive way – which by steps leads one to God. God's pristine and eternal programme is one which leads to himself as Ground and End. Significantly, this resounding statement of how human freedom is both bounded and boundless – bounded by the divine constraints, and boundless in that God, the true infinite, is its delight and goal – comes immediately prior to the narration of the Son's exaltation and Lucifer's fall. A creaturely freedom which refuses all bounds will initiate that alternative history which we understand now includes our own.

But we are made for God and heaven, and God's purposes are not finally frustrated. I close with my personal favourite from many exalted passages in this extraordinary Christian epic. Speaking of the fall, Milton's God says:

> I can repair
> That detriment, if such it be to lose
> Self-lost, and in a moment will create
> Another World, out of one man a Race
> Of men innumerable, there to dwell,
> Not here, till by degrees of merit rais'd
> They open to themselves at length the way
> Up hither, under long obedience tri'd

191

And Earth be chang'd to Heav'n, and Heav'n to Earth,
One Kingdom, Joy and Union without end.

(VII.152–161)

In all its essential features the vision of *Pardise Lost* remains one which richly commends itself to both mind and heart.

A closing note: apart from the many ways in which all readers must, in honesty, acknowledge the Christian character of Milton's great epic, there is a way in which the Christian reader can expect a special engagement with the poem. I shall refer to this as *resonance*. Have we not all had the experience of finally encountering an elusive X or a Y or a Z, and then, when coming across one of these in a poem or story, saying to ourselves, 'Oh, I recognize that. I now have a feeling for that.' Certainly it happens in the reading of Scripture. After a notable experience of, say, the Holy Spirit in a small-group setting, one may read John's gospel and find that whenever the Holy Spirit is mentioned the language has a special charge of meaning. The reference is now fully resonant for the reader. Much the same is true for the Christian reader of *Paradise Lost*. Deep calls to deep, spirit to spirit. The committed reader will find that his or her personal Christian belief and practice mean a special resonance for all manner of references made in the poem. To take just one example, the Son who is epic champion in Book III, creative Word in Book VII and promised Saviour in Book III and the closing prophecies is also the reader's living contemporary, a known presence.

Milton's Puritan contemporaries stressed a devotional approach to the Bible which I find relevant here. One came to the written Word as if entering God's throne room. One prepared, humbly and expectantly, to meet the God of heaven and earth. The Christian reader of *Paradise Lost*, a poem which exalts the God of all time and space, can expect something similar. The believing heart resonates and responds to the spiritual realities Milton himself honoured.

A select reading list

C. S. Lewis' little book is a natural place to begin in the secondary material, for it is accessible, witty and explicitly Christian in its approach. Stanley Fish's study involves the reader-response method and argues brilliantly that Milton's strategy throughout was to impress upon the reader his or her own fallenness. A. J. A. Waldock presents a temperate version of the so-called Satanist reading of the poem. Diane Kelsey McColley presents Milton's Eve as a character who can withstand the scrutiny of the feminist critic. E. M. W. Tillyard offers a wise discussion of Milton's several heresies. Regina Schwartz provides a fine-spun and sensitive though somewhat difficult approach to the biblical framing of Milton's poem.

Lawrence Babb, *The Moral Cosmos of Paradise Lost* (East Lansing, MI.: Michigan State University Press, 1970).

Harry Blamires, *Milton's Creation: A Guide Through Paradise Lost* (London: Methuen and Co., 1971).

Joseph E. Duncan, *Milton's Earthly Paradise: A Historical Study of Eden* (Minneapolis, MN.: University of Minnesota Press, 1972).

J. M. Evans, *Paradise Lost and the Genesis Tradition* (Oxford: Oxford University Press, 1968).

Stanley Fish, *Surprised by Sin: The Reader in Paradise Lost* (New York: St Martin's Press, 1967).

C. S. Lewis, *A Preface to Paradise Lost* (Oxford: Oxford University Press, 1942).

Diane Kelsey McColley, *Milton's Eve* (Urbana, IL.: University of Illinois Press, 1983).

Regina M. Schwartz, *Remembering and Repeating: Biblical Creation in Paradise Lost* (Cambridge: Cambridge University Press, 1988).

E. M. W. Tillyard, *Milton* (New York: Collier Books, rev. edn. 1966).

A. J. A. Waldock, *Paradise Lost and Its Critics* (Cambridge: Cambridge University Press, 1962).

George Whiting, *Milton and This Pendant World* (Austin, TX.: University of Texas Press, 1958).

A. N. Wilson, *The Life of John Milton* (Oxford: Oxford University Press, 1983).

11

Romantic poetry and the Wholly Spirit

J. R. Watson

'Romanticism', said T. E. Hulme, 'is spilt religion'.[1] The description seems loaded against the Romantic poets (as we might have expected from a friend of the classical-minded Ezra Pound): it suggests a moment of literary time in which something which had been held carefully, even reverently, was knocked over, making a mess, diffused. And it is certainly possible to view the treatment of religious matters by the Romantic period poets in this way: as the dilution of cherished and traditional belief systems into new and lesser ones, concerned with such things as nature, society and the self. And there is some truth in the idea that the period saw what M. H. Abrams has called 'the secularization of inherited theological ideas and ways of thinking',[2] a process in which the Romantic period poets reshaped some of the systematic theologies into new forms. In that process, however, they created literary artefacts which are not secular so much as newly or differently sacred, consecrated – in a certain way, though not an entirely orthodox one – through the authenticity of individual experience and the integrity of recording it.

Poetry becomes an exploration of the self, but it does not cease to be a spiritual quest: as Coleridge put it, 'the poet, described in *ideal* perfection, brings the whole soul of man into activity'.[3] The process is intensely serious, as the German philosopher K. W. F. Solger suggested:

> Philosophy, art, and religion are the three necessary parts of a harmonious culture. Philosophy without art is means without purpose; art without philosophy is end without beginning; and both without religion are utterly

debased, vile and godless: philosophy becomes insolence
and violence, and art arrogant amusement.[4]

All the writings of the Romantic period poets, including Byron,
suggest that for them art was anything but arrogant amusement:
rather it was a desperately important and serious quest for a
system or systems of belief which would satisfy their individual
needs. In a way, and a way that has not been sufficiently studied,
it was a natural consequence of Protestantism and the Reformation, of the preference for conscience and reason over tradition
and teaching. Where it agrees with Reformation teaching is in the
sense of its own rightness: the hermeneutic tradition of the
Romantic period poets, like that of the sixteenth- and seventeenth-century Reformers, reads the Bible and justifies its own
position. Where it differs from the Reformation tradition is in the
latitude which it allows, validating its beliefs in a wide variety of
experiences. It is impossible to argue that it is, or is not,
sufficiently orthodox: for that would depend on what degree of
orthodoxy is regarded as necessary. I like to think of the Romantic
poets as concerned with sacred things, and certainly not as
secular: the essay which follows is an attempt to justify this belief.

The processes of Romantic period poetry, as many critics have
shown, involve a subtly and infinitely complicated dialogue with
the past, and nowhere more so than in the creation of belief-
systems. The most important of these was the Bible, the book
itself: 'The Old & New Testaments', said Blake, 'are the Great
Code of art';[5] and the Bible was not only the Great Code itself, but
a cause of other writings, so that the Romantic search for
wholeness of soul goes on in confrontation and re-appropriation
of earlier religious texts. The most important of these was *Paradise
Lost*, because of its epic aspirations and its Protestant hermeneutics, as was shown in the last chapter; but there were many others.
The essay which follows, therefore, acknowledges that the
Romantic period poets were searching for wholeness, the whole
soul of which Coleridge spoke, and which Blake thought of as
resurrected humanity; and insists that in the process, the texts that
were produced have an intricate relationship with others that
have been produced before. It is the kind of intertextuality of
which Bakhtin writes:

> Any speaker is himself a respondent to a greater or lesser
> degree. He is not, after all, the first speaker, the one who
> disturbs the eternal silence of the universe. And he

presupposes not only the existence of the language system he is using, but also the existence of preceding utterances – his own and others' – with which his given utterance enters into one or other kind of relation (builds on them, polemicizes with them, or simply presumes that they are already known to the listeners). Any utterance is a link in a very complexly organized chain of other utterances.[6]

Bakhtin's inclusiveness admits both agreement and disagreement, building on and polemicizing against. It is these engagements which will be discussed in the essay which follows.

1. *The rushing mighty wind*

'The wind bloweth where it listeth,' said Jesus to Nicodemus, 'and thou hearest the sound thereof, but canst not tell whence it cometh, and whither it goeth; so is every one that is born of the Spirit' (Jn. 3:8).[7] As a text for a discussion of the English Romantic poets, this will do as well as any: for the wind is important, both for itself – as a natural breeze – and as a traditional symbol for the Holy Spirit at Pentecost, and also as a Romantic metaphor. *The Prelude* begins with a benign and gentle wind:

> O there is blessing in this gentle breeze,
> That blows from the green fields and from the clouds
> And from the sky; it beats against my cheek,
> And seems half conscious of the joy it gives.
>
> (I.1–4)[8]

The breeze comes from everywhere – fields, clouds, sky; the poet cannot tell whence it cometh and whither it goeth. His knowledge of it is from his own sensations, the wind on the cheek: that is what gives the moment authenticity, and that is where the reader of Romantic poetry has to begin, with the authenticity of individual experience. For Wordsworth, *The Prelude* is a record of his own feelings and his personal development: any beliefs which he has are those which he has discovered for himself as a part of his life-experience. In 'Lines Written a Few Miles above Tintern Abbey' he writes:

> For I have learned
> To look on nature, not as in the hour

> Of thoughtless youth; but hearing often-times
> The still, sad music of humanity,
> Nor harsh, nor grating, though of ample power
> To chasten and subdue. And I have felt
> A presence that disturbs me with the joy
> Of elevated thoughts . . .
>
> (88–95)

'For I have learned . . . And I have felt': Wordsworth is writing his testimony here, asserting the validity of his own experience. In that sense he is following the traditions of self-analysis found in Rousseau (in *The Confessions*) and, before that, in Puritan spiritual autobiography.[9] The difference between Wordsworth and the Puritans is that his autobiography is directed to an understanding of himself and his poetic gift, rather than being a record of God's grace to the repentant sinner.

The Puritan autobiographical writers of the seventeenth century understood the working of God's grace through the preaching of the Word and the singing of metrical psalms, and shaped their lives accordingly: they saw their lives as illustrations of a pattern that was demonstrated in the conversion of St Paul or in the conversation between Jesus and Nicodemus: 'Except a man be born again, he cannot see the kingdom of God' (Jn. 3:3). The Romantic poets saw their experience in parallel terms to those of evangelical patterns – involving dedication, commitment, inspiration, even holiness, what Keats called 'the holiness of the heart's affections'. But it remains their own experience, and starts from there: in the opening section of *The Prelude*, Wordsworth goes on to echo Milton:

> The earth is all before me – with a heart
> Joyous, nor scared at its own liberty,
> I look about, and should the guide I chuse
> Be nothing better than a wandering cloud
> I cannot miss my way.
>
> (I.15–19)

Milton had ended *Paradise Lost* with the lines:

> The world was all before them, where to choose
> Their place of rest, and Providence their guide . . .

But Adam and Eve have just been told of the redemption, and

they leave Paradise with hope as well as in penitence: they leave, too, with Providence as their guide in choosing where to live, and how to live. Wordsworth opens out the choice: his freedom may mean that he has nothing better as a guide than a wandering cloud. He is an existentialist *avant la lettre*, although this does not, of course, exclude the awareness of the workings of divine providence. At the end of the poem on the growth of his own mind, Wordsworth spoke of something which he thought of as a universal possession:

> The feeling of life endless, the one thought
> By which we live, infinity and God.
> *(The Prelude*, XIII,183–184)

This final book of *The Prelude*, with its description of the climbing of Snowdon (deliberately held back from its chronological place to form a climax to the poem), is evidence of Wordsworth's awareness of a higher power; and the act of climbing, the gradual ascent from Beddgelert, through the mist, up into the moonlight, is a physical enacting of the movement of the mind upwards, from the physical towards the metaphysical. Wordsworth sees the two things as intricately connected: poetic minds 'deal / With all the objects of the universe', but they are also *exalted* by those objects – 'the enduring and the transient both':

> They build up greatest things
> From least suggestions, ever on the watch,
> Willing to work and to be wrought upon.
> They need not extraordinary calls
> To rouze them – in a world of life they live,
> By sensible impressions not enthralled,
> But quickened, rouzed, and made thereby more fit
> To hold communion with the invisible world.
> Such minds are truly from the Deity . . .
> (XIII.98–106)

Again the language is religious, that of quickening and communion; and Wordsworth's sense that there are minds which are truly from the Deity is a concluding reflection on the complex, multi-episodic history of his own mind as recorded in *The Prelude*. His childhood and school time, his education at Cambridge, his visit to the Alps in 1790, his time in London, and (above all) his first-hand experience of the French Revolution, these all contribute to the strange and yet familiar self that he recognizes as his own individual nature. This accumulated experience is relevant not only to some major social and historical ideologies (revolution, education, society); its transformation into poetry, the imaginative *understanding* of it, is evidence of a power that is outside society and beyond politics. Wordsworth speaks of it as a creativity, using the wind of *The Prelude*'s first four lines as a metaphor:

> For I, methought, while the sweet breath of heaven
> Was blowing on my body, felt within
> A corresponding mild creative breeze,
> A vital breeze which travelled gently on
> O'er things which it had made, and is become
> A tempest, a redundant energy,
> Vexing its own creation.
>
> (I.41–47)

'Redundant' here means 'exuberant': the wind that blows is 'vexing', as the sense sublime in 'Tintern Abbey' 'disturbs'. In both cases, however, the movement is benign. The wind here is a power

> That does not come unrecognised, a storm
> Which, breaking up a long-continued frost,
> Brings with it vernal promises, the hope
> Of active days, of dignity and thought,
> Of prowess in an honorable field,
> Pure passions, virtue, knowledge, and delight,
> The holy life of music and of verse.
>
> (I.48–54)

For Wordsworth, as for Keats, there is something holy here, an occupation which (in Wordsworth's case) is both prophetic and priestly:

> To the open fields I told
> A prophecy; poetic numbers came
> Spontaneously, and clothed in priestly robe
> My spirit, thus singled out, as it might seem,
> For holy services.
>
> (I.59–63)

The wind which bloweth where it listeth is a wind of a holy spirit
– not *the* Holy Spirit, but the spirit within someone that is holy:

> . . . for there's not a man
> That live who hath not had his god-like hours,
> And knows not what majestic sway we have
> As natural beings in the strength of Nature.
>
> (III.191–194)

The wind blows on the cheek: the correspondent breeze within is
an energy that is channelled into the holy life of music and of
verse. Wordsworth has come to a belief through his own
experience, his prophetic word to himself. Later in his life he was
to accommodate this, without much difficulty, to the teaching of
the church and the gospel of grace, which appear in alterations to
later versions of *The Prelude*, in *The Excursion*, and in the
Ecclesiastical Sonnets. In these later poems, the wind no longer
bloweth where it listeth, but in directions carefully signposted by
centuries of teaching, church history and devotional practice.

For Shelley, the wind also blew, but he jealously guarded the
authenticity of his own experience, preferring to remain ignorant,
like Nicodemus, of whence it came or whither it was going. The
wind is there, sure enough: in the 'Ode to the West Wind' it blows
through the wood near Florence as a destroyer and preserver, part
of the great process of nature which is found in autumn and
winter, spring and summer. Yet it is also something which
encourages Shelley to feel an identification with it, as a
correspondent breeze, with an intense urgency:

> Be thou, Spirit fierce,
> My spirit! Be thou me, impetuous one!
> Drive my dead thoughts over the universe
> Like withered leaves to quicken a new birth!
> And, by the incantation of this verse,
> Scatter, as from an unextinguished hearth
> Ashes and sparks, my words among mankind!
> Be through my lips to unawakened earth
> The trumpet of a prophecy! . . .
>
> (61–69)

Shelley, like Wordsworth, saw his words as a prophecy: being one
with the wind, he will inspire the world, make it a better place. In
A Defence of Poetry, similarly, he spoke of poets as prophets:

Poets, according to the circumstances of the age and nation in which they appeared, were called, in the earlier epochs of the world, legislators or prophets: a poet essentially comprises and unites both these characters. For he not only beholds intensely the present as it is, and discovers those laws according to which present things ought to be ordered, but he beholds the future in the present, and his thoughts are the germs of the flower and the fruit of latest time.

2. The letter killeth, but the spirit giveth life

Although this is close to the model of an Old Testament prophet such as Ezekiel – poet and guide to society – it is difficult to see Shelley as ever coming to terms with religious orthodoxy, as Wordsworth did in later life, if only because his prophetic inspiration was more political than Wordsworth's: he regarded the society in which he lived, in the years following the failure of the French Revolution and the fall of Napoleon, as corrupt and repressive: the massacre of 'Peterloo' in 1819 confirmed his anger and despair, and strengthened his determination to attack monarchy and tyranny (with which he associated the church). His reading of the New Testament, however, made him a fervent admirer of the person and life of Jesus Christ, whom he saw as one who had a similar relationship with the church and the society of his own time. 'For his Christianity,' said Leigh Hunt,

> he went to the Epistle of St James, and to the Sermon on the Mount by Christ himself, for whose beneficent intentions he entertained the greatest reverence . . . His want of faith, indeed, in the letter, and his exceeding faith in the spirit, of Christianity, formed a comment the one on the other, very formidable to those who chose to forget what Scripture itself observes on that point.[10]

Hunt is thinking of 2 Corinthians 3:6: 'the letter killeth, but the spirit giveth life'; and the Sermon on the Mount preaches a way of life rather than the old law – poverty of spirit, meekness, mercy, purity, peacemaking, hunger after righteousness. It blesses those who are persecuted for righteousness' sake, while it also condemns revenge, judgmentalism and hypocrisy. Shelley preached to his own society about the danger of revenge, and his greatest hero, Prometheus, forswears hatred, even for the tyrant who has had him chained to the rock and tortured. He disdained power, and distrusted money, for they might 'stain . . . / A poet's free and heavenly mind' ('An Exhortation'): and his deepest loyalty and admiration were for the person of Jesus, together with the beauty of Greek thought as found in the works of Plato. The 'Hymn to Intellectual Beauty' demonstrates this with an intricate negotiation of the territory of the mind which is at once rejecting official teaching and asserting individual intuition: Shelley criticizes the 'vain endeavour' of accepted morality, and the 'poisonous names with which our youth is fed', presumably the names of kings and tyrants in history but also perhaps the teaching of religion in schools. At the end of the poem, however, he describes himself as one who is bound by the spirit of intellectual beauty 'To fear himself, and love all human kind'. This last line comes as a surprise: we might have expected 'love himself' and 'fear all human kind'. But the Shelleyan opposite is close to the teachings of Jesus – 'Thou shalt love thy neighbour as thyself' (Mt. 22:39), 'Love one another, as I have loved you' (Jn. 15:12) – and to the meaningful paradoxes of the spiritual life: 'He that loveth his life shall lose it; and he that hateth his life in this world shall keep it unto life eternal' (Jn. 12:25). Shelley is coming to the same point as Jesus but claiming it as his own pattern for life: he is not concerned with the teaching of the church, but he is bound, under the spell of intellectual beauty, to *live* the gospel.

3. Church and state

Shelley's admiration for Jesus, and his partial identification with him (found in *Adonais*), was based on the concept of Jesus as an anti-authoritarian figure who was crucified by an alliance between a corrupt church and an oppressive imperial state. He did not like to think of Jesus as the Son of God, because this gave him privileges: and in the notes to *Hellas*, he described Jesus' character as 'deformed' by the association with God, 'a Power, who tempted, betrayed, and punished the innocent beings who were called into existence by His sole will'. Such unorthodoxy was encouraged, for Shelley and others, by a refusal to take the church seriously: this was partly for political reasons, for the church had become associated with the forces of reaction and counter-revolution during the French Revolution. An earlier example may be found in Coleridge: in the notes to 'Religious Musings', begun in 1794 and completed in 1796, he recorded with indignation that in Parliament in 1784 the Duke of Portland, advocating war against the new French Republic, said that he 'considered the war to be merely grounded on one principle – the preservation of the Christian religion'.

In his early years, Coleridge was as anti-clerical as Shelley. In 'Religious Musings' he wrote of 'Disease', 'Envy' and 'Want', and then of

> Warriors, and Lords, and Priests – all the sore ills
> That vex and desolate our mortal life
>
> (215–216)

and after 'sore ills' his note adds

> By a Priest I mean a man who holding the scourge of power in his right hand and a bible (translated by authority) in his left, doth necessarily cause the bible and the scourge to be associated ideas, and so produces that temper of mind which leads to Infidelity – Infidelity which judging of Revelation by the doctrines and practices of established Churches honours God by rejecting Christ.

Coleridge looked for the millennium, the day of judgment and the end of all things (Rev. 6 – 8), but saw it in his own terms, as the coming of a new political system of justice and truth. Similarly, Wordsworth, hoping for the French Revolution as the beginning of a new world, remembered the pain which he felt when separated from a village community at prayer:

> It was a grief –
> Grief call it not, 'twas any thing but that, –
> A conflict of sensations without name,
> Of which he only who may love the sight
> Of a village steeple as I do can judge,
> When in the congregation, bending all
> To their great Father, prayers were offered up
> Or praises for our country's victories,
> And, 'mid the simple worshippers perchance
> I only, like an uninvited guest
> Whom no one owned, sate silent – shall I add,
> Fed on the day of vengeance yet to come!
>
> (X.264–275)

Wordsworth is here living out the predicament of the Romantic poets: their individual response to the expected patterns of teaching and experience was authentic, but it cut them off from others, from the community which they would have loved to celebrate and liked to belong to. In its most acute form, this disturbs the fragile contact between the poet and his audience: from primitive times onwards, poets have spoken to audiences and for communities, as the psalmist did in ancient Israel. Now the poets were speaking for themselves, in a role which is closer to the prophetic. Sometimes they were ignored, as Blake was; or they did not publish, as Blake did not, in any traditional way, or as Wordsworth did not with *The Prelude*. The most distinctive example is Blake, who fought like a tiger against his predecessors and against the established church ('God & his Priest & King' in 'The Chimney Sweeper', from *Songs of Experience*).

Blake was a supporter, as the other first-generation Romantic poets were, of the actual revolutions of his own time, but his deeper hope was for a transformation of the inner self, away from what he saw as conventional morality and religion towards a finer ideal of human living. One of his most celebrated early engravings, 'Albion Rose' or 'Glad Day', shows a young man dancing, his whole posture one of physical delight; and his last prophetic book, *Jerusalem*, celebrates the death of the old self and the new vision of humanity. And because he was so conscious of the possibilities of human life, its potential for vision and its hope for the good society, Blake was a determined enemy of all those elements which he saw as thwarting the full development of people – the chains of the body (slavery, exploitation of all kinds, poverty), and the chains of the mind, what he called in 'London' the 'mind-forg'd manacles'. Thus he wrote about the horrors of prostitution, about little boys who were sold to become chimney-sweepers, about children who were neglected and taken into charity schools. The causes of these evils were those elements of human behaviour condemned by Jesus, human selfishness and greed: Blake detected them not only in personal and individual cruelties but also in the influence of the big corporations who governed the London financial markets:

> I wander thro' each charter'd street
> Near where the charter'd Thames does flow
> And mark in every face I meet
> Marks of weakness, marks of woe.

The streets are 'charter'd', bought up by big companies: so is the river, which should be pure and clear and free. Blake's city is in striking contrast to the holy city seen in Revelation 21 – 22: 'And I John saw the holy city, new Jerusalem' (21:2). The angel also shows John the river:

> And he shewed me a pure river of water of life, clear as crystal, proceeding out of the throne of God and of the Lamb.   (Rev. 22:1)

The contrast with the London of the 1790s could not be stronger: and Blake weeps over London as Jesus wept over Jerusalem:

> And when he was come near, he beheld the city, and wept over it, Saying, If thou hadst known, even thou, at least in this thy day, the things which belong unto thy peace! but now they are hid from thine eyes.
>   (Lk. 19:41–42)

In the same chapter, the scribes and Pharisees were seeking to destroy Jesus, and Blake's attitude to the contemporary church was to see it as part of a repressive system, involving kings, lords, priests, the makers of laws and the enforcers of tyranny (Blake had a particular loathing, shared by many radicals of his time, for the government of William Pitt, which passed harsh laws against sedition and anti-government writing). It is possible that when he speaks of the 'mind forg'd manacles', which he hears in the cries of the Londoners around him, he was thinking of the repressions of the political system.

4. *Innocent play*

In opposition to this is the vision of *Songs of Innocence* (1793), where the piper with a child-like spirit describes a world before the knowledge of good and evil, in which children play in innocence, and the old people look on with delight (sometimes the innocence of the children means that they are imposed upon, as they are in 'The Chimney Sweeper'). When they are tired they can return to their mothers – 'like birds in the nest / Are ready for rest'; it is all natural and good. 'The Divine Image' is found in the working of the attributes of God, which are not truth, justice, and righteousness, but mercy, pity, peace, and love:

> To Mercy, Pity, Peace, and Love
> All pray in their distress;
> And to these virtues of delight
> Return their thankfulness.
>
> For Mercy, Pity, Peace, and Love
> Is God, our father dear,
> And Mercy, Pity, Peace, and Love
> Is Man, his child and care.

God is a father, but in Blake's theology he is not remote and unknowable: he is in the world, as Jesus was. Indeed, 'God is Jesus' (Blake inscribes this on his engraving of *Laocoön*), rather than the angry God of the Old Testament giving the law to Moses. God as Jesus is the point of 'The Lamb', a brilliant summation of the ideas of God as creator and as redeemer. In the first verse, the question is asked about the origins of things – 'Little Lamb, who made thee?' – pointing towards the account of creation in the first chapter of Genesis. The answer is given in verse 2:

> Little Lamb I'll tell thee,
> Little Lamb I'll tell thee;
> He is callèd by thy name,
> For he calls himself a Lamb:
> He is meek and he is mild,
> He became a little child:
> I a child & thou a lamb,
> We are callèd by his name . . .

This is Jesus, the Lamb that 'taketh away the sin of the world' (Jn. 1:29) and 'the Lamb that was slain' (Rev. 5:12). We have leapt from the first book of the Bible to the last in two simple verses. The significance is that Blake is here joining the two: God is Jesus, creator and redeemer. He is versifying an incarnational theology based on John 1:3: 'All things were made by him; and without him was not anything made that was made.'

Blake's aim was wholeness, a God who was not far off and mysterious but who included all goodness, the human qualities of mercy, pity, peace and love: he aims for a divinity that is human, and a humanity that is divine. Later he was to construct a mythology in which humanity was (alas) divided, split into four, with Urizen (reason) dominant, together with Luvah (passion), Urthona (imagination) and Tharmas (pity). It is the reunion and balance of these four which Blake seeks, and 'Glad Day' is a visual representation of this ideal.

In *Songs of Innocence*, Blake was writing a book for children, but it is also a book for those adults who would understand and learn from children (like all the Romantic period poets, Blake believed that children had much to teach adults). He clearly had in mind some of the eighteenth-century books which had been written for children, such as Charles Wesley's *Hymns for Children* of 1742, and especially Isaac Watt's *Divine Songs Attempted in Easy Language for the Use of Children*, first published in 1715.

Blake's piper wrote his happy songs 'Every child may joy to hear'. The piper's message is universal, addressed to all children, whereas Watts' child is exclusive and narrowly Christian:

> Lord, I ascribe it to thy Grace,
> And not to Chance, as others do,
> That I was born of Christian Race,
> And not a Heathen, or a Jew.

Blake answers this in 'The Divine Image', where the appeal is to the 'new commandment' of Jesus 'that ye love one another', a command which Blake (as Shelley was later to do) extended to all mankind:

> And all must love the human form
> In heathen, turk or jew.

The addition of 'turk' may have come from the Third Collect for Good Friday in the *Book of Common Prayer* ('Have mercy upon all Jews, Turks, Infidels, and Hereticks . . .'), but the universalism of his vision is also in direct opposition to Watts' poem and to his child's complacent exclusion of others.

For there are two kinds of gospel system in opposition to each other in the poems of Watts and of Blake. The argument between them is not just a matter of hermeneutics but of a whole systematic theology. For Watts, the human situation was seen through the standard Puritan doctrine of the fall and the redemption; and the instruction is to believe in the Lord Jesus Christ and be saved. Watts' child praises God because he was taught to read the Bible, so

> That I am brought to know
> The danger I was in,

> By Nature and by Practice too
> A wretched Slave to Sin.
>
> That I am led to see
> I can do nothing well;
> And whither shall a Sinner flee
> To save himself from Hell?
> ('Song VIII')

Blake's child, on the other hand, is 'innocent', and that word 'innocent' challenges the Calvinist system of original sin, Watts' 'By Nature'. The Puritan attitude to children spoils childhood: what might have been an innocent time is seen, in Watts' adult retrospect, as a time of wickedness, in which the inescapable, hereditary sin of Adam is found in every action; and the only escape is through belief in the saving power of Jesus Christ. Blake's children, on the other hand, are unable to conceive of such a scheme of things; they are 'innocent' of such theories:

> I have no name
> I am but two days old –
> What shall I call thee?
> I happy am
> Joy is my name, –
> Sweet joy befall thee!
> ('Infant Joy')

In its happy confusion and pre-grammatical state, the child gives two answers to the question 'What shall I call thee?' – 'I happy am' (as though 'happy' were its name) and then 'Joy is my name'. This is the innocence of spring, of natural things, of abundance, of merriment and delight, all expressed in an innocent language, a childish prattle:

> Little Boy
> Full of joy.
> Little Girl
> Sweet and small.
> Cock does crow
> So do you.
> Merry voice
> Infant noise
> Merrily Merrily to welcome in the Year.
> ('Spring')

Blake's lightly punctuated text and short lines, its floating phrases, allow a freedom of interpretation, a shifting kaleidoscope of impressions which is quite different from the stability of Watts' text. Watts' child sings in the language which the adult has taught him. Both Blake and Watts write as adults but use the voices of children, but Watts' children speak like little adults, in a kind of piping hymnology.

Watts' child is not unaware of the beauty of the created world. Indeed, he is knowledgeable about it, and its source:

> I sing th'Almighty Power of God,
> That made the Mountains rise,
> That spread the flowing Seas abroad,
> And built the lofty Skies.
>
> ('Song II')

But the instinctive reaction of Watts' child is to flee from God, in an attitude of fear, presumably because of awe, or a sense of sin and unworthiness. For him, God is a mystery, as he is even to the angels:

> Not angels that stand round the Lord
> Can search his secret-Will;
> But they perform his heavenly Word,
> And sing his Praises still.

It is as if the angels obey blindly, unable to understand the secret will of God, but performing his word and singing his praises notwithstanding and for ever ('still'). Blake's caricature of this is found in 'The Human Abstract', where 'the Eye altering alters all', and sees the virtues of 'The Divine Image' as the product of selfishness, fear and inequality. This is because they are seen with an eye, which, like Watts', beholds God as remote and inaccessible: the poem is a 'human abstraction' from the available data, and a view which is incomplete because it takes God away from earth and hides him; whereupon

> the Catterpiller and Fly
> Feed on the Mystery.

Another way of expressing Blake's antagonism towards Watts' idea of the hidden God is found in 'The Little Boy Lost', where the child loses his father-figure, who flies away in a vapour.

When the child is really lost, God appears, in 'The Little Boy Found', in the guise of his father. Blake's point is that God is found *in* parental love, not in the distant relationship of God as the mysterious 'Father' in heaven, the 'Nobodaddy' of Blake's later writings.

The result of God's remoteness is that Watts' child is very conscious of sin; whereas Blake's divinity resides in the human breast, Watts' is a Saviour but also a punisher of wrong-doing. His child is familiar with the concept of judgment, and has the terrible imagination of a medieval doom-painting:

> There is beyond the Sky
> A Heaven of Joy and Love,
> And holy Children, when they die,
> Go to that World above.
>
> There is a dreadful Hell,
> And everlasting Pains,
> There Sinners must with Devils dwell
> In Darkness, Fire, and Chains.
>   ('Song XI')

The child is disciplined by fear, and speaks in the language of a priestly religion, which promises him a place in heaven if he is good (or 'holy', that is conforming to the priestly concept of good behaviour) and in hell if he is bad. The 'priestly care' of this kind of religion is grotesquely caricatured by Blake in 'A Little Boy Lost' from *Songs of Experience*, where the priest takes the little boy 'And bound him in an iron chain' before destroying him:

> And burn'd him in a holy place,
> Where many had been burn'd before:
> The weeping parents wept in vain.
> Are such things done on Albion's shore.

The burning of the child in the holy place is the destruction of the natural child in the name of religion; the poem is Blake's response to Watts' 'Song XXIII', entitled 'Obedience to Parents', where Watts promises dreadful punishments to disobedient children:

> Have we not heard what dreadful Plagues
> Are threatened by the Lord

211

> To him that breaks his Father's Law,
> Or mocks his Mother's Word?
>
> What heavy Guilt upon him lies!
> How cursèd is his Name!
> The Ravens shall pick out his Eyes,
> And Eagles eat the same.

Blake's technique, as Alicia Ostriker has acutely observed,[11] is to condemn Watts by producing a dramatic presentation of these religious figures of speech; but he also humanizes Watts' remote parents, and shows them as weeping rather than as stern law-givers. The priest destroys the family as well as the child, and the implication is that Watts' conception of parental authority and total obedience is a religious recipe for the destruction of love.

The natural and innocent child is destroyed in the name of religion. Similarly, the garden of love, where the child used to play, has become a chapel, with 'Thou shalt not' written over the door, and with priests in black gowns walking their rounds. Watts' children live within this chapel-world, taught what to do and what not to do:

> Happy's the Child whose youngest Years
> Receive Instruction well;
> Who hates the Sinners Path, and fears
> The Road that leads to Hell.
>
> ('Song XII')

Blake's response to this is in 'The School-Boy', where 'to go to school in a summer morn / O! it drives all joy away', and the child pleads with his parents for a natural development, on the analogy of summer and fruit:

> O! father & mother, if buds are nip'd,
> And blossoms blown away,
> And if the tender plants are strip'd
> Of their joy in the springing day,
> By sorrow and cares dismay,
>
> How shall the summer arise in joy
> Or the summer fruits appear?

The image of the bud is used in direct contradiction to Watts' use of it in 'The Advantages of early Religion':

When we devote our Youth to God
'Tis pleasing in his Eyes;
A Flower when offer'd in the Bud
Is no vain Sacrifice.

('Song XII')

The word 'Sacrifice' has implications which Blake explores in the dreadful image of child sacrifice found in 'A Little Boy Lost' (where the child is indeed lost, destroyed). The image of the priest's 'trembling zeal' as he takes the little boy away to be burned is one of a perverted and monstrous cruelty; but such violence is part of a regime of fear in which 'many had been burn'd before'. Watts' book has a series of poems, 'The All-seeing God' (IX), 'Solemn Thoughts of God and Death' (X), 'Heaven and Hell' (XI) and 'The Danger of Delay' (XIII), all of which are designed to put the fear of God into the minds of children:

What if the Lord grow wroth, and swear
While I refuse to read and pray,
That he'll refuse to lend an Ear,
To all my Groans another Day?

What if his dreadful Anger burn,
While I resist his offered Grace,
And all his Love to Fury turn,
And strike me dead upon the place?

Watts' place is echoed in Blake's 'holy place', and of course this is exactly what the priest does in the name of God – he strikes the child dead upon the place.

Children prefer play to work, or going to church. And play was of great importance to Blake, who anticipated D. W. Winnicott in his awareness of its importance in healthy development. Winnicott's thesis 'that in playing, and perhaps only in playing, the child or adult is free to be creative'[12] has an obvious relevance to poems such as 'The Ecchoing Green', 'Laughing Song' and 'Spring'. Watts' child is reminded that spending time in play may mean that he forgets to pray:

Why should I love my Sport so well?
So constant at my Play?
And lose the Thoughts of Heaven and Hell,
And then forget to pray?

('Song XXIV')

A certain amount of play is permitted, but there is no doubt that religious duty comes first; whereas play is allowed within certain limits, as in 'Innocent Play':

> Abroad in the Meadows to see the young Lambs,
> Run sporting about by the side of their Dams
>   With Fleeces so clean, and so white;
> Or a Nest of young Doves in a large open Cage,
> When they all play in Love without Anger or Rage,
>   How much we may learn from the Sight!

But Watts' reading of the word 'innocent' is a limited one, and the children can play only if they are gentle, and are not going to get dirty:

> If we had been Ducks, we might dabble in Mud:
> Or Dogs, we might play till it ended in Blood;
>   So foul, or so fierce are their Natures.
> But Thomas and William, and such pretty Names,
> Should be cleanly and harmless as Doves, or as Lambs,
>   Those lovely sweet innocent Creatures.

As in 'Song XVI', 'Against Quarrelling and Fighting', which begins 'Let Dogs delight to bark and bite', children are exhorted to control their anger:

> But, Children, you should never let
>   Such angry Quarrels rise;
> Your little Hands were never made
>   To tear each others Eyes.

It is clear that the word 'innocent' has very different meanings for the two writers. For Watts it means innocent of certain kinds of 'bad' behaviour. His child is dignified:

> Away from Fools I'll turn my Eyes,
>   Nor with the Scoffers go;
> I would be walking with the Wise,
>   That wiser I may grow.

It is verses such as this which help to explain Blake's protest, in *The Marriage of Heaven and Hell*, that the tigers of wrath are wiser than the horses of instruction. For Watts' verse is holding up a certain kind of behaviour for approval, a code of conduct which depends on self-control, discipline and self-interest. It is also, as generations of children have learned through suffering, a way of pleasing the adults.

Watts' book was very successful, coming off the press in edition after edition: Blake's *Songs of Innocence* was almost unknown in his own day. His defiance extended to a refusal to take part in the kind of mass-produced book-making, and the mass-produced morality that went with it, so that each copy of *Songs of Innocence* was coloured by hand and issued separately. Blake's confidence in himself and his methods is strange and sublime: he could not have expected that one day the whirligig of time would bring in its revenges, so that everyone would read Blake and no-one would read Watts. That confidence, however, is the confidence of a prophet: he saw the society around him as repressive and corrupt, and he saw Watts' book as one element in it.

His dialogue with Watts represents a revisionary writing which is useful because it is so clear; it is a struggle between a traditional view of religious and moral conduct – as evidenced in Milton, in Puritan experience, in Watts' version of Calvinism – and another view of the world, that sees religion as grounded in human need and experience, Tillich-like, and which recognizes freedom and life as primary needs, not just for society but for an individual's religious and spiritual well-being. Instead of doctrine, the search is for openness and readiness; instead of mystery, for compassion and love; instead of piety, energy. It is, above all, a search for wholeness, for a complete humanity; for a spirit of wholeness, a wholly spirit (though for Blake it must never be separated from the body) rather than a Holy Spirit.

5. Life more abundantly

Jesus said, 'I am come that they might have life, and that they might have it more abundantly' (Jn. 10:10). It is that sense of 'life' which the Romantic poets fight for, the sense of joyous and free living which Blake thought of as wholeness and resurrected humanity, and which Wordsworth and Shelley (in the fourth act of *Prometheus Unbound*) associated with the energy of nature. In Book II of *The Prelude*, Wordsworth describes himself at the end of his childhood, before going to Cambridge, as having received so much life from nature:

I was only then

Contented when with bliss ineffable
I felt the sentiment of Being spread
O'er all that moves, and all that seemeth still.
O'er all, that, lost beyond the reach of thought
And human knowledge, to the human eye
Invisible, yet liveth to the heart,
O'er all that leaps, and runs, and shouts, and sings,
Or beats the gladsome air, o'er all that glides
Beneath the wave, yea, in the wave itself
And mighty depth of waters.

(II.418–428)

This is a characteristic Romantic rewriting of a biblical text, in this case Revelation 5:13:

> And every creature which is in heaven, and on the earth, and under the earth, and such as are in the sea, and all that are in them, heard I saying, Blessing, and honour, and glory, and power, be unto him that sitteth upon the throne, and unto the Lamb for ever and ever.

It is in this purposeful rewriting of earlier texts, this twisting of the Holy Spirit into the spirit of wholeness, that marks out the Romantic negotiation of sacred areas of thought and feeling. In the process, as M. H. Abrams has masterfully shown in *Natural Supernaturalism*, the Romantic poets re-enact certain patterns of religious experience – prophecy, conversion, dedication: Abrams sees this as 'the assimilation and reinterpretation of religious ideas, as constitutive elements in a world-view founded on secular premises'.[13] This essay has been presenting a Romantic religious poetry which would blur the sacred/secular divide which Abrams proposes: the search for self-fulfilment and wholeness, for the good society, and for the beautiful in humanity and in nature, is parallel to the religious quest; and it is not so secular as Abrams suggests, because it is built upon a perception of the character of Jesus that is clearly found in the gospels. What is not found (and in this sense Abrams is correct) are the interpretations of the gospel by Paul, Luther and Calvin, in which human sin is redeemed by the sacrifice of Jesus Christ on the cross, and his subsequent resurrection; and salvation is by faith and not by works or by the fulfilling of the law. 'Salvation' is likely to be thought of as being saved from selfishness or failure, or pointlessness: Keats spoke of 'a system of salvation',[14] but he did not mean Christian salvation. And resurrection, for Blake, is likely to refer to a rebirth of society in a new and better form, as a transformed nation ('Albion Rose') responds to a better understanding and a new vision.

That vision is not secular, so much as unconcerned with doctrine, hostile to the church (as associated with a corrupt establishment), and selective in its use and interpretation of Scripture and of traditional teaching. Its strength is its psychological insight and its social responsibility. These poets set out, as religious writers do, to change the world, even to 'redeem' it; and they seek a new world, a holy city, whose builder and maker is the imagination. Blake saw Jesus as the imagination: 'All things are comprehended in their Eternal Forms in the divine body of the Saviour, the True Vine of Eternity, the Human Imagination.'[15] Blake is here rewriting John 15:1 ('I am the true vine, and my Father is the husbandman') to serve his own hermeneutical purposes, just as he re-wrote Christian doctrine to correspond to his vision of the divine humanity and the human divinity, in which 'Energy is eternal delight'. Those who saw Jesus change the world in thirty-three years might have agreed.

12

Time for Hardy: Jude and the obscuring of Scripture

David Barratt

Everywhere the vastness and terror of the immense night which is roused for a brief while by the day . . . There was no Time, only Space.

(D. H. Lawrence, *Sons and Lovers*)

1. Introduction

The previous chapter on Romantic poetry questions the extent to which it was 'secular' as opposed to 'sacred'. J. R. Watson points up a growing opposition within the nineteenth century, one which interestingly becomes entwined with the root meaning of 'secular', as 'of the time or age' (Latin *saecularis*). If we turn now from poetry to the novel, we could say that the enterprise of humanism within the nineteenth-century novel was to define human happiness and freedom in terms of time, and can therefore rightly be called secular humanism as much as liberal humanism. In trying to do this, it saw unnecessary borders and limitations in terms of social institutions, mores, values and traditions.

The enterprise was not usually seen as incompatible with Christianity, however, as Christian values and beliefs formed an agreed subtext, to be occasionally made explicit, as in Austen, Dickens or Charlotte Brontë. Even an agnostic such as George Eliot was prepared to accept ethical structures which doubled as Christian, even while discarding Christian theology. But Hardy, along with other late-nineteenth-century writers, took his cue from such radical Romantics as Shelley and Swinburne, and was prepared to challenge Christianity as being inimical to any possibility of happiness and freedom. He did this by directly challenging Christian institutions and values, and then by substituting 'a different gospel'. This denied theodicy, seeing impersonal forces at work, indifferent to the suffering of humanity. Hardy's pessimism is a partly evolutionary one: the belief that while individuals may be becoming in and over time more spiritually responsive (defined partly in terms of the desire for personal happiness and fulfilment in [love] relationships), the universe remains as 'crassly obtuse' as ever. Society forms the middle term here between the individual and universal Nature: it is almost as obtuse and unchanging as universal Nature, but because it comprises individuals, it can change in the end, although always too late for his heroes and heroines. This is sometimes referred to as his 'ameliorism'.

Hardy clearly invites a response from Christian readers. For one thing, in his youth he seriously thought of entering the Christian ministry (as does Jude), and was well acquainted with the Greek New Testament. To that extent, the Bible works as a constant subtext for him. Then, too, he is provocative of and directly challenging to Christian beliefs, nowhere more so than in *Jude the Obscure*. A possible response for Christian readers is to 'burn the book' – in exasperation or a frustration too easily focused on Hardy's use of coincidences, plot manipulations, melodramatic devices, and so on. This is hardly a discerning response, and if you, like me, really like Hardy, it can all become quite problematic.

Do we, then, agree with Hardy on some points? His attack on the late-nineteenth-century Church of England is not misplaced, for instance. But even when we agree with him here, have we really touched the heart of the novel? Is Jude's failure to enter the church really central to his decline and fall? Other such points of agreement would, I think, often turn out to be equally peripheral. We need a response that is both much more wholehearted and much more to the wholeness of the novel.

So on the one hand, if 'all truth is God's truth', we as Christian readers need to see in what ways Hardy's revelation of truth is consistent with biblically revealed truth, to 'deconstruct' one in terms of the other. Certainly, as with most deconstructive strategies, Hardy's fiction will stand visibly full of ambiguities, contradictions and ambivalences that seem to undermine intentions. Yet we need to realize that these intentions are never set up as a systematic set of beliefs, any more than the gospels were (Hardy call them 'impressions'). So as discerning readers, we must guard their integrity as imaginative truth and fictive whole, and not denigrate them logically for something they are not in essence.

A balanced response or deconstruction might best start from the commonsense notion that undermining or fall occurs if you cut off the branch on which you are sitting – at least if the cut is made between you and the trunk! The application would be that Hardy still needed Christian revelation as his trunk, as did George Eliot before him, and D. H. Lawrence after. This thesis validates, I believe, a Christian deconstruction conducted explicitly in Christian terms and subjected to a normative biblical critique, one yet still fair to Hardy, especially as I take it we would want to see such deconstructed 'impressions' as pointing to deeper realities, rather than as mere decentred playthings.

2. Tense and tension

In his introduction to *Jude the Obscure*,[1] C. H. Sisson writes:

> Jude and Sue are figures in the new uneasiness deprived
> of their past. It is Sue's part to welcome a future which
> she does not understand and finally to swerve back into
> a pseudo-past which has its own unreality.

Looking at Hardy's last novel, Sisson focuses on a central feature which has become increasingly urgent for Hardy. In *Tess of the d'Urbervilles*, for example, Hardy contrasts the restlessness of modernity (as exemplified in Angel, Alec and Sandbourne) with the presentness of Tess herself, a spiritually discerned dimension which she finally enters into as 'rest' in the last chapters. Although parallels to the New Testament letter to the Hebrews are not immediately obvious, if we look at such central concepts as striving to enter into a promised land (seen as a final rest), pilgrimage and faith (or loss of it), then there are clear similarities to be seen. In *Jude*, references to the new Jerusalem are more than allusions to the New Testament view of the future: they are conscious parodies of or antipathies to it. Time and tense, therefore, for Hardy, had become points of confrontation with Christian Scripture.

This would seem to be a good entry point, then: a deconstruction of Hardy's 'impression' that Christian concepts of time inhibit human freedom and the search for happiness, but that the language used figuratively to express such concepts can be re-routed for secular purpose. Both Rowland Cotterill and J. R. Watson in previous chapters have conducted examinations of other such 're-routings' in a fairly informal way. I want to propose a more specific methodology. In Auerbach's classic text on Realism, *Mimesis: The Representation of Reality in Western Literature,*[2] his first two chapters compare reality in ancient Greek and biblical literature. Differences highlighted essential characteristics of both literatures. As Leland Ryken points out in chapter 8 above, Auerbach's methodology helped restore the idea of the literariness of the Bible in a systematic and rigorous way, unlike earlier 'Bible as literature' attempts.

The attempt to compare biblical and non-biblical texts can open up both in new ways, as well as providing a point of reference for looking at the secular text. It can then be used as a critique of the secular, though with caution in order to avoid reductionism (keeping the integrity of the text, as I put it earlier). Many Marxist and Freudian readings tend to be reductionist, for example. There must be rigour in examining the biblical text as literary product, rather than merely abstracting theoretical and metaphysical insights of a non-literary, non-rhetorical sort. Above all, we must avoid reading into the secular text what we think it ought to be saying. So much has been said elsewhere in this collection; so much Auerbach exemplifies in practice.

His first stage is to compare by close analysis several specific relevant passages. In the case of Hardy's novels, we could compare 2 Peter 3 with the opening of *The Return of the Native*; or, turning to *Jude the Obscure*, we could compare Acts 13:16–41 with *Jude*, Part 2, chapter 2; or Hebrews 3:7–47 with the opening pages of *Jude*, Part 4, chapter 1. All deal with time as the central concept, and an analysis should show significant differences in the metaphysical and technical force of its realization. The second stage of his methodology is to use insights gained from close analysis and move to some generalizations in attempting more of an overview of the texts as a whole. It will be here that the deconstructive insights and techniques I suggested in the introduction will be particularly applicable and manifestable. From there, the third and most tentative stage is to conduct a more general critique of Hardy's own form of secular humanism.

But before turning in detail to *Jude*, I am going to attempt a brief trial of the first stage of this methodology by looking at the comparison of 2 Peter and *The Return of the Native* suggested already. There is nothing arbitrary about the selection of texts: Peter conducts a specific discussion about the nature of time, a much wider discussion than just the second coming. References to time are as frequent in the epistle as they are in those to the Ephesians or the Hebrews. In his first letter Peter speaks of prophetic time as part of a wider salvation history (1:11); time before the foundation of the world (1:20); judgment time (4:17); future time (4:13); and after time (5:4), where the emphasis is on revelation and manifestation, that is, a sense of hiddenness that is now being uncovered prophetically. Time contrasts are made: transcience *versus* permanence (1:24); 'once' *versus* 'now' (2:10; *cf.* 3:5–6). Salvation time on the cosmic scale is paralleled by our personal or autobiographical salvation history (2:9–12; 5:10).

This sense of prophetic time is picked up in 2 Peter 3:2, and its analysis could easily be put alongside an analysis of the first chapter of *The Return of the Native*.[3] At first glance, we might well think that Hardy is one of the 'scoffers' of Peter's second letter, since the suggestion is made that Egdon Heath 'has gone on as it has since the beginning of creation'; what it 'now was, it always had been . . . (it) had been from prehistoric times as unaltered as the stars overhead'.[4] Egdon almost seems to take God's place in its pagan substitutions of the biblical text: 'The sea changed, the fields changed, the rivers, the villages, and the people changed, yet Egdon remained' (*cf.* 1 Pet. 1:24–25). Such deliberate echoing of biblical rhythms is a perfect example of the Bible 'trunk' or sub-text, and could be a jumping-off point for an analysis or deconstruction and comparison that would pick up on the various ambiguities, contradictions and perhaps evasions in the Hardy text as he both uses and abuses the biblical text.

What could well emerge is the undermining of the Hardyean text. For example, Egdon's permanence is the sign of consolation 'to the mind adrift on change and harassed by the irrepressible New' (also Jude's problem).[5] Yet its true, night, form is phantom-like, as in 'midnight dreams of flight and disaster'.[6] This contradiction produces not faith, but fears and memories of nightmare. Egdon's unchangingness ultimately takes us into a sort of dark night of the soul in its indifference to human activity. Consolation is at a fearful price, which we are never convinced Clym has paid, and therefore has little to preach in his final gospel.[7]

3. Working history

Turning to *Jude*, I want to pick up on the suggested comparison between Acts 13:16–41 and *Jude*, Part 2, chapter 2. Both passages seek to rediscover in history a meaning for the present moment. Differences of recuperation may well be significant in the ongoing narratives of both texts. But they need, as with Auerbach, analysis in their own right before comparison can be made. In the New

Testament, there are many reworkings of Old Testament history, Stephen's defence (Acts 7:2–53) being one of the best examples. Paul's evangelistic sermon at Pisidian Antioch (Acts 13:16–41) converts the genre of historical writing to that of oral persuasion. His use of history is linear but unspecified. Speaking to Jews and Gentile converts, he takes a good deal for granted. *When* things happened is not important; what is, is God's sovereignty. He 'chose', 'made prosper', 'led out', 'overthrew'. This is the normative Old Testament understanding reflected in many Psalms.[8] History relates to God's acts on behalf of (and despite) Israel, his chosen people. Paul, however, does not start at creation any more than Stephen does. But the latter is more specific: 'The God of glory appeared to our father Abraham' (Acts 7:2). Stephen actually takes forty-five verses to cover what Paul covers in four. Even given the probability that this was a summary, the contrast is striking. Paul introduces a specific time period – 450 years (Acts 13:20). Not symbolic or remarkable of itself, it yet gives the factual solidity that Paul requires.

In Acts 13:21 ('The people asked for a king'), Paul avoids the original problematic felt by the prophet Samuel. (Stephen actually omits the episode altogether, even though it fits in remarkably well with his thesis that the Israelites always resisted the Holy Spirit; 7:51.) What is important for Paul is David as paradigm and progenitor of Jesus (13:23). Paul's account is much less confrontational than Stephen's, much less provocative. His audience comprises brothers, not persecutors, and he limits the wrongdoers in 13:27 to the Jews at Jerusalem, rather than Jews as a class.

The same verse introduces the central historical concept of prophetic time. The key word is 'fulfilled'. The point about prophetic time is that it does not give a future timetable – there is a hiddenness about it, a secrecy; its fulfilment needs both discernment and proclamation which points back in time, not in a causal mode, but as demonstration of God's sovereignty. He does what he says he will do (compare Stephen's phrase 'as the time drew near for God to fulfill his promise', 7:17). This is purpose and divine pattern, repeated again in 13:29, climaxing in God's supreme act, he 'raised him from the dead' (13:30). This now forms the core of the Christian message (13:32–33), reinforced in terms of prophetic fulfilment (13:33–35). Only at 13:38 does Paul turn away from historical and prophetic time to theology, returning quickly in conclusion to prophetic time: 'I am going to do something in your days' (13:41).

Paul's sense of time is linear, the site of the demonstration of

God's sovereignty and salvation. It is thus purposeful, but needs revelation and proclamation. It is hopeful: Paul's hearers can become part of Israel, though there is the possibility of exclusion for the scoffer (13:41). As Professor Kaufmann shows in his discussion of *Paradise Lost*, Milton's use of time fits closely with Paul's usage, except in the former's use of mythic time.

It is interesting that when Paul preaches to a non-Jewish audience at Athens (Acts 17:22–31), his subject matter is quite different, starting at creation and building up a natural theology before eventually moving on to God's sovereignty in salvation history: 'in the past . . . now . . . he will judge' (17:30–31).

Turning now to *Jude*, Part 2, chapter 2, we find that Jude's arrival to fulfil his long-cherished vision of being a student at Christminster has been described in the previous chapter. It is now evening, when he imagines 'ghostly presences' of former scholars all around him. In the morning he has to find (manual) work until such time as his vision can be fulfilled. In searching for such work, he has a moment of revelation, which in fact he rejects in favour of his former vision. Hardy suggests that this revelation was 'a true illumination', but not sufficiently grounded. 'The deadly animosity of contemporary logic and vision towards so much of what he held in reverence was not yet revealed to him.' In other words, a further revelation is needed, since as yet it is unproclaimable. It is worth noting that the language of the Bible would not see any opposition between 'vision' and 'revelation' unless the former were entirely false prophecy. Is this what Hardy had in mind?

At first sight, there might seem little to compare between the two passages. But they are both structured in terms of comparing a past time to a present one, with concepts of discernment and revelation central. Jude is seen as unenlightened and therefore doomed to futility. However, Hardy does not condemn him for this, or see him in any way unbelieving – quite on the contrary, his ignorance and naïvety are more than balanced by his genuine feel for his craft and his immediate task of renovation of 'old poetry'.

What is thrown up by Hardy, in contrast to Paul's sermon, is an ambiguity. Its prevalent expression is in irony, uncertainty, even contradiction, as opposed to the sense of fulfilment in Paul's account. While the present may be a site of the revelation of new things and a passing away of the old, for Hardy these new things are themselves questioned as stemming from 'the modern vice of unrest'. Hardy here introduces a term new to the biblical account, that of modernity. Jude, while in love with the past, is still under the sway of the modern. He can only resolve this as provisionality:

his personal vision is a vice, therefore. Hardy has already led us to such a conclusion. He contrasts Jude's daylight perceptions ('the more or less defective real') with his previous night's 'perfect and ideal'. Yet Hardy has described in the previous chapter such perceptions as 'ghostly presences', spectral memories, a phantom and insubstantial history (compare the descriptions of Egdon Heath at night), signed by 'rottenness of stones' and 'decrepit and superseded chambers'. What we have, therefore, is a classic Hardyean dual perception (compare Tess overhearing Angel's harp playing in the garden). For Jude, Hardy suggests, the past is an illusion bound to lead to tragic unfulfilment; but the present, as the modern, offers nothing either. 'Contemporary logic and vision' are presumably bound to the same futility of unrest.

Where should Jude's salvation lie, then? Hardy's 'gospel' here, I believe, is more unconsciously ambiguous than that of the double perspective. On the one hand, Hardy suggests that Jude's craft puts him in touch with his origins – Jude 'stroked the mouldings as one who knew their beginning' – and the true nature of his medium, stone. He can thus renew and regenerate them. But this sense of permanency and solidity is undermined by Hardy's insistence that Jude would merely be perpetuating a discarded fashion: that this is not the true shape of the future. Neither does Hardy distance himself from Jude's perception that such work is mere imitation, producing 'modern prose', not 'old poetry'. Ultimately, Jude has nowhere to go. If he stays as a manual worker, he is consigned to the archaic; if he seeks his personal vision, he will again be led to a different form of the archaic. Unlike Paul, Hardy cannot find a prophetic word in the past to be fulfilled as a 'new thing' 'today'. The 'modern' is the parodic equivalent of the 'now' moment of God, and so hope stumbles into unrest and unfulfilment. Jude is consigned to tragedy, as must all people who have the sensitivity and idealism that makes Jude heroic in the Hardyean cosmos.

4. Patterns of time

We turn now to the second stage of comparison, the move to the general. It is possible in seeking an overview of the biblical concept of time to find references to natural time (the seasons, days and nights) and personal time (biography); and, of course, to historic and mythic time (though no sharp divide is set up here at all). But what subsumes them all is the concept of covenant time, at the heart of what is often termed 'salvation history'. Thus Isaiah writes:

> In the time of my favour . . .
>   and in the day of salvation . . .
> I will keep you and will make you
>   to be a covenant for the people,
> to restore the land . . .
>   (Isaiah 49:8)

This last phrase typifies the Old Testament – historical time is the account of the land, a site for God's covenant to be worked out incarnationally with his people. Seasonal time is subsumed in this, as in Deuteronomy 11:13 – rain at the right time is part of covenant conditions. Time comes to mean God's time, the right time, *chairos*.

In the New Testament, the geographical disappears gradually, and prophetic time is foregrounded (as it had begun to be in the last third of the Old Testament). As we have seen, this is essentially fulfilled time – the covenant promises are revealed, or replaced by newer, more universal promises. The revelation is sometimes seen as intervention – God moving into secular affairs, even though the secular fails to realize this. Hence grows a sense of hiddenness as well as manifestation. A new set of tensions is created to replace the Old Testament ones of obedience and disobedience. At the furthest extreme, this hiddenness is extended to the end time of Christ's second advent: 'No-one knows about that day or hour . . . only the Father' (Mk. 13:32–33; *cf.* Acts 1:7), this being linked to its suddenness (as in the thief imagery and much parabolic material). The sense of 'the right time' is still central – 'The time has come' (Mk. 1:15); 'at the appointed season' (Tit. 1:3); 'God . . . set a certain day, calling it Today' (Heb. 4:7, quoting Ps. 95:7–8). This sense of 'today' is crucial; it is far more dramatically used than our rather abstract 'the present' (*e.g.* Heb. 5:5, quoting Ps. 2:7; Heb. 3:7, 13, 15). It correlates with 'now', as in 'but now that you know God' (Gal. 4:9), or, as in Paul's sermon in Athens, 'In the past . . . but now . . . for he has set a day when he will . . .' (Acts 17:30–31). The 'now' has existential force despite the linearity of time here: the time of repentance is when we hear the gospel: that is the choice by which our time by faith becomes incorporated in God's covenant time. Just as Christ's coming was a fulfilment of prophetic time, the 'now' moment by faith fulfils that to us.

The New Testament emphasizes covenant time over against mythic time. 'Before time began' is the dramatic phrase Paul uses (1 Cor. 2:7, literally 'Before the ages'; *cf.* 1 Pet. 1:20). The mysterious reference to Melchizedek in Hebrews 7:3 demonstrates this too – Christ's priesthood is not only covenanted before time, but eternally present (*cf.* Heb. 1:10–12, quoting Ps. 102:25–27). One of the fascinating things for me in reading Stephen Hawking's *A Brief History of Time*[9] was the concept of negative or imaginary time, from which one could predicate a condition of eternity, positive time needing a beginning (a 'big bang'). The Old and New Testaments hold both in dual perspective.

The other New Testament phrase that includes an idea of presentness is 'the (or 'these') last times' (as in Acts 2:17; Heb. 1:2; 1 Pet. 1:20). 'Last' is far more ambiguous than 'recent', since it also means 'end', and this ambiguity is constantly exploited in the New Testament (*e.g.* Jn. 2:8) – eschatology constantly intrudes; the sense of an ending. The story must finish soon, so much has been fulfilled. We need to read on without delay. Hence the urgency of Paul's preaching and Peter's exhortation, as God's book is being written to completion.

In *Jude*, Hardy's perception of time is bleakly and ironically contrary to the biblical view. 'Life's time's fool,' he writes. The move from the impersonality of time in the opening of *The Return of the Native* to the pessimistic ambiguities of the passage examined in *Jude* in the last section should be seen as significantly contrary to the biblical movement. As has been seen, ambiguities derive from the contrast of historical time to modernity. Other sorts of time, typical of earlier novels by Hardy, are minimized, particularly seasonal or natural time, so strong a structuring device in *Tess* or the pastoral *Under the Greenwood Tree*. Mythic time likewise is little mentioned in *Jude*, unlike in *The Return of the Native*. On the other hand, we have a form allegorized in the strange figure of Little Father Time, a device many readers find alienating and even shocking.

But there are continuities with earlier novels, especially in the tracing of historical time back to Roman and British (*i.e.* pre-Anglo-Saxon) time, and especially the use of personal history. Hardy's use of memory in his poetry to establish a time–place graph of biographic time is one of its most striking features, well explored by J. Hillis Miller.[10] In the last novels, this nexus is much more complex. Generational patterns are also stressed, though not in the strange way of *The Well-Beloved*, where the protagonist falls in love with three generations of women.

What patterns emerge, then? The whole nineteenth-century tradition formed plot, theme and character by discovering such patterns. Some are archetypal: love sought, half-gained, lost and regained is one such. In *Jude*, the additional step of 'lost again' is what turns comic into tragic pattern. With most nineteenth-century novelists, the transitions are part of a moral patterning. Time is a moral dimension in which characters learn, reflect, mature and change. Those characters unable to use time morally are doomed to frustration or ridicule.

It is easy to trace the development of this through Austen, Dickens and George Eliot – indeed, on to E. M. Forster and D. H. Lawrence (F. R. Leavis' 'great tradition'). One of the ambiguities with Hardy is whether he fits this moral patterning of 'sowing and reaping' in terms of moral cause and effect, or whether such terms function subversively. Jude can thus be interpreted as having his life patterned by his own moral choices; but alternatively by being overtaken by forces beyond him, which he tries to make sense of or order, but which efforts must be seen ultimately as illusion. Such forces may be expressed as timeless (as Fate or Destiny), or within time (traditional or modern, for example). Hardy's generational patterning in *Jude* can likewise be seen as either determining forces or as moral warnings which Jude fails to heed. One of the fascinations with a good Hardy text is its openness to such alternative readings, and the subtle tensions set up between the ambiguities. The feeling is ultimately, for me, that of Greek tragedy rather than of biblical time. Sue says, 'It makes me feel as if a tragic doom overhung our family, as it did the house of Atreus.'[11] In any case, biblical thinking does not foreground such moral patterning in individual lives, stressing either people's election or their crises of faith. Choice and repentance remain subsidiary, though necessary, to this. And generational patterns ('to the third and fourth generation') in the Old Testament are replaced in the new by individual responsibility for sin (though Je. 31:30 foreshadows this). Hardy's move away from overarching moral patterns is not therefore unbiblical in itself. As with biblical thought, it opens up a space for the spirit and for supernatural forces – the sacred, possibly. The novelist's difficulty in general here is not to play god too obviously. George Eliot can be so accused, especially in her use of coincidence. Hardy's repetitions and coincidences are more problematic, in that they often appear to have moral patterning in the exposure of past guilt (for example, illegitimate babies – a favourite Victorian device), yet the 'feel' is more that of Hardy justifying his view of an impersonal, even blind, set of forces controlling life. In *Jude*, Hardy tends to avoid such coincidences, though the allegory of Little Father Time seems as crude and unjustified, if not more so. If 'in all things God works together for the good of those who also love him' (Rom. 8:28), and if the redemption of time is possible, as T. S. Eliot so eloquently explores in *Four Quartets* from a biblical perspective, then for Hardy nothing works for good to his chosen heroes and heroines. Time, therefore, remains unredeemable, the ironic medium for illusion, false hopes and futility. Without a sense of divine destiny, secular humanism has little to prevent such development.

Looking more specifically at *Jude*, we have seen Jude's vision of the past (the Christminster ideal) as illusion, an archaic rottenness which finally kills him. He lies at the end destroyed both by his craft as a mason and by his need to identify with Christminster. Yet it is more than this: he is also killed by his love for Sue, trying to see her one last time in the driving rain, and her desertion, caused likewise by her archaic (it is suggested) moral guilt. Sue's unrealities, however, are not timebound in the same way as Jude's: her love for the classical has little to do with her dislike of the flesh, her 'spirituality'. The classical pastoral joy they briefly experience[12] is also seen as illusion.

Other forms of the historical can be equally destructive. Philotson's hobby of Roman antiquities symbolizes his dessicated spirit. In terms of time as speed, the old 'foot-time' is associated with Vilbert the quack; with Jude and Sue walking and missing their train,[13] with Sue's subsequent expulsion from training college; and with Jude's walking to work and back, only to be seduced by Arabella. As in *Tess*, walking between places is fraught with danger; it symbolizes not so much man as pilgrim (the biblical view), but man without protection, vulnerable and rootless.[14] Christminster is the new Jerusalem for Jude, but is revealed as the ultimate anti-pilgrimage. Even if Bunyan's Pilgrim finds as many dangers on the way, it is true pilgrimage.

Hardy's references to the destruction of the past by the present, however, do suggest some value for it. The first chapter suggests that, however decayed the past, it represents something more substantial than the modern. He focuses on the church rebuilding, something Hardy knew about at first hand. The replacing of the old Marygreen church with Victorian Gothic seems to him (and us) tasteless, false, inauthentic. It is in this new church that Sue remarries, and where she and Jude have their last encounter. Its architect, 'a certain obliterator of historic records',[15] actually runs down from London by train. The immemoriability of the burial site is replaced by 'eighteenpenny cast-iron crosses warranted to last five years'. The modern is cheap and temporary. Modern agriculture equally obliterates landscape, depriving the fields 'of all history beyond that of a few recent months'.[16] What makes landscape significant are landmarks,[17] which in Marygreen have been systematically destroyed by modernity, evacuating any meaning derived from place.

All this makes the Victorian notion of progress very problematic for Hardy. He responds with the same ironic ambiguity already noted with regard to the past. Sue's modernity is contradictory, for example, as seen in her crypto-feminism in her search for new experience, her inability to live with the past, her views, the shape of her desire, and her unconventionality and anti-legalism.[18] She seeks to be a free spirit. Yet she also claims to be classical, to revert back to Greek joyousness, while her views on sex seem to be an extension of Victorian prudery!

Jude's modernity can also be seen as an extension of Victorian self-help, even if undermining Samuel Smiles' sub-texts. Yet the oft-repeated assertion that Jude is ahead of his time[19] is not, in itself, unreasonable as we look back with a century's hindsight. But to construe Jude's tragedy as being that of a progressive soul thwarted by a reactionary age will hardly do from what has been shown of Hardy's contradictions. Jude's attempts to enter Christminster are not only too reactionary, but too disorganized and too ignorant to warrant tragic status.

5. *This present age: some conclusions*

For the final stage of our methodology, we need to try to form some conclusions, however tentative. Compared to the certainties of the biblical text, the ambivalencies undermining the Hardy text are striking. The Bible has no idea of societal progress into the future: the last days, if anything, will be marked by degeneracy (2 Pet. 2). The only authentic progress is in Christlikeness (*e.g.* Eph. 4:14–15), and the growth of the kingdom of heaven (*e.g.* Mt. 13:31–33). The only ambiguity here is whether these concepts are just inward, or societal as well; the uncertainties are in terms of how soon is the end of the age.

With Hardy, the existential 'now' of salvation drama is lost, in *Jude* at least, under the weight of the idea of progress and the need to reify the present as the modern. Hardy's triumph is almost in spite of himself, by being able to penetrate to the timeless in his tragic patterns, and by being able to capture something of the sense of modern time as symbol rather than idea of character. To my mind, the best example of such symbol is that of railway time.

Although railway journeys occur in other novels (*A Pair of Blue Eyes*, *The Well-Beloved*), here there is an accelerating pattern. Sue herself sees railway stations as the sign of modernity, rejecting meeting Jude at the cathedral to meet him at the railway station. But it fails them – they miss the train back; it takes Sue away,[20] causing separation, disorientation, and finally the fracturing of the continuum between countryside and personal identity. The 'series of crooked railways'[21] merely brings futility and a sign of inauthenticity as Jude meets the hymn composer. Railway time increasingly rules all meetings, and closes down choices.[22] It brings anonymity closer; when Little Father Time arrives at Aldbrickham, there is no-one to meet him. A Kafkaesque vision glints fleetingly at this point. It is impossible to be a pilgrim by rail. Although there is a promise of termini and destination, railways actually bring circularity and disjuncture.

The linearity of biblical time is not intercepted by such notions of speed. Time, as we have seen, is a relativity (2 Pet. 3:8) – a view unknown to Hardy scientifically, even if it is remembered theologically. His Darwinian science will have suggested long past time, to be compared to the shortness of human life, but left him ignorant of cosmology's fraction of a second timing for the 'big bang' of creation. Biblical relativity anticipates both. But because it is personal, 'with God', then it is safe, purposed, loving, and not the iron track of impersonal forces.

Hardy's typical refuge from this is to seek permanence in personal history. For example, Philotson reads Sue's handwriting as memory, not as notes on history.[23] Jude carves his initials and vision on the milestone, seeking to fix time to landmark, to signed place. The biblical echo of 'What do these stones mean?' (Jos. 4:6, 21) becomes increasingly ironic as each return marks another step towards a memorial of failure. Similarly, Christminster becomes 'the place of vanished dreams'.[24] Other attempts to revisit personal history become squalid.[25] In the end, Jude's final return to Christminster with Arabella forms a mocking merging of history and autobiography – the Martyrs' burning place becomes that of his martyrdom. But in his drunken haze, it is merely self-regarding. The absence of Christian meaning for Jude quite literally leads to loss of personal signification. It is an anti-martyrdom,[26] and as with *The Mayor of Casterbridge*, the tone at the end changes to pathos, the possibilities of (heroic) significant ending having been undermined by the failure of the enterprise to establish this permanence of place and history. In a sense, it is exactly what a biblical understanding would predicate.

Hardy's resonances, then, which make him such a powerful writer, do not lie in the setting up of a humanist critique of traditional thought or values, or in the tracing of progress of great souls of the type posited by Carlyle, Arnold and other Victorian humanists. They lie in the tensions felt through every character, plot and symbol, that such efforts are futile at best, inauthentic at worst. This is the bleakness. But this is balanced by the memory of absence, or rather, the traces of an absent Christian gospel, where purpose and love are life-giving redemptive structures. In our examination of time, we can see Hardy seeking to reconstruct biography in such terms of purpose, vision and love, but, in the absence of personal salvation history, meaning and direction are lost, and futility leads to pathos rather than to redemptive martyrdom. Linearity is maintained, but pilgrimage – the journey through time to a pre-envisioned, holy place – is increasingly impossible: the new Jerusalem cannot even be maintained as personal construct, let alone as spiritual reality.

Hardy's prophetic voice, then, can place itself in prophetic time: it calls from the wilderness of the alienated human spirit, wanting, but not knowing, a messiah. The literary journey from *Jude the Obscure* to *Waiting for Godot* is inevitable in the history of secular humanism. A discerning Christian reader sees in Hardy the truth of the futility of uncovenanted time, which, as T. S. Eliot saw, is therefore unredeemable, however great the sacrifice made.

Some follow-up work

You may like to try some follow-up exercises. For example, you could compare the 'today' passages in Hebrews (Heb. 3:7–47) with the opening pages of *Jude*, Part 4, chapter 1. Or you could take the famous suicide scene (*Jude*, Part 6, chapter 2) and compare it with the annunciation scenes in the gospels (Mt. 1:17 – 2:24; Lk. 1–2). Key notions of consolation, hope and death intermingle in quite different patterns.

Moving away from time to place, the opening of *The Return of the Native*, chapter 4 of *The Mayor of Casterbridge*, or the description of Tess walking to Talbothays for the first time (*Tess of the d'Urbervilles*, chapter 16), could be compared to the pilgrimage metaphors of Hebrews (Heb. 11:8–12; 12:18–24; 13:12–14). Tess's flight (chapters 42–43) could be compared to Jacob's flight (Gn. 28).

A more difficult exercise would be to apply a more explicit postmodern critique to *Jude*. I have tended to treat the novel as a proto-modernist text in the emphasis on alienation of hero from his world; and on the emphasis on the secular humanist attempt to retain identity in the face of the collapse of Victorian certainties. Madan Sarup, quoting Jameson, suggests that we as a society have now become incapable of dealing with time, and can only produce pastiche. The postmodern also deals with the fragmentation of the individual, as well as categories of absence, traces of lost presence. I have hinted at some of these, but you may like to see *Jude* as anticipating such postmodernist motifs, and concentrate on them in comparing the same biblical passages to *Jude*.[27]

Some useful books on Hardy

D. L. Collins, *Thomas Hardy and his God: A Liturgy of Unbelief* (Basingstoke: Macmillan, 1990).

A. Enstice, *Thomas Hardy: Landscapes of the Mind* (Basingstoke: Macmillan, 1979).

I. Gregor, *The Great Web: The Form of Hardy's Major Fiction* (London: Faber, 1974).

F. Hardy, *Life of Thomas Hardy* (Basingstoke: Macmillan, 1928–30).

J. Holloway, *The Victorian Sage: Studies in Argument* (Archon, 1962).

D. Kramer (ed.). *Critical Approaches to the Fiction of Thomas Hardy* (London: Macmillan, 1979).

J. H. Miller, *Distance and Desire* (Oxford: Oxford University Press, 1970).

B. Qualls, *Secular Pilgrims of Victorian Fiction* (Cambridge: Cambridge University Press, 1981).

C. H. Salter, *Good Little Thomas Hardy* (Basingstoke: Macmillan, 1981).

13

How feminist can a handmaid be? Margaret Atwood's *The Handmaid's Tale*

Elizabeth Clarke

For anyone who is a Christian, or a feminist, or both, *The Handmaid's Tale* is an extremely rewarding text, particularly if you are the kind of critic who takes both theory and theology seriously, as I do. In naming the dystopia as Gilead and using key texts from the Bible, Margaret Atwood immediately raises one of the most important theological and literary issues: how should we read the sacred text which is at the heart of Christianity – a question which the previous two chapters have also posed? The institution of the handmaid itself is the result of a literal reading of one of the less savoury practices in the Bible: the offering of the handmaid as a sexual partner to an important man whose wife is barren. The best-known of these is Hagar, Abraham's handmaid, and feminists have isolated this story as one of the most degrading to women in Scripture.[1]

The narrator of *The Handmaid's Tale*, Offred, is such a handmaid in a future society where Aids, pollution, radiation and abortion have reduced the birthrate to alarming levels. A right-wing coup in the north-east corner of the US has installed a totalitarian regime which has a fundamentalist approach to the Bible, and imposes a partriarchal order on society and family alike. In this society, a handmaid is a woman who has proved her fertility by bearing a child but is not in a legitimate relationship, according to the regime. Offred's marriage has been dissolved, because it was her husband Luke's second: he has been imprisoned, or killed, and she has been made into a 'national resource', available to the highest-ranking officers as a concubine. Offred has been deprived of her own name and is known only as the possession of the head of the household, Fred. The spellcheck on my wordprocessor insistently suggests that 'Offred' is an incorrect version of 'offered', an apposite pun that Margaret Atwood may or may not have intended.

Thus, in the corrupt power structures and practices of Gilead, Margaret Atwood demonstrates the dangers for women of an extremely literal view of Scripture. One of the epigraphs to the novel is Genesis 30:1–3 (Authorized Version), which recounts Rachel's despairing offer of her maid as sexual partner to her husband. The bizarre practice she suggests – 'she shall bear upon my knees, that I may also have children by her' – is adopted and extended by the Gileadean regime to the act of conception, thus imposing physical and mental humiliation on both handmaid and wife, and also, it must be said, on the husband. As Arnold E. Davidson points out, 'The Biblical fundamentalism of Gilead poses crucial questions about the interpretive use of literary texts, for that society's most appalling practices all have their scriptural justification'.[2] 'They can hit us, there's Scriptural precedent,' says Offred of the wives.[3] Most feminist theologians would agree that such a literal reading of much of the Bible is not possible for a church that rejects patriarchy.[4] Margaret Atwood does not appear to be attacking the Bible as such, but the authoritarian and fundamentalist use of it. In Gilead, the Bible itself is kept locked away, lest private readings undermine the one authorized interpretation.[5] As we shall see, Offred's personal reading of Scripture, independent of the official religion, plays a very positive role in *The Handmaid's Tale*.

Although Gilead has been described as a 'demonic misrepresentation of Judaic-Christian religion', its practices are not 'Christian' in any recognizable sense. In fact, some extremely familiar Christian denominations are presented as actively resisting the Gilead regime. The Quakers courageously smuggle women out of Gilead, and Offred's friend Moira, who benefits from their help, is very positive about their particular Christian values, which involve a commitment to political and social intervention typical of modern Quakers. More surprising, perhaps, is the discovery that the Baptists are actually involved in armed revolt against Gilead! However, the point is made: Atwood is deliberately not targeting Christian denominations. If anything, she is warning against the consequences of the backlash against feminism that characterizes the Moral Majority movement in the

United States. The portrayal of what could happen if a right-wing patriarchal movement came to power might make some Christian readers hostile to feminism think again. Atwood singles out Serena Joy, a woman who had been a famous leader in an anti-feminist organization, and who now regrets the loss of the vocation and prominence she had denied to other women. There are plenty of Serena Joys in the present Christian church. As in Gilead, in a patriarchal system which is set up for the benefit of men at the expense of women, some women seek male approval in suppressing feminism more viciously than the men.

A feminist 1984?

Thus *The Handmaid's Tale* is not an attack on Christianity itself, although it could be interpreted as attacking hierarchies within some parts of the Christian church. Having some respect for the outdated concept of 'authorial intention', I asked Margaret Atwood why she wrote it. The answer, when it came, was obvious: she is trying to rewrite each novelistic genre for women, and *The Handmaid's Tale* is a women's *1984*. This idea is consonant with the feminist project of rewriting key myths in the culture, including stories from the Bible: such texts are rewritten so that the female point of view and 'feminine' values are inscribed, modifying the largely masculine emphases of our heritage. The similarities between *The Handmaid's Tale* and *1984* appear in a close reading of the text. Orwell's slogan, 'Big Brother is watching you', is replaced by the similarly ominous 'Under his eye'. His subversive organization is called 'The Brotherhood', whereas it is 'The Female Railroad' that helps dissidents in Gilead. Both texts share the standard format of the dystopia:

> First, the narrator experiences hopeless despair in the face of the brutal regime, then feels some hope through discovering the possibility of resistance . . . and begins to perceive cracks in what seemed to be the unassailable power . . . This political hope is strengthened by personal hope in the form of a love affair, a testament to continuing human emotion in the face of the dehumanization of the regime. Finally, there is the possibility of escape.[6]

Apart from the final characteristic – there was never any possibility of escape for Winston Smith – the plot structure of both novels is identical. The two texts seem to be written with a similar seriousness of purpose. It is clear that *1984* was a warning by a man with a concern for truth who perceived in post-war society the disquieting signs of totalitarianism: in some ways, *1984* is not fiction, but journalism. Margaret Atwood also insists that her novel is 'true': 'There's not a single detail in the book that does not have a corresponding reality, either in contemporary situations or historical fact.'[7] Subsequent discoveries about political control of women's fertility in the Ceausescu regime in Romania lent credence to her claim. Such concern for truth is particularly attractive to the Christian reader, but Orwell and Atwood have different answers to the question, 'What is truth?'

In *1984*, the epitome and encapsulation of truth is in the formula 2+2=4: 'If that is true, all else follows,' says Winston Smith. In *The Handmaid's Tale*, Offred's 'owner', the Commander, denies women access to this formula: 'Women can't add . . . for them, one and one and one and one don't make four.'[8] Surprisingly, Offred accepts this chauvinist statement, but rewrites it into a demonstration of women's concern for the individual.

> What the Commander said is true. One and one and one and one doesn't equal four. Each one remains unique, there is no way of joining them together. They cannot be exchanged, one for the other. Nick for Luke or Luke for Nick.[9]

The Commander meant to show women's stupidity in being unable to grasp abstract concepts, an attitude even the beloved Luke appears to share.[10] Offred, however, is not interested in such abstract, formulaic definitions of 'truth': people are more important in *The Handmaid's Tale*. In general, Margaret Atwood's story is more optimistic than Orwell's, perhaps because she has more faith in human beings, particularly women, and their ability to communicate in the face of all laws to the contrary.

Orwell's nightmare, worked out through his invention of 'Newspeak', is that language can be manipulated to control thought. Language is also highly regulated in Gilead. There is no word for 'sterile', for example, since childlessness is assumed to be the woman's fault; but this does not stop any of the women, including the Commander's wife, thinking that the Commander is impotent. Denied language, the handmaids communicate non-verbally: sign language, body language, symbols. The fragility of human words is exemplified for Orwell by the way that writing can vanish into ashes in a second. The women in Gilead encode their communication in more physically substantial media. The graffiti scratched in Offred's room by her predecessor, for example, are a powerful focus for hope. Winston Smith's diary will never be read, but Offred summons a reader into being by the very strength of her faith. 'By telling you anything at all I'm at least believing in you, I believe you're there, I believe you into being. I tell, therefore you are.'[11] Witnessing to the truth is the key activity in *The Handmaid's Tale*: passing on personal testimony at whatever cost.

Atwood's novel is thus more optimistic and more open to interpretation than Orwell's narrative, which reaches absolute closure, with the destruction of 'the last man in Europe'. The 'open' ending is a feature of Margaret Atwood's fiction: rewriting the 'thriller', in *Bodily Harm*, she designed an ambiguous ending for another narrative genre that traditionally demands closure. She would probably agree with T. Mark Ledbetter that an open ending is less 'masculine':

> it seems to me male to superimpose a story of meaning and order on a world chaotic and meaningless. Males love denouement – persons in power seek conclusion, self-defined conclusion, as the means of maintaining power.[12]

Most novels about a dystopia follow one person, usually a man, in his attempts to fight a viciously totalitarian regime. This perhaps rather 'masculine' plot, describing what is essentially a power struggle, demands a conclusion: the hero either succeeds or fails. But Offred does not fight, and we do not even know whether she escapes the wrath of the regime. Perhaps Margaret Atwood is deliberately refusing to use her authorial power to impose a neat solution, in what she would see as an example of the male desire for mastery. The film of the book, presumably designed for a wider market than the feminist novel, had a completely different ending: Offred killed the Commander and escaped amid a satisfying inferno of blown-up buildings. In a patriarchal society, people, not just males, love denouement.

2. Feminist or postfeminist?

This is one of the reasons some feminists have objected to the whole idea of reappropriating patriarchal texts: rather than writing oneself out of patriarchal culture, the argument runs, feminist writers can write themselves into it, because they have to accept the basic plot structures of the originals, and the values encoded in them.[13] Indeed, some feminist critics do not see *The Handmaid's Tale* as a feminist text in any real sense. One (male) critic questioned its feminism in these terms: 'We hardly see men behaving badly at all, and what we do see is counterbalanced by women behaving badly in all sorts of ways.'[14] This is a total misunderstanding of the project of feminism, which is to combat the power structures of patriarchy, not to attack individual men: the ultimate example of how to 'hate the sin and love the sinner'. Gayle Greene, in a more thoughtful analysis, points out that the relationship between Offred and her feminist mother 'epitomizes the relationship of feminists to postfeminists'.[15] In fact, *The Handmaid's Tale* contains within itself a critique of radical western feminism, which is seen as having helped to produce Gilead by its sentimentality about women and its separatist attitudes. Offred's comments to Moira in the pre-Gileadean world of free speech imply that radical feminists are naïve to shut themselves away in separatist enclaves and hope that patriarchy will disintegrate of its own accord.[16] Atwood offers us no alternative but our own, deeply flawed society, which Offred constantly looks back to with nostalgia. The message, if there is any, to a twentieth-century readership is to value what you have. It is difficult for a western feminist, or a Christian, to learn anything from Offred's actual behaviour: she collaborates with the Commander, she engages in an illegal affair with the chauffeur, she chooses personal survival over the demands of the pro-women's resistance. None of this is the stuff of radical feminism. It is true that Offred locates heroism in the attitude of her radical feminist friend Moira, but she distances herself from these qualities, and fears them even as she admires them: 'Moira was like an elevator with open sides. She made us dizzy.'[17] Traditional women's virtues, such as the patience and silent endurance which Offred displays, do not resonate with western feminists, although the feminist theologian Sara Coakley is currently developing a feminist theology which stresses exactly those qualities.

In fact, it is in its implicit and explicit comment on academic discourse that *The Handmaid's Tale* can be seen at its most radical, and at its most relevant to the feminist critic. The epilogue to Offred's story is presented as the proceedings of a rather dry academic conference. Thoroughly immersed in the subjective and personal narrative of *The Handmaid's Tale*, the reader might be inclined to skip it, if it did not occur at a particularly crucial part of the narrative, just as Offred is being taken away, to freedom or execution. The characters in the epilogue are academic scholars of the future studying the text we have just read as an historical text from the Gileadean period. The discussion of the text as physical artefact – actually a cassette tape rather than a written document – forces us to think of the conditions of its composition, an issue which we usually prefer to suspend along with our disbelief. Since Offred could not possibly have recorded any kind of text during her servitude as a handmaid, she must have been rescued by the subversive organization, Mayday. Thus the ending of *The Handmaid's Tale* is actually not as open as it may first appear. Offred has in fact told us all this, but in our desire for suspense and denouement we have ignored it: 'When I get out of here, if I'm ever able to set this down, in any form, even in the form of one voice to another, it will be a reconstruction.'[18] After all, we are accustomed to the novelistic convention that the reader can be allowed inside the narrator's head, and have probably not stopped to think about the difficulties of authorship under Offred's circumstances.

This epilogue allows Atwood to make explicit a comparison of male and female discourses. We very soon learn that the male scholars are far from satisfied by the remarkable text which has come into their possession. Professor Pieixoto's paper, 'Problems of Authentication in Relation to *The Handmaid's Tale*', raises the question of the authority of the text we have just read. Clearly, one of his problems is that the author of the text is female, writing apparently at the whim of a capricious female goddess:

> She could have told us much about the workings of the Gileadean empire, had she the instincts of a reporter or spy. What would we not give, even now, for twenty pages or so of printout from Waterford's private computer! However, we must be grateful for any crumbs the Goddess of History has designed to vouchsafe us.[19]

Female discourse is trivialized by a pejorative comparison with factual, investigative writing: even the impersonal workings of a computer would be preferable to Offred's account. Professor Pieixoto would much rather deal with the notebook of a (probably male) reporter than with one woman's personal story. At this point, the reader who has followed Offred through the vicissitudes of life under the Gileadean regime resists the disqualification of her style of writing, while acknowledging the fictional nature of the account. We know about Gilead in a way that the Professor obviously does not know, or he could not continue with his sexist jokes and chauvinist discourse. And thus one of the most important issues in feminist literary criticism and feminist theology is raised: is women's writing really different from men's?

3. Psychoanalysis and 'essentialism'

It is French feminist criticism which has explored this issue most thoroughly using psychoanalysis to explain categories of 'male' and 'female', particularly in relationship to writing.[20] Lucy M. Freibert thinks that the whole project of *The Handmaid's Tale* is a theoretical one, in this sense: Margaret Atwood 'deconstructs western phallocentrism and explores those aspects of French feminist theory that offer women some measure of hope'.[21] The ideas which Freibert wants to take from French theory include women's ability to tell stories, take risks, reclaim their bodies, find their voices, and reconstruct society. This is a rather simplified digest of French theory, but it does demonstrate some of the potential of psychoanalytic theory for a Christian feminist. After all, if, thanks to feminism, women finally find their voices, it should be in order to make a positive difference to society.

'Telling stories' is central to *The Handmaid's Tale*. It is what Offred represents herself as doing in the activity of authorship. She explores different possibilities for the role of storyteller in her narrative. She offers different versions of an event; she breaks off one story and resumes another, she fully admits the provisionality of all her accounts. What she does not do is threaten to abandon the story altogether, even if it is painful, or question the enterprise of telling stories, in the way that Professor Pieixoto explicitly does. When Offred is taken to Jezebel's, the brothel for men of status, all she wants to do is to talk to the women, even though there is no appropriate word for the sharing of women in a sisterly relationship: 'fraternize' is the only word she has.[22] Meeting Moira in the washroom, she demands to know everything that has happened to her. 'What's the point?' says Moira, but she does not need to answer her own question, and immediately begins to tell her story. Offred's report of Moira's story shows the limits of her role as storyteller. She fills it out;[23] she makes it sound as like Moira as she can; but she can't make the story end differently, because it didn't happen that way.[24] In this novel, the limits of the author's imagination are the limits of truthfulness, which rules out one meaning for the phrase 'telling stories'. Moreover, there is a compulsion to tell this particular story, simply because it is the truth about the narrator.

> I keep on going with this sad and hungry and sordid, this limping and mutilated story, because after all I want you to hear it, as I will hear yours too if I ever get the chance, if I meet you or if you escape, in the future or in Heaven or in prison or underground, some other place.[25]

This compulsion is partly the need to testify, the need that led Winston Smith to address his diary 'to the future'. Margaret Atwood has described her own sense of responsibility to write novels which bear witness to political realities.[26] But for Offred, telling her story is not merely an account of the sins of the Gilead regime. As Professor Pieixoto registers but does not understand, Offred's storytelling is an intimate disclosure of her self as inscribed in language, and rather than an authoritative statement of the truth, it is one half of what she hopes will be a mutual process, the giving and receiving of personal stories.

However attractive the idea of female storytelling is to a Christian mentality in which personal testimony carries weight, it is not really central to French feminist concerns, which have been summed up in the concept of *l'écriture féminine*. There is some agreement that, although women occupy a privileged position because of their relationship to their own bodies, it is possible for men to take part in this kind of discourse. Hélène Cixous, in *The Laugh of the Medusa*, offers a vision of women 'writing their bodies':

> What woman hasn't flown/stolen? Who hasn't felt, dreamt, performed the gesture that jams sociality? Who hasn't crumbled, held up to ridicule, the bar of separation? Who hasn't inscribed with her body the differential, punctured the system of couples and opposition? . . . A feminine text cannot fail to be more than subversive. It is volcanic.[27]

This is a rather more radical version of what Lucy M. Freibert meant when she suggested that in *The Handmaid's Tale* women 'reclaim their bodies' and 'find their voices'. Perhaps it is in the texture of Offred's narrative voice that the subversively feminist project of Margaret Atwood's novel consists. Most of Margaret Atwood's novels are very obviously concerned with the body, particularly the fragmented body: Roberta Rubenstein lists the grim litany of dismembered parts in *The Handmaid's Tale*.[28] One of the most interesting aspects of Offred's narrative is her sense of alienation from her own body. It is clear that this is a product of strictly imposed patriarchal values:

> My nakedness is strange to me already . . . Did I really wear bathing suits at the beach? . . . I avoid looking down at my body, not so much because it's shameful or immodest but because I don't want to see it. I don't want to look at something that determines me so completely.[29]

Offred mourns the loss of a united consciousness that included her female body. The patriarchal version of body-consciousness is a false one that alienates because only certain parts of the female body are valued: the handmaids are seen as 'two-legged wombs'. Now, her body is still a place of refuge, but a perilous one. The remnants of that healthy feminine consciousness are articulated in Offred's ability to image the distorted world which is her body:

> I sink down into my body as into a swamp, fenland, where only I know the footing . . . I used to think of my body as an instrument, of pleasure, or a means of transportation, or an implement, for the accomplishment of my will . . . There were limits but my body was nevertheless lithe, single, solid, one with me. Now the flesh arranges itself differently. I'm a cloud, congealed around a central object, the shape of a pear, which is hard and more real that I am and glows red within its translucent wrapping. Inside it is a space, huge as the sky at night and dark and curved like that, though black-red rather than black. Pinpoints of light swell, sparkle, burst and shrivel within it, countless as stars. Every month there is a moon, gigantic, round, heavy, an omen. It transits, pauses, continues on and passes out of sight, and I see despair coming towards me like a famine . . . I listen to my heart, wave upon wave, salty and red.[30]

Surely Offred's description of her womb, fantastic and ominous as it is, constitutes 'writing the body' – *l'écriture féminine*. This

244

writing is perhaps so powerful because Margaret Atwood is not only a woman, but also a poet: one of Julia Kristeva's key ideas is that poetic language, whatever the gender of the poet, has always shared the characteristics of women's writing.[31]

However, being defined by her body is Offred's limitation rather than her liberation. The argument against the psycho-analytic description of female sexuality which is the basis for French feminist theory is that to link the concept of 'woman' with a particular biology predestines women to subordination. *The Handmaid's Tale* all too graphically portrays this point of view. This is the danger of essentialism, a 'sin' of which one part of the feminist movement is continually accusing the other: the categor-izing of men and women as essentially very different. Extreme essentialists, who tend to be separatist in outlook, limit women's resistance to patriarchy to the extra-symbolic realm outside of language, thus in effect silencing women.[32] In fact, Offred is desperate to re-enter the male world of discourse, the 'symbolic order' in psychoanalytic terms. Her monthly treat is the television news, and she longs for something to read: the single word 'Faith', embroidered on her cushion, occupies her usefully for ten minutes. She plays Scrabble with the Commander, which is surely a 'masculinist' activity – using mechanical verbal skill to defeat an opponent! However, the relationship with words described here is not the cerebral mastery which characterizes the symbolic order for French feminists:

> The counters are like candies, made of peppermint, cool like that. Humbugs, they were called. I would like to put them into my mouth. They would also taste of lime. The letter C. Crisp, slightly acid on the tongue, delicious.[33]

Offred has a physical enjoyment of words. When she is finally able to take up a pen and write, the sensation is again physical, almost sexual:

> The pen between my fingers is sensuous, alive almost, I can feel its power, the power of the words it contains. Pen is Envy, Aunt Lydia would say, quoting another Centre motto, warning us away from such objects. And they were right, it is envy. Just holding it is envy. I envy the Commander his pen. It's one more thing I would like to steal.[34]

In this humorous redefining of Freud's term 'penis envy', which he saw as the affliction of every little girl, Offred firmly delineates what she envies men for: not their sexuality, but their physical ability to write. Authorship is just one more activity which has been denied to women in Gilead. Like many male authors of the western tradition, such as Gerard Manley Hopkins, the rulers of Gilead have posited a direct link between the penis and authorial inspiration.[35] This white male tradition is truly phallocentric. Women's discourse, however, does not stop for lack of pen or penis. As *The Handmaid's Tale* testifies, women continue to communicate under the most difficult of circumstances; and Offred becomes an author, even though she can only compose in her head. The story, however, is not an abstract one: it is firmly incarnated in her own physical experience. Finally, the story too becomes a body, if, like Offred's sense of her own body, or perhaps of Luke's, a mutilated one:

> I'm sorry there is so much pain in this story. I'm sorry it's in fragments, like a body caught in the crossfire or pulled apart by force. But there is nothing I can do to change it.[36]

4. A feminist post-structuralist text?

One way of avoiding essentialism is to see the categories of 'man' and 'woman' as social and linguistic constructs which have no real meaning in themselves. Thus one of the projects of feminist post-structuralism is to analyse gender descriptions in the light of society's power structures, and to 'deconstruct' the traditional categories. This is part of the larger post-structuralist enterprise which is to see all meaning as produced by social and linguistic struggles, and therefore not fixed or determinate. There are gestures towards post-structuralism in this novel: as we have seen, Offred is aware of the slippage between language and meaning. However, the sense of inevitability of this story – that the author is limited by what happens in a world outside of the discourse – finally does not allow the novel to be read in this way. Although, as we have seen, Offred (and Atwood) plays with her power as author, she is in fact careful to make distinctions between what is real and what is not. The story is a reconstruction, not a deconstruction: it is an attempt to get as near to 'reality' as possible, an attempt which fails only because there are not enough words to describe it.[37] Although she is particularly aware of the power of metaphor, a power that creates, she is careful to distinguish between the meaning thus verbally created, and reality:

> I look at the one red smile. The red of the smile is the same as the red of the tulips in Serena Joy's garden, towards the base of the flowers where they are beginning to heal. The red is the same but there is no connection. The tulips are not tulips of blood, the red smiles are not flowers, neither thing makes a comment on the other. The tulip is not a reason for disbelief in the hanged man, or vice versa. Each thing is valid and really there.[38]

Offred cannot afford the post-structuralist luxury of viewing the world as a collection of discourses which are all equal in status. In order to survive, Offred has to make careful distinctions between things that she observes in the real world. This involves making value-judgments to which one is prepared to testify – risking one's life if necessary, as Offred did, in love and in authorship. Personal testimony such as Offred's, however, has become passé for some forms of feminist theory, in a move which has important implications for Christian criticism. One of the most interesting but painful books I have read recently is a collection of autobiographical writing by feminist scholars, many of them with a post-structuralist sense that their identity is not an essential given but a construction of the social discourses around them.[39] An account of personal experience, therefore, loses its authority. This is Linda S. Kauffman apparently telling her own story of her father's rebellion against a fundamentalist Protestant family. She interrupts at the point when he gambled the family's money away after becoming a Bible salesman:

> Is it even possible to write against the grain of individualism? When you read my opening gambit, didn't it make you (whether you know me personally or not) want to know more? That is precisely my point: there is something fatally alluring about personal testi-mony . . . Society tames the feminist through the story in particular, the use of personal testimony in general.[40]

The difficulty of saying 'I' in such circumstances is acute, leading contributors to this volume to some obscure strategies in trying *not* to tell their own stories.

The Handmaid's Tale depends on its first person narrative strategy, Offred's capacity to say 'I', even though she can never give voice to her true name. This novel is fiction, but it demonstrates the value of bearing witness. As we have seen, the irony implicit in the epilogue teaches the reader to value such personal testimony over the academic scholarship represented there. Margaret Atwood has commented on the detachment with which scholars tend to treat even the most intense of human experience, and in her account of this conference she satirizes these unpleasant aspects of academic discourse.[41] However, although the sexist jokes and tasteless wit are unpleasant, there is a more sinister aspect to this 'objectivity', as Arnold E. Davidson points out:

> The supposed 'objectivity' of the scholarly enterprise of the Twelfth Symposium on Gileadean Studies is a chilling postscript to a story in which women (and others too; blacks, Jews, homosexuals, Quakers, Baptists) have been totally *objectified*, rendered into objects by the State. And implicit in that question is a more immediate one. Do we, as scholars, contribute to the dehumanization of society by our own critical work, especially when, as according to the distinguished professor of the novel, 'our job is not to censure but to understand'?[42]

This plea for committed scholarship is one that feminists, and Christians, should take seriously. The Twelfth Symposium on Gileadean Studies, all too recognizable as contemporary academic discourse, is an example of how not to do it.

There are many 'feminisms', as I hope this essay shows, and just as many feminist critical practices. All of them claim to have women's rights as their preoccupation and political change as their goal. A Christian feminist who shares these aims has to distinguish between various feminist theories, and she must make the choice unsupported by the sacred text, which offers little help in developing feminist readings.[43] My own practice is to value women's personal stories, while acknowledging the significance of the cultural context in which they speak. Even in a fictional account, practical and rhetorical strategies for resisting the institutional sin of patriarchy may be found. In *The Handmaid's Tale* Margaret Atwood shows us rhetorical ways of resisting a supremely patriarchal society, although practical options, as we have seen, are problematic. To the academic, her plea is for a literary criticism which is not an intellectual game but which takes into account the circumstances of the human beings who are authors. To the ordinary woman, storytelling is important, even if only to herself, in the necessary activity of remembering. Texts may also be a source of resistance, even if they exist only in the memory, and one of the most powerful and most memorable texts is the Bible.[44] One of the most moving parts of the book is where Offred rewrites the Lord's Prayer:

> My God. Who Art in the Kingdom of Heaven, which is within.
> I wish you would tell me Your Name, the real one I mean. But *You* will do as well as anything.
> I wish I knew what you were up to. But whatever it is, help me to get through it, please. Though maybe it's not Your doing; I don't believe for an instant that what's going on out there is what You meant.[45]

The Bible, which post-Christian feminists have entirely discounted as the ultimate patriarchal text, is a classic source of succour for those fighting oppression. No woman's writing can start again with a clean sheet, in feminism's utopian dream of a break with the masculine order of discourse, or in Christianity's vision of a Spirit-inspired speech which will entirely bypass human chauvinist conventions. The response to this limitation should not be silence: there are stories to tell, texts to be written, or rewritten. 'Women must continue to struggle to tell the stories otherwise. The possibilities are endless.'[46]

Questions and topics for further study

1. Is there a particular biblical text which you can 'rewrite' into a narrative which can sustain women in a situation of discrimination or oppression?
2. Think of the endings of novels you have read. Do you agree that a desire for a satisfying ending, 'closure' in a narrative, is essentially a masculinist phenomenon?
3. Can you distinguish between critics you have read who are 'committed', and those who are 'objective'? Does the gender of the writer make a difference, and is the former kind of criticism inherently better than the latter, as Margaret Atwood seems to be suggesting?
4. Try reading another text as a feminine rewriting of a masculine

genre: *The Color Purple* as a version of Alex Haley's *Roots*, for example, or feminist science fiction as a redefinition of male-authored, technology-centred science fiction.

5. Is the only alternative to the post-Christian feminist the Christian post-feminist?

14

Why wait for an angel? Thomas Pynchon's *The Crying of Lot 49*

John Schad

I define *postmodern* as incredulity toward metanarratives.[1]

In the previous chapter, Elizabeth Clarke selected a text to work out the theoretical material of her colleague, Elisabeth Jay. In the same sort of way, I want to take a literary text to work out some of the implications of Kevin Mills' chapter, 'Words and presences'.

1. Radical uncertainty

Postmodernism is characterized, above all, by incredulity, a perpetual questioning of not just the grand narratives, or meanings by which we make sense of our lives, but also of any certainty, or truth. For the Christian, for one who follows one who declared, 'I am . . . the truth' (Jn. 14:6),[2] such radical scepticism must itself be subject to scepticism. The problem, though, for the Christian reader of contemporary literature is that so often our reading seems to echo the postmodern call to uncertainty.

This is, perhaps, particularly true of *Lot 49*, since not only is the novel itself an unresolvable problem, but its central figure, Oedipa Maas, finds her very world to be a riddle without solution. If you have not yet read *Lot 49*, let me put you in the picture, or rather the question.[3] The novel, which is set in 1960s California, opens with Oedipa learning that she has been named as an executor of the late Pierce Inverarity. In exploring this estate she seems to discover more and more clues suggesting the existence of an anarchic organization called the Tristero, which seems to have its own secret system of communication and, indeed, a secret symbol described as 'a muted post horn' and reproduced thus: ⊸◁

'Communication is the key,'[4] declares the incomprehensible Nefestis. He refers, of course, to his improbable machine and its supposed reception of the messages of Maxwell's demon, nevertheless Nefestis' dictum is pertinent to the whole novel. For we are given a world crammed with all sorts of communications, or messages – not only letters, newspapers, books, acronyms and signs on walls, but also phone calls, television, radio and neon signs. However, just as Oedipa, the protagonist, 'wait[s in vain] . . . for the Demon to communicate',[5] so we often wait in vain for these communications – if only because there are so many – ever to be fully understood or even received. The television, for instance, may be on but not necessarily watched; the phone may ring at three in the morning but there is no real message; and, in the supermarket, 'muzak' plays – music, of course, to be heard but not listened to.[6] In a sense, then, the whole of San Narciso (the novel's fictional Los Angeles suburb) shares the condition of the homeless who spend the night 'swung among a web of telephone wires' and 'thousands of unheard messages'.[7] Indeed, when Oedipa looks down at the geometric street layout of San Narciso she thinks of 'the time she'd opened a transistor radio . . . and seen her first printed circuit'.[8] The American city, it seems, is not so much a place as a vast network for the circulation of disembodied messages – hence 'Telegraph Avenue'.

This is, of course, what cultural theorists have come to call the postmodern universe, a world dominated by the constant flow of unauthored and unaddressed messages, or signs. Such a world may well be frighteningly empty – when Oedipa rings from a pay booth but gets no reply: 'The phone buzzed on and on, into hollowness.'[9] However, just as the novel also gives us the '*miracle of communication*'[10] so postmodernist theory, for all its talk of absence, often bears witness to the stubborn persistence of some kind of sacred presence. As Philippa Berry remarks, 'The trace of the holy survives within postmodernism in persistent echoes of that cultural legacy to which it declared itself the murderous heir.'[11] Echoing Berry, several critics and theorists[12] have recently argued that the holy has survived the disruption of all the guarantees and assurances of traditional western culture – in particular the guarantee that words yield meanings, that messages have content, that letters have destinations. In short, Roland Barthes may well have got it wrong when, in 1968, he famously declared that 'to refuse to fix meaning is, in the end, to refuse

God'.[13] Though the texts and signs among which we live may not make sense, that does not necessarily mean that there is no God; the Christian God is not wedded to sense, or meaning – or at least meaning as something definite, or univocal (one-voiced).

2. An alternative 'mode of meaning'?

This is something, indeed, of which *Lot 49* reminds us. For it is charged with the possibility that there might just be 'another mode of meaning';[14] moreover, the novel is positively fascinated with that moment in which the gospel bursts out in not one considered voice but many and spontaneous tongues – namely, Pentecost. Not only does *The Courier's Tragedy* (the Jacobean play that is being performed and researched during the course of the novel) include a grotesque and 'frightful Pentecost' of literal 'tongue[s] aflame',[15] but, as Edward Mendelson has pointed out, Pentecost comes *forty-nine* days after Easter.[16] Admittedly, the Christian reader might, at first, read these intimations as just one more instance of postmodernism rewriting Pentecost in its own, multivocal image. We might, though, suggest that *Lot 49* simply serves to defamiliarize the biblical event, to rediscover the shock of a God who speaks through many to many and in many voices.

Clearly, our sense of God is going to be considerably defamiliarized by a novel which gives us not only a 'zany paraclete' but an 'epileptic Word' and a Jesus (the character Jesús Arrabal) who is an anarchist.[17] To be more specific, these teasing formulations disrupt our received and largely Enlightenment sense of a God whose actions and speech are consistent with reason and order. The chief biblical source for such a rational account of God is, of course, the prologue to John's gospel where Christ is identified as the *Logos*, meaning – for the later Greeks[18] – reason, or concept; *Lot 49*, however, with its 'epileptic Word' gestures toward a quite *un*reasonable, or *dis*ordered *logos*. And indeed, the communications of the holy do seem quite as bizarre as all the other communications. Oedipa's first 'revelation', for instance, is an 'odd, religious instant'[19] experienced in a Chevvy along a San Narciso freeway, and her last, we anticipate, is in an auction room; in between she is prey to 'all manner of revelations'.[20] That the Word is not, in *Lot 49*, its usual, privileged self is clear enough; but lest we miss the point, the novel's single most important sign, its Word as it were, first appears to Oedipa on the wall of a public convenience. For the gospel of John we may read the 'ladies' john'.[21]

Strange, though, as it may seem, such an exchange does not necessarily represent a loss or reduction, since, as Oedipa tells herself, there is a 'high magic to low puns'.[22] In other words, the very fact that the American slang for 'toilet' should happen to coincide with the name of the fourth gospel does not so much bring down Scripture as – to lapse into a fittingly bizarre phrase – raise up urinals. To pick up on earlier discussions, from chapters 11 and 12, we might say that the 'sacred' has nothing to lose and much to gain from sharing the same symbolic world as the 'secular'. This is, of course, a crucial point in a novel in which these two realms, or discourses, constantly interrupt each other. The disc jockey, for instance, 'cue[s] . . . the next record with movements stylized as the handling of . . . [the] chalice might be for a holy man'; the movie *Cashiered* features 'father, son, and [a] St Bernard'; and in the laundromat 'the odour of chlorine bleach [rises] . . . heavenward, like an incense'.[23] Moreover, in this context the very verb 'to communicate' becomes charged with a second, eucharistic sense (according to the Anglican Prayer Book, in taking the bread and wine we 'communicate'). As then the Word grows epileptic, as the sacred is exposed to all the fitful disorders of the novel's sheer intertextuality (its radical mixing of narratives and voices), so that sacred shares in the 'high magic of low puns'. According to David Seed, Oedipa 'seek[s] . . . the Word' though 'finds only words',[24] but if *Lot 49* teaches us anything it is that this is a distinction which overlooks the potential within 'mere' words for the high magic of the sacred.

Can, then, the Christian reader relax in the assurance that since she has a God whose name is Word, or speech,[25] that same God only increases with the novel's multiplication of words and signs? In short, if communication is indeed a miracle or sacred magic, are all words made in the image of *the* Word, or at least the epileptic Word? I think not; *Lot 49* knows too well that, as the quasi-Marxist Michel Foucault has argued, words and meanings are never purely or simply themselves but are always distorted by power.[26] For even as Oedipa, in her pursuit of the Tristero, increasingly finds San Narciso's world of signs charged with alarming connections and coincidences, so she comes to suspect the dead hand (or dead letter) of Pierce Inverarity; is she simply being set up by the novel's most powerful character? She is beset, if you like, by the Foucauldian conviction that this world of signs – however Californian, however 'free,' however postmodern – finally reveals not truth, but power or will. As Oedipa remarks of the radio circuit, there is 'a hieroglyphic sense . . . of an intent to communicate';[27] there is, in more senses than one, a *will* to communicate – namely Pierce's. In fine, Oedipa the interpreter comes to fear that the 'high magic' of coincidence and connection might turn out to be no more than low cunning, something 'willed' into existence.

This anxiety, of course, is rather too close for comfort for anyone who reads the novel with an eye to its theological patterns. We scarcely need reminding that what makes these patterns possible might just be an intent, or will – this time, our own. Like Oedipa we are compelled to ask if, caught in an hermeneutic circle, our interpretations are merely projections – as Oedipa herself puts it, do we merely *'project a world'*?[28] If so, then like the Cardinal in *The Courier's Tragedy* – who has his big toe cut off and is 'made to hold it up like a Host [consecrated bread] and say "This is my body"'[29] – do we 'communicate' not with God but only with ourselves? Indeed, given the place-name San Narciso (Saint Narcissus) the novel inevitably prompts the suggestion that the fate of the Christian (whose biblical name is, of course, 'saint') is necessarily narcissistic. This suggestion is underlined by the description of the appropriately named *Echo* Courts; for here the narrator casually remarks upon 'the stillness of the pool',[30] and in doing so prompts, albeit for a moment, associations not only with the mythological pool in which Narcissus (Echo's beloved) becomes enamoured of his own reflection, but also the biblical pool of Bethesda where the waters are still until the angel descends.[31] We have to wait, of course, until the very end of the novel for even the possibility of 'a descending angel';[32] in the meantime, then, it is as if we (the readers of theological patterns) are – like Narcissus – seated beside a still pool gazing at our own reflection, the projection of our own world.

However, though pool-gazing may be the tragic end of the story of Narcissus, it is not the end of the story of Bethesda. For according to the gospel narrative, though the stillness of the pool means no angel, it does not prevent the arrival of Christ. Thus, while the novel leaves us still waiting, in effect, for the angel to descend, is it just possible that, by the high magic of analogy, we have already been visited by Christ? Is it possible that we are like Oedipa who, come the end of the novel, is still waiting for the answers to her questions and *yet* (almost without knowing it) has met Jesus, Jesús Arrabal the anarchist? Are we who await so eagerly, and yet vainly, for an end to the novel which will complete our theological speculations, overlooking the fact that we have already met the very subject of those speculations? To be blunt: why wait for an angel when the novel has already given us a Jesus? The theological point of the Bethesda sub-text, perhaps, then, is this: that we must not be so preoccupied with the 'promise of hierophany'[33] that we miss the Christ who has already come to us; the Christ, indeed, who – to borrow a favourite formulation of Jacques Derrida's – we have 'always already' encountered. Exactly what it might mean to say that Christ is never purely or simply present (in both senses of the word) will become clearer as we continue. What *is* obvious now is that we are reminded of the danger of not recognizing Christ. We are reminded of the danger of being like Oedipa, who at first misunderstands and then completely passes over Mr Thoth's claim that he 'feel[s] him close to me'. 'Your grandfather?' she asks. 'No, my God.'[34]

3. *The hint of community*

The irony of still seeking what one may in fact have already found does, of course, haunt Oedipa's quest for the Tristero. For in passing through the San Narciso underworld and all sorts of marginalized and dispossessed groups – the gay night-club, the 'busful of Negroes',[35] the Inamoratti, and so on – does she perhaps encounter the very community of which the Tristero is an elaborate metaphor? ('It was a Negro neighbourhood. Was The Horn so dedicated?')[36] Is it possible, then, that the Tristero exists not so much *beyond* the urban web of hints, clues and muted post horns but *among* them? If so, we are confronted with the more general and philosophical possibility that all human discourse, however hollow or contentless, entails within itself the faint outline of mutuality, or community.[37] To put it another way, just as Oedipa, when poring over the single mention of 'Tristero' in one edition of *The Courier's Tragedy*, pursues 'the . . . face of the word',[38] so the whole question of the Tristero promises to lay bare the faces *among* the words. The Tristero, that is to say, names the decidedly *un*postmodern possibility that community is the inner *telos* of communication, that signs – however opaque – do not come between people but bring them together. And perhaps that is the real 'miracle of communication'.

We come closest, no doubt, to just such a miracle when, in a dream-like passage, Oedipa encounters 'a circle of children in their nightclothes' playing a jump-rope game involving not only a post horn chalked on the sidewalk but the chant 'Tristoe, Tristoe, one, two, three'; thus, quite unknowingly, they at once perpetuate the circulation of the Tristero sign and form a kind of society: they 'told her they were dreaming the gathering ... and needed nothing but their own unpenetrated sense of community'.[39] For all the haunting beauty of this gathering, it is formed, we presume, without parental consent and so is charged with a subversive, almost Blakean, energy. And much the same can be said of all the communities intimated by the Tristero; it comes to possess, that is, something of the danger and threat of the myriad counter-cultural movements within 1960s America. To invoke 'the high magic of low puns,' while communications in *Lot 49* entail the vague promise of *revelation*, the community inscribed within those communications entails the promise or threat of *revolution*. This revolution is not necessarily that 'anarchosyndicalist'[40] insurrection which Jesús Arrabal represents, but the revolution which goes by the philosophical name of Otherness, or alterity – that is, all that is not familiar or, as it were, not-the-same. The Tristero is given this name by Emory Bortz when explaining how, for the Scurvamhites, only one part of creation 'ran off the will of God' while the rest ran off 'some opposite Principle': they 'felt,' concludes Bortz, that 'Trystero ... symbolize[d] the Other quite well'.[41] Oedipa develops this theme when, just a few pages later, she remarks of the Tristero that 'a network by which X number of Americans are truly communicating' quite independently of 'the official government delivery system' would, if it does exist, constitute 'a real alternative to the exitlessness, to the absence of surprise to life, that harrows the head of everybody American'.[42]

Exitlessness is not, though, a peculiarly American fate but rather one shared by those of us who read *Lot 49*, particularly if we are Christians. The novel, that is, threatens not only to characterize us as a kind of (San) Narcissus looking 'out' on nothing save our own theological speculations but also, come the very end, to start all over again: 'Oedipa settled back', we read, 'to await the crying of lot 49.'[43] Caught in a novel which promises no way out, we share, it seems, in the exitlessness of America – an America which has so completely dreamt the world in its own image[44] that there is nothing that is not America, and therefore no way out of America. All this, of course, is brought more sharply into focus by the Tristero since, as Oedipa concludes, 'there either was some Tristero beyond the appearance of the legacy America, or there was just America'.[45] In short, this postal system which operates quite apart from the official state system symbolizes not just a very general Other but also, and more specifically, America's Other. After all, in contrast to Oedipa's America where 'the oldest building' dates from only just 'before World War II',[46] and life is dominated by property and inheritance, the Tristero has an history which goes back to sixteenth-century Europe and is a community that styles itself as 'El Desheredado, the Disinherited'.[47] In short, 'Tristero's empire' comes to represent both a time that is other than now and an economy that is other than our own, other than property-based; it is structured not by a law of the same or continuity, but of difference and discontinuity. In this sense the Tristero is like the mirror in which Oedipa 'tried to find her image' but 'couldn't'.[48]

While Oedipa's interpretive pursuit of the Tristero mystery is always haunted by the possibility of narcissism, then, her encounters with the miscellaneous outcasts who people the urban maze of post horns are quite different. The facially deformed welder, the scarred negro woman, and the soap-eating night watchman[49] – to name but three – are very obviously *not* made in either her visual or her socio-economic likeness. They represent, that is, an 'alternative to the exitlessness' of Oedipa's hermeneutic circle. This is never more obvious than when she meets the old sailor with the post-horn tattoo; in pausing, touching and even holding the old man she encounters for once not just another clue, or sign, but the person of the sign – or, if you like, 'the face of the word'. In doing so, indeed, she not only looks into a face that is, for once, not her own but also thereby opens up a profoundly ethical space within the conspicuously *post*-ethical continuum of California; for when she whispers, 'I can't help . . . I can't help,'[50] even while holding and rocking the old man, we cannot avoid reading, 'I can't help *but help.*'

4. A memory of Christ

The rude otherness of the Tristero here locates, it seems, something whose existence the novel might otherwise teach us to doubt – instinctive generosity. And it is a generosity that we are moved to value not just as ethical but also as Christian. Oedipa's outstretched arms acquire, that is, a certain Christlikeness in the sense that, although the stamp on the sailor's letter portrays, as usual, 'a jet flying by the Capitol dome . . . at the top of the dome stood a tiny figure in deep black, with its arms outstretched. Oedipa wasn't sure what exactly was supposed to be on the top of the Capitol, but she knew it wasn't anything like that.'[51] To quote an earlier question of Oedipa's, 'A cross? Or the initial T?'[52] Has Oedipa once again met a Jesus? 'Inasmuch as you have [served] one of the least of these my brethren,' declares Christ, 'ye have done it unto me' (Mt. 25:40). This particular Tristero outcast seems to constitute not just 'the face of the word' but also the face, as it were, of the Word. Here the Tristero names the possibility not only that communication entails community but also that the poor give us Christ.

By the end of the novel, though, the Tristero outcast does not simply give or embody Christ but, to be more precise, represents a *memory* of him – a memory of Christ. For when Passerine 'spread[s] his arms' we do not simply speculate, with Oedipa, whether this gesture is that of 'the priesthood' or 'a descending angel';[53] our response is more complex, since we are also reminded of the sailor's stamp and that 'tiny figure . . . with arms outstretched'. Once again, theological speculation – this time, of priesthoods and angels – is to some extent foreclosed by the possibility that we, like Oedipa, have already come across Jesus, that he is encountered not so much through interpreting as remembering.

To remember, of course, is not an easy thing to do among the almost exclusively post-war architecture of San Narciso; nevertheless, the Tristero mystery simply compels Oedipa to remember, to develop an historical consciousness. Not only does she trace and research its 400-year history, but in the middle of her night 'spent . . . finding' everywhere 'the . . . Tristero post horn',[54] we read the arcane declaration that '*She was meant to remember*' – 'I am meant to remember,' she echoes.[55] Who or what she is to remember is not clear, but two pages further on into 'the night's profusion of post horns',[56] we read that 'Oedipa . . . had remembered Jesus'[57] – not, we should note, 'Jesús'. Remembering Jesus is, of course, written into the novel in the form of its preoccupation with that 'perpetual memorial', the eucharist – like the name 'Oedipa *Maas*' (originally 'Mass'),[58] the novel's fascination with 'the intent to communicate' possesses, as we know, a double significance. After all, as well as the disc jockey handling records like a 'holy man' 'handling' a 'censer',[59] and Wharfinger's cardinal holding up his amputated toe 'like a Host',[60] there is that haunting remark at the end of chapter four: 'As if the dead really do persist, even in a bottle of wine'.[61]

If, though, the novel as a whole 'remember[s] Jesus' in an eucharistic sense, the Tristero also remembers him in the punning sense of re-membering, or re-fleshing; for, strange as it may seem, the Tristero may be interpreted, *among other things*, as the *body* of Christ – that is to say, the church as described by St Paul (1 Cor. 1:12–27). It is no accident that what we anticipate to be the

Tristero's final revelation of itself is comically reduced to the body: ' "Your fly is open," whispered Oedipa. She was not sure what she'd do when the bidder revealed himself.'[62] My point is simply that the reader's own investigation of the Tristero puzzle is also interrupted by a body, the metaphorical body of Christ. We tend to share, that is, Oedipa's difficulty in distinguishing the Tristero's 'initial T' from 'a cross' if only because, as Mendelson has pointed out, the word 'Calavera' in the founding Tristero's name – Hernando Joaquín de Tristero y Calavera – is the Spanish form of 'Calvary'.[63] Moreover, at times the church and the Tristero seem inextricably intertwined – witness the curious involvements of both the Vatican and the Scurvamhites in the text of *The Couriers's Tragedy*. At other times, it is more that church and Tristero seem equally ubiquitous: as we know, at the laundromat with a post horn tacked to the bulletin board 'the . . . chlorine . . . rose . . . like an incense';[64] again, in Bortz's library Oedipa reads about the Tristero brigands at a 'tabernacle' ('canopied niche' or 'receptacle for . . . eucharistic elements', *Oxford English Dictionary*); and yet again, Jesús' anarchist party operates not only under the sign of the post horn stamped on to their newspaper but also, 'like the church we hate' (to quote Jesús), in the name of rebirth – the paper is called *'Regeneración'*.[65] In short, just as Oedipa fears that the Tristero has been inscribed, or rather 'encrypted'[66] into Inverarity's will, so, we might say, church – by association with 'crypt' – is written into the Tristero.

5. A kind of church?

The notion that an alternative system of communication might constitute a kind of church is with us from very early in the novel – the disc jockey *cum* celebrant is, we read, 'really tuned in to the voice, voices, the music, its message, surrounded by it . . . as were all *the faithful* it went out to'.[67] We have, then, some idea of what Mendelson means when he remarks that 'the Tristero [also] carries with it a sense of sacred connection and relation'.[68] Needless to say, though, the church described by the Tristero is not one with which we are particularly familiar; it is, rather, one we are 'meant to remember,' one that requires an historical consciousness. For it is the early, pre-Constantine church that most obviously constituted an 'underground' system of communication, employing – like the Tristero – both acronym and cryptic ideogram. For W.A.S.T.E., that is, we might read, ICHTHUS, and for the sign of the post horn we might substitute the sign of the fish.

Admittedly, to do so is to indulge in Christian interpretation of the kind that the novel gently characterizes as a form of narcissism, as gazing in the pool at Bethesda. However, what distinguishes the church as the focus of a Christian interpretation of *Lot 49* is that it can survive the discrediting of that interpretation. For just as the Tristero is not so much a puzzle that Oedipa fails to resolve, as a community that she has already encountered, so the church, for the Christian reader, is quite obviously not so much a sub-text to be deciphered as the very community, or body, out of which she reads. In other words, *Lot 49* finally returns the Christian reader to that body.

Indeed, and more excitingly, perhaps the same may be said of any reader who, at Passerine's (anti-)climactic gesture, is reminded of the 'tiny figure' on the airmail stamp; for if readers are thereby caused to 're-member Jesus', then – by 'the high magic of low puns' – do they in some sense bring into being the very body of Christ? For the reader who would not, before reading the novel, have called herself a Christian, this possibility might well come as a surprise, perhaps even a revelation. For the avowedly Christian reader it is surely a call to draw back from our pool-gazing to remember the strange and estranged body of Christ – to embrace, as it were, the alcoholic sailor.

Postscript

In response to the editors' invitation to 'demonstrate how I arrived at a Christian reading', let me offer the following remarks.

First, I am not sure how helpful it is to speak of a 'Christian reading'; can the way that I read ever be 'Christian' in the same way that I am? In one sense, then, the answer to how I arrived at a Christian reading (if I ever did) is by being a Christian – being a Christian not only when reading but also when not reading. Indeed, to read as a Christian is often to *be called* not to read; as *Lot 49* reminds us, though Christ is the Word (and thus a text, or complex of meanings, with which I must engage), the Word has a face, he is someone I must encounter.

To start again, then: how did I, as a Christian, read *Lot 49*? To be honest, my first and intuitive impulse was always to save the text, to read it as a crypto-Christian novel. At times, I suspect, this led to wilful misreading – looking for Christian patterns at the expense of apparently counter-Christian moments. In so far as this was the case, I was neither a discerning nor a Christian reader. Nevertheless, at the same time as seeking to save the text I also sought to lose it; that is, to allow the novel to rewrite the text that is Christianity without my beliefs foreclosing that process. If one name for the Christian God is Word or speech, then in one sense there is, in language, no outside of God. I could, therefore, suspend belief in the sure hope that, whatever Thomas Pynchon's intentions, I would somehow encounter the high magic of the living and epileptic Word amid all the chances, changes and low puns of *Lot 49*. In so far as this was what happened, then my reading may be characterized as a kind of Christian deconstruction.

Questions for further thought

1. Consider the novel's interest in the Word, or communications, of God, alongside Derrida's dictum that 'the letter *can* always *not* arrive'.[69]
2. In the light of my suggestion that 'for the gospel of John we may read the "ladies' john" ', consider the possibility that the novel is concerned with a specifically female *Logos*, or Scripture.
3. Since Oedipa, we read, 'left The Greek Way',[70] is it possible that she enters what Derrida has called 'the [Jewish] other of the Greek'?[71] In what senses is this a Jewish novel?

Part 3

For further reading:
a survey

15

For further reading: a survey

David Barratt

Introduction

Many chapters have contained their own bibliography or suggestions for further reading. Instead of making a comprehensive list of such titles, the editors felt it would be much more helpful to produce a final survey, not as a complete guide to what a Christian student might read, but to indicate, first, the great range of helpful critical and theoretical material now available; and, secondly, to inculcate the quality of awareness that we are looking for as discerning readers. Lists of recommended books, by themselves, cannot possibly do this. Of course, it needs to be understood that the choices of works cited are limited to the experience of the reviewer(s); and also, unfortunately, by their availability – usually a more frustrating factor to the reader, discerning or not.

The approach I have adopted in this final chapter is to divide the field into two, following the structure of this book. First, then, I shall look at theoretical or general approaches to Christian poetics, categorizing according to the theological standpoints of the writers. I shall then look at specific critical studies, of texts or periods, this time categorizing in terms of whether it is the text or the writer that is Christian.

1. Theoretical positions

I want to look at four main positions identifiable among Christian literary scholars: the Reformed; other evangelical positions; Catholic and other traditional positions; and lastly, non-aligned, liberal or unorthodox stances.

The Reformed position is much more easily identifiable in North America than in the UK, partly because of the network of Reformed colleges which has successfully institutionalized and supported scholarship stemming from orthodox Calvinist theology, and partly because the Reformed churches themselves are much more extensive there, producing many more students of literature. One of our co-editors, Leland Ryken, is a distinguished example of such American Reformed literary scholarship, as are other contributors, such as John D. Cox and Donald T. Williams.

An older sister of this book is the volume Leland Ryken co-edited with Clarence Walhout, entitled *Contemporary Literary Theory: a Christian Appraisal* (Grand Rapids: Eerdmans, 1991). Various Reformed scholars, mainly teaching at colleges within the Reformed network, have each addressed a specific of modern literary theory. Some of the chapters overlap with those in this book, for example, John D. Cox's 'New Historicism', or the one on feminist literary criticism. But it differs in method in not having specific textual studies or application. Inevitably it lacks some of the diversity of this volume, but gains in overall focus.

Professor Ryken has edited or co-edited other books, for example, *The Christian Imagination: Essays on Literature and the Arts* (Grand Rapids: Baker, 1981). This is a most useful collection of statements by major Christian writers and critics. It is often difficult to track down some of this material – to have so much so easily to hand is a gift. One of his first books has been more widely available in the UK since it was published by IVP in the USA and the UK: *Triumphs of the Imagination: Literature in Christian Perspective* (Downers Grove and Leicester: IVP, 1979). It was certainly the first book of his that I read. On rereading it, I feel the book has weathered well, since it simply answers the sort of basic questions any Christian student of literature asks himself or herself, rather than embroiling itself in current trends. A more recent book by Professor Ryken is *Realms of Gold: The Classics in Christian Perspective* (Wheaton: Harold Shaw, 1991), which looks at nine texts that occur frequently in student syllabi, such as *Great Expectations, Macbeth, The Stranger*. The book forms part of the Wheaton Literary Series. In it, Ryken asks, as T. S. Eliot before him, 'What is a classic?' concentrating more on good and bad readings. His own enthusiasm for each of the texts discussed, his 'friendship' with them, combines easily with his specific theoretical concerns. Another title of his in this series is *The Liberated Imagination: Thinking Christianly about the Arts* (Wheaton: Harold Shaw, 1989), which sets literature in the wider context of the arts.

Both books stress the concepts of imaginative truth and the centrality of the aesthetic.

An older book on the subject within this tradition is Calvin Seerveld's *A Christian Critique of Art and Literature* (St Catherine's, Ontario: Association of Reformed Scientific Studies, 1963). In its four lectures it sets out a Reformed approach much more theologically than Ryken, with particular reference to the Dutch thinkers Dooyeweerd and Kuyper. Concepts of common grace and Christian community are clearly discussed, and the need for moral dimensions to all literary criticism. Seerveld is perhaps more of an art critic, as of course was H. R. Rookmaaker, whose *Modern Art and the Death of a Culture* (London and Downers Grove: IVP, 1970, reissued Leicester: IVP, 1994) is still a benchmark in Reformed art criticism and apologetics.

Other titles that can be cited here include Francis A. Schaeffer's *Art and the Bible* (Downers Grove: IVP; London: Hodder and Stoughton, 1973). Although Schaeffer mainly wrote apologetics, this booklet remains an excellent pioneer on thinking Christianly about the arts. Philosopher Nicholas Wolterstoff writes as an aesthetician in *Art in Action: Towards a Christian Aesthetic* (Grand Rapids: Eerdmans, 1980), and has been viewed as a progressive voice to those impatient with older attitudes toward 'high art'.

Gene Edward Veith, Jr, has provided a wide-angle view of both literature and art from a biblical perspective in his companion volumes *Reading Between the Lines: A Christian Guide to Literature* and *State of the Arts from Bezalel to Mapplethorpe* (Wheaton: Crossway, 1990, 1991). For a British offering, especially for the theologically minded, comes Jeremy Begbie's *Voicing Creation's Praise: Towards a Theology of the Arts* (Edinburgh: T. and T. Clark, 1991), an acute and readable attempt to put truth, beauty and creativity in art into a Christian framework. It is mainly focused on the visual arts but can easily be adapted to literature. As a non-Reformed comparison and at a more informal level comes Richard Harries' *Art and the Beauty of God* (London: Mowbray, 1993), which argues for a central place for beauty in Christian truth, and for Christian truth in artistic beauty, in an Anglican tradition going back to Herbert and earlier.

In the absence of strong Reformed scholarship in the UK in the arts, British evangelical thought has been slow to produce work that fully engages secular academic thought. In the last ten years there have been signs of catching up. Here, one of the most important contributors to an evangelical poetics has been Michael Edwards, already cited by several contributors to this book. He is not only a theoretician and a teacher, equally at home in French and English literature (he has held chairs in both), but also a poet. I would like to commend his *Towards a Christian Poetics* (Grand Rapids: Eerdmans; Basingstoke: Macmillan, 1984), and suggest you read this, if nothing else.

Edwards derives the main inspiration for his thinking from T. S. Eliot – not so much Eliot the critic, but Eliot the poet, to whom he devotes a whole chapter. It is the redemptive 'possibility' of language in Eliot, in the *Four Quartets* especially, that Edwards lays hold of. His thinking has also been influenced by the great Canadian critic Northrop Frye, especially in his approach to genre and figures of speech. His chapters on tragedy, comedy and story could well be compared to those in Frye's *Anatomy of Criticism*. Behind both of these there echo also the philosophies of Pascal and Wittgenstein. The foundation of his poetics is therefore philosophical and literary rather than systematically theological.

Out of Pascal's paradox of the 'grandeur' and '*misère*' of mankind, Edwards creates a dialectic, resolvable in terms of triades. The third term in each triade (as man/sinner/Christian or Creator/Judge/Redeemer) represents the possibility of the Christian gospel, which then becomes the possibility of literature. Unlike much traditional and liberal Christian poetics, Edwards grounds his in the fall, rather than in creation and/or the incarnation. Story comes out of our exile from Eden. He takes Eliot's brief references to Pentecost in the *Four Quartets* to develop the possibility of language after the *misère* of the serpent and Babel.

Edwards' poetics are forward-looking; their hope in the possibility of transformation. The concept of possibility is further explored in his later book *Poetry and Possibility* (Basingstoke: Macmillan, 1988), which again deals with fallenness and origins, adding a further concern over inspiration. Edwards poses the question, 'In what way can Poetry counter the Fall?' – a question that goes back to St Augustine and Sidney. This is poetry's possibility, and in this Edwards begins fittingly with a chapter on *Paradise Lost*, and the possibility of regaining paradise through the poem.

The third volume of this trilogy, *Of Making Many Books: Essays on the Endlessness of Writing* (Basingstoke: Macmillan, 1990), according to the blurb,

> . . . elaborates a counter-culture to the current reductive
> and deluded materialism . . . He has explored afresh the

movement of history, the nature of self, the place of the human in a non-human world open at all points to the divine. The view he presents is explicitly Christian, but it also contains a critique of the customary metaphysics of Christianity.

In fact, this third volume is more a collection of essays, some of which build on chapters in the earlier books; for example, a further chapter on Eliot (also to be found in *Ends of Time*, cited later).

The second major contributor to the British side of an evangelical response to postmodern theory is Valentine Cunningham, who contributed our second chapter. His *In the Reading Gaol: Postmodernity, Texts and History* (Cambridge, MA. and Oxford: Blackwell, 1994), cited by several contributors, is a large and lively attempt to bring historicist and post-structuralist modes of reading to order, by exploring the word/world nexus/disjuncture in particular. His approach is quite dissimilar to Michael Edwards'. Edwards puts forward his thesis explicitly as a Christian theory, inviting readers to suspend disbelief to examine it on its merits; Cunningham's Christian foundations are implicit. He engages directly with secular theory, especially Derrida, and only in the final chapter does his thesis unfold theologically: that the whole postmodernist enterprise is parasitic on the Holy Scriptures, which thus becomes an absolute/telos, however much this is supressed. Whilst Edwards centres on the fall and Pentecost, Cunningham centres on Babel and the incarnation, his literary exempla largely from the nineteenth-century novel. He prefers George to T. S. Eliot. His style is of the polymath, punning and allusive, immensely stimulating. His readings of novels are novel indeed.

On the whole, evangelical publishers, especially in the UK, have not been noted for producing much imaginative literature, let alone literary or critical theory. One exception has been Ruth Etchell's *A Model of Making* (London: Marshall, Morgan and Scott, 1984). Miss Etchells has taught both literature and theology in her academic career. The book is a discussion of what might be the characteristics and insights of a specifically Christian criticism. Unlike Edwards, but more typically of Christian theorists, she takes the basic model of God as creator for both writers and critics. The book is written much more straightforwardly than either Edwards' or Cunningham's, and is thus a more obviously introductory volume to the subject.

Outside the Reformed and Evangelical traditions, there lies a range of positions that could be included under the term 'mere Christianity' – the term C. S. Lewis used to describe Christian positions that espouse traditional Christian doctrine, refusing liberal deviations, while yet not willing to be more specifically labelled. Such a position is to be seen in Harry Blamires' *The Christian Mind* (London: SPCK, 1963), in which he shows how secularly many of us still think, even though we profess Christianity and even teach or study within a Christian institution. (Blamires taught English in a church-related college.) He suggests specific marks of Christian thinking. Even though written thirty years ago, there is still much that is challenging today. His books on literary history and criticism are all clearly written and informed with a Christian sympathy: for example, his *A Short History of English Literature* (London: Routledge, 2nd edn. 1989) and *A History of Literary Criticism* (Basingstoke: Macmillan, 1991).

Most readers will connect the term 'mere Christianity' not only with C. S. Lewis but also 'the Inklings', his group of associates at Oxford. From there, we need to include also such critics as T. S. Eliot and Dorothy L. Sayers, and then move further out still to include a number of Roman Catholic critics who continue to embrace orthodox positions. There are a number of things that need to be taken into account here: very often, the more specifically Christian ideas of the former group are expressed in short essays, or almost peripherally in some larger argument; or they are not focused narrowly on poetics, but on culture or the arts in some wider sense.

This is a point Donald T. Williams makes in chapter 3, where he reviews the best Lewis material to look at. Likewise, he cites Tolkien and Sayers, and I can do no better than refer readers back to chapter 3.6 and the very full endnotes (p. 289). For a fuller bibliography, see Colin Duriez, *The C. S. Lewis Handbook* (Eastbourne: Monarch, 1990) – it goes up to 1988. It is interesting that both Lewis and Sayers have been more influential in the USA than in Britain. Leland Ryken writes of Sayers' *The Mind of the Maker*: 'I know of no book that has been more widely cited among American evangelicals who have written on artistic theory.'

T. S. Eliot's literary theory and influence were in place before his conversion to Christianity. If anything, his most profound Christian thinking is done in his later poetry, as both Edwards and Blamires note. His more general Christian thinking is in terms of culture rather than literature, but his *The Use of Poetry and the*

Use of Criticism (London: Faber, 1933) is more specific, as are his essays 'The Function of Criticism' and 'Literature and Religion' (in *Selected Essays*, New York: Harcourt, new edn. 1960). I have examined Eliot's important views on tradition in an essay 'When Does the Funeral Take Place? A Christian Reading of Literature and Tradition', where I compare his views to those of Lewis and an Anglo-Catholic critic, A. E. Dyson. The essay is to be found in the modest prototype to this present volume, D. Barratt and R. Pooley (eds.), *Reading Literature: Some Christian Approaches* (Leicester: UCCF Associates, 1984), obtainable through IVP in Leicester or Downers Grove. We think it is still worth reading.

There are, of course, many books about this group of Christian writers, some of which do justice to their literary criticism and thinking, such as David Newton de Molina (ed.), *The Literary Criticism of T. S. Eliot* (London: Athlone, 1977), or, about the Inklings, Charles A. Huttar (ed.), *Imagination and the Spirit* (Grand Rapids: Eerdmans, 1979). The latter is a set of essays presented to Clyde Kilby, and so reflect the interests of that distinguished American Christian scholar – hence the essays on the Inklings.

Moving on to Catholic poetics, an early offering still accessible is William Lynch: *Christ and Apollo: the Dimensions of the Literary Imagination* (Notre Dame and London: University of Notre Dame Press, 1960). As is typical of certain Catholic poetics, it is based on scholastic or Aristotelian theory. For example, Lynch uses the four medieval levels of imagery and Duns Scotus' concept of *haeccitas* (developed by G. M. Hopkins as 'inscape'). Lynch sees the Hebrew imagination opposed to the gnostic one; the Catholic position stems from the former, as 'men of the finite', against the latter's 'men of the infinite'. The 'geometry of descent and ascent' is explored in another chapter, with the final two chapters focusing on the all-penetrating power of the theological and the Christian imagination. A non-Catholic book that might be compared to this is John Coulson, *Religion and Imagination* (Oxford: Oxford University Press, 1981).

Of Catholic writers, one that may not be known to so many British students is Flannery O'Connor. Her *Mystery and Manners* is cited in the bibliographies to chapters 1 and 3, and is strongly to be recommended. Her essays could well be set alongside those of Eliot and Lewis.

If much Catholic writing derives from Aristotelian theory, we ought to balance this with the equally enduring Platonic tradition. Despite Plato's own scepticism on the place of poets in his ideal republic, his pervasive idealism has been attractive to many

Christians, and in the anti-Aristotelian reaction of the Renaissance this found expression in the work of Sidney, Spenser and Milton, among others. The Romantic movement built on this, a line of Platonic poetics being traceable through Wordsworth, Coleridge and George MacDonald, to become once more a specifically Christian theory in Lewis and A. E. Dyson. The latter's *Between Two Worlds: Aspects of Literary Form* (Basingstoke: Macmillan, 1972) is a particularly clear expression. It takes a number of texts for analysis, beginning appropriately with Milton's *Comus*. His thesis deconstructs modernist expressions of hopelessness in literature by positing that the very act of creation is one of hope and vitality. To deny this is to become irrational. He traces a direct correlation in the western literary tradition between a decline in sanity and a move away from the Christian doctrines of fall and grace. His anti-Romanticism stands in great contrast to C. S. Lewis, but his claim that 'only a Platonic or Christian universe can give the imagination a fitting home' is one that Lewis would certainly agree with.

In this more general survey of Christian poetics, I would like to finish with critics and theorists who embrace other, often more liberal, theologies. This would also be a fitting place to mention the work of the Conference for Theology and Literature in the UK, the brain child of David Jasper, then of the University of Durham, where its conferences are regularly held. It has helped to coordinate the work of academics, particularly in the growing number of joint theology and literature departments in British universities. Its journal *Theology and Literature* appears quarterly, and papers read at its conferences are collected into book form after the usual lapse of time at publishers. The first such volume, edited by Jasper, was *Images of Belief in Literature* (Basingstoke: Macmillan, 1984), and gives an idea of the range of theological diversity among its contributors, no particular standpoint being assumed or required. Contributions I would recommend are those from Helen Wilcox, Michael Edwards, Stephen Prickett and T. R. Wright. Some of the later volumes I shall mention in the second part of this chapter.

Besides these volumes, the conference has given impetus for a new series from Macmillan, under the title of *Studies in Literature and Religion*, edited, of course, by Jasper himself. Again, I will mention several shortly, but two can be mentioned here: David Jasper's *The Study of Literature and Religion* (London: Macmillan, 1992) – stimulating, speculative and brief, though its anti-dogmatic tendencies may disturb some Christian readers; and

Paul Fiddes' *Freedom and Limit: A Dialogue between Literature and Christian Doctrine* (London: Macmillan, 1991). Fiddes is, in fact, a theologian. As with Edwards, there are chapters on theory, genres and authors. He accepts an Edwardsian dialectic, though disagreeing that it should be sited in the fall, and about what its terms should be. Fiddes' paradigm is Kierkegaard rather than Pascal. It is certainly one of the more literarily sophisticated books by a theologian so far reviewed.

T. R. Wright is one of the co-editors of the conference journal. His *Theology and Literature* (Oxford: Basil Blackwell, 1988), mentioned already by Roger Pooley (p. 20) and Kevin Mills (p. 127), is actually part of a theology series. In a clear, non-technical way, a search is made for a poetics of faith. Wright particularly considers 'in turn the extent to which narrative, poetry and drama have been involved in the theological task of exploring the Christian faith'. He thus renews a task of the 1950s. While much less exciting than Edwards' work, it is a lot easier to grasp. But be aware of Kevin Mills' caveat.

Another contributor to the conference volumes is D. Z. Phillips, a moral philosopher by profession. One of his best-known books is *Through a Darkening Glass: Philosophy, Literature and Cultural Change* (Notre Dame: University of Notre Dame Press; Oxford: Basil Blackwell, 1982). It is actually a series of essays, many of which deal with belief systems rather than religion *per se*. He sees literature as a 'source of reminders' for a philosophy trying to understand why people's hold on certain beliefs and values weakens. One of his theses is that the study of literature destroys the myth of progressive enlightenment. Far from moving towards a more fully rational belief system, modern reductionism distorts much clear past expression of truth, both moral and religious. Phillips is a philosopher who sees the study of literary texts as essential, in that philosophic generalities often lead to a sense of meaninglessness, while the concreteness and specificity of literary texts give us a distinct, insightful sense of significance.

Frank Palmer's *Literature and Moral Understanding: a Philosophical Essay on Ethics, Aesthetics, Education and Culture* (Oxford: Clarendon, 1992) takes Phillips' work a little further. Chapters include 'Fiction *v.* Fantasy: Pretence and Make-Believe'; 'Moral Responses to Fictional Characters'; 'Bad Morality, Bad Art?' Despite the weighty title, the style is clear; he poses and answers many of the questions the discerning Christian student asks, as Leland Ryken's *Triumphs of the Imagination*.

In the USA, the Conference on Christianity and Literature is a major professional group with over a thousand members. Its journal is *Christianity and Literature*, which is somewhat more focused theologically towards a conservative stance. There is also a second journal, *Religion and Literature*. One of the earliest and most prolific of the American 'religion and literature' scholars was Nathan Scott, Jr, many of whose studies are on modern literature, usually from a fairly liberal perspective. His *Poetics of Belief* (Chapel Hill and London: University of North Carolina Press, 1985) is one of his most recent books, more theoretically based than some. Probably his best known is *The New Orpheus: Essays Towards a Christian Poetic* (New York: Sheed and Ward, 1964). The stance is inclusive, to seek reconciliation rather than to find opposition or dialectic, and, to readers brought up on postmodernism, it may seem a little dated.

I would like to mention briefly three other pre-postmodernist books to conclude this first section. First, Vincent Buckley: *Poetry and the Sacred* (London: Chatto and Windus, 1968). This has separate chapters on various writers such as Donne, Blake, Yeats and Eliot, but no central thesis. Helen Gardner's *Religion and Literature* (London: Faber, 1971) contains one section on the nature of tragedy, the other on the nature of religious poetry. Both Buckley and Gardner are respected representatives of an older British mainstream academic tradition; both write from broad Christian sympathies. For an overall perspective of such fairly recent Christian criticism, Norman Cary's *Christian Criticism in the Twentieth Century* (Port Washington, NY.: Kennicat Press, 1975) is a very useful survey, recommended by Donald T. Williams, though not easily available in the UK.

2. Specific studies

In this second section I want to deal with specifics, in some cases supplementing bibliographies already supplied. For example, Professor Ryken reviews approaches to the Bible as literature, and mentions other books for further reading. His contribution to a Reformed and evangelical approach to the Bible cannot be over-estimated. In addition to his books already cited, readers should be aware of his *Words of Life: A Literary Introduction to the New Testament* (Grand Rapids: Baker, 1987) and *The New Testament in Literary Criticism* (New York: Frederick Ungar, 1984), which he edited, and describes as 'a roadmap to both the agreement and disagreements among literary critics of the New Testament'. There is a companion volume, *The Hebrew Bible in Literary Criticism*, edited by Alex Premingen and Edward L. Greenstein. Perhaps more easily obtainable in the UK is the volume by a co-editor of Ryken, Tremper Longman III, whose *Literary Approaches to Biblical Interpretation* has been made available under the Apollos imprint of Inter-Varsity Press (Leicester: Apollos, 1993).

The two great texts on the Bible as literature, it seems to me, must be Northrop Frye's *The Great Code: The Bible as Literature* (New York: Harcourt, Brace, Jovanovich, 1981; London: RKP, 1982), and Robert Alter's *The Art of Biblical Narrative* (London: Allen and Unwin, 1982; New York: Basic Books, 1985), both appearing coincidentally in the same year. Frye has not pursued his interest, but Alter has, building up an impressive range of studies, especially *The Art of Biblical Poetry* (New York: Basic Books, 1981; Edinburgh: T. & T. Clark, 1985).

For those readers wishing to look at British contributions to this field, a starting point might be David Greenwood's essay in *Reading Literature: Some Christian Approaches* (*op.cit.*). I would then tentatively suggest Gabriel Josipovici: *The Book of God: A Response to the Bible* (New Haven and London: Yale University Press, 1988). The preface contains a personal account of how Josipovici turned to the Bible in search of authority and tradition, the loss of which in contemporary literature he had explored in his earlier *The World and the Book*. He concludes that the Bible remains open in a way that the most modern of modernist texts cannot attain. This is a much more positive account of its 'secrecy' than Frank Kermode's *The Genesis of Secrecy* (Cambridge, MA. and London: Harvard University Press, 1979). Other British offerings that might be mentioned are Stephen Prickett, *Words and the Word: Language, Poetics and Biblical Interpretation* (Cambridge: Cambridge University Press, 1986), and those cited by Kevin Mills in his endnotes to chapter 7 (pp. 296–297).

Having looked at literary studies of the sacred text, I want to move on to other Christian literary texts, whether written on by Christian or non-Christian critics. A discerning Christian reader is obviously going to look for approaches that will open up the text Christianly. The critics' personal stances here are less immediately important. Christian critics can write in a muddled, unhelpful way; non-Christians can write perspicaciously; it is their willing servanthood to the text that matters. For example, I would recommend A. D. Nuttall's *Overheard by God: Fiction and Prayer in Herbert, Milton, Dante and St John* (London: Methuen, 1980), even though Nuttall is an admitted unbeliever. His central question, 'What would God think of this?', is handled sympathetically, and acts as a challenge to Christians. For example, he asks: why are believers so complacent about the 'scandal' of Christianity in St John's gospel?

As Christian readers, we also need to claim our 'birthright', a point A. E. Dyson made many years ago in an editorial in the *Critical Quarterly* (13.4): many of our major English writers were writing in the Christian tradition, even if much mainstream (secular) academic criticism would now marginalize this or re-route it to other traditions. Part of our critical reading, therefore, needs to be a recapturing of this tradition. Perhaps this has best been done so far for the sixteenth and seventeenth centuries. For example, Donald Williams and Leland Ryken have both cited Barbara Lewalski's *Protestant Poetics and the Seventeenth-Century Religious Lyric* (Princeton: Princeton University Press, 1979). C. A. Patrides' *The Grand Design of God: The Literary Form of the Christian View of History* (London: RKP, 1972) could be put alongside this – despite its title, it concludes at the end of the seventeenth century. Two of our contributors have done essays on Herbert: Donald T. Williams in the *Christian Scholar's Review* (19.3), cited in the bibliography to chapter three; and Elizabeth Clarke, in *The Glass* (the journal of the Literary Studies Group; no. 8, Autumn 1993).

U. Milo Kaufmann has supplied a useful Milton bibliography in his chapter (pp. 192–193); perhaps it could be supplemented by a mention of C. A. Patrides, *Milton and the Christian Tradition* (London: Oxford University Press, 1966); and Leland Ryken and James Sims (eds.), *Milton and the Scriptural Tradition: The Bible as Poetry* (Columbia: University of Missouri Press, 1984). I would also emphasize Milo Kaufmann's recommendation of Stanley Fish's *Surprised by Sin: The Reader in Paradise Lost* (New York and London: St Martin's Press, 1967), which, it has been claimed, has been the most influential book on *Paradise Lost* for the past three decades.

The nineteenth century has also proved a rich site to quarry Christian material from, though very often in its 'faith and doubt' form. For example, another of our contributors, Elisabeth Jay, has compiled *Faith and Doubt in Victorian Britain* (Basingstoke: Macmillan, 1986), where she allows the Victorians to speak for themselves. One of the best offerings on the faith/doubt axis is Lance St John Butler's *Victorian Doubt: Literary and Cultural Discourses* (Hemel Hempstead: Harvester Wheatsheaf, 1990). Butler is a post-structuralist, and refuses the easy 'gradual loss of faith' approach, questioning more fundamentally why Christianity could not find a language that was 'free of signs inimical to faith', while agnostics 'were extraordinarily reliant on the language of the religion they rejected' (one of the points I make in my chapter on Hardy).

I have always found J. Hillis Miller's *The Disappearance of God: Five Nineteenth-Century Writers* (Cambridge, MA.: Harvard University Press, 1975) very stimulating reading as an attempt to use literary criticism to form a description of the spiritual history of the period. A more recent book that also does this is Michael Wheeler's *Death and the Future Life in Victorian Literature and Theology* (Cambridge: Cambridge University Press, 1990), which is a model linking of literature, art and theology in a specific historical locus. There is a major re-examination of *In Memoriam*, *The Dream of Gerontius*, *The Wreck of the Deutschland* – all key Christian texts – and of *Our Mutual Friend* in terms of imagery and analogy.

Another seminal work which Professor Watson uses in his chapter on Romanticism is M. H. Abrams, *Natural Supernaturalism* (New York: Norton, 1971). The most Christian of the Romantics, Coleridge, is covered in David Jasper's *Coleridge as Poet and Religious Thinker* (Basingstoke: Macmillan, 1985). Jasper has also edited, with T. R. Wright, *The Critical Spirit and the Will to Believe: Essays in Nineteenth-Century Literature* (Basingstoke: Macmillan; New York: St Martin's Press, 1989), one of the Durham conference collections, somewhat fragmentary and really only for advanced students. The chapters by Prickett, Michael Wheeler and Elisabeth Jay (on 'Doubt and the Victorian Woman') are of especial interest.

It is rather more difficult to categorize works on twentieth-century literature here. I have already cited works on such specifically Christian writers as Eliot and the Inklings, to which I would like to add Harry Blamires' *Word Unknown: A Guide through Eliot's Four Quartets* (London: Methuen, 1969). But the general approach is often of finding religious ideas and themes in texts whatever the belief stance of the authors. I prefer, therefore, to leave recommendations for this period to the last sub-section which deals with specifically Christian criticism.

But before doing this, we might just briefly turn to genre studies of Christian texts. David Daiches, *God and the Poets* (Oxford: Clarendon, 1984) is a series of lectures, starting with Job and *Paradise Lost*, with a final chapter on 'Poetry and Belief'. *Paradise Lost* is also cited in Leopold Damrosch, Jr, *God's Plot and Man's Stories* (Chicago and London: University of Chicago Press, 1985), one of the better accounts linking Christian narrative and the rise of the novel. Damrosch sees Puritan narrative as central here, and sympathetically traces Puritan experience and art through Milton and Bunyan into the early eighteenth-century novel. A book covering similar ground is one mentioned in the opening chapter (p. 283, n.7), McKeon's *The Origins of the English Novel*.

Colin Manlove has written pre-eminently about fantasy. His *Christian Fantasy* (Basingstoke: Macmillan, 1992) is a slightly pessimistic account of the genre from medieval times to the present, including chapters on Kingsley, Lewis and Tolkien. Accounts of these Christian fantasists are also to be found in his *The Impulse of Fantasy Literature* (Ohio: Kent State University Press, 1983; Basingstoke: Macmillan, 1984), and in his *C. S. Lewis: His Literary Achievement* (New York: St Martin's Press; Basingstoke: Macmillan, 1987). Tolkien's essay 'On Fairy-Stories' is essential reading. It is to be found, *inter alia*, in his *Tree and Leaf* (London: Chatto and Windus, 1964).

In terms of drama, there are a number of accounts of the rise of drama in Christian liturgy of the medieval church. The attempted twentieth-century revival of Christian verse drama is well explored in William Spanos, *The Christian Tradition in Modern British Verse Drama: The Poetics of Sacramental Time* (New Brunswick: Rutgers University Press, 1967).

Lastly, I turn to critical material generated by Christian scholars. Particular interests of such academics and critics vary widely – they certainly cannot be accused of writing to a narrow agenda. Concerns include relating literary concepts and thematic material to theology; linking religious biography to an author's work; tracing intertextualities (biblical and other); and tracing Christian implications in genre studies. Christian undergraduates in secular institutions can take comfort that today there are numbers of Christian scholars in their chosen field of study. There always have been those, of course, going back to St Augustine, whose fourth book *On Christian Doctrine* deals with biblical stylistics, and Sir Philip Sidney, whose *The Apology for Poetry* or *Defence of Poesy* (best UK edn. G. Shepherd, ed., Manchester: Manchester University Press, 1973) appeals to the Bible as paradigm for the whole enterprise of literature.

But Christian students can be forgiven if they do feel alone. Let this book encourage them. Most of its contributors have produced academic books in their own right: for example, John Schad, *The Reader in the Dickensian Mind: Some New Language* (Basingstoke: Macmillan, 1992); Roger Pooley, *English Prose of the Seventeenth Century, 1590–1700* (London and New York: Longmans, 1992), the third part of which deals with religious prose; or Elisabeth Jay,

Margaret Oliphant (Oxford: Oxford University Press, 1995). Other books and articles by contributors have already been cited earlier in this chapter or elsewhere.

Obviously, there still needs to be discernment, as I have said. C. S. Lewis pointed out that a Christian faith does not necessarily make one a better critic *per se*, but it will give one a greater sympathy for certain writers and texts, and different insights and approaches. Having said this, I do not want to fall into the trap of listing large numbers of 'OK' Christian critics as if they were infallible guides; but I do think it would be helpful to mention a few texts, perhaps as examples of discerning thinking and writing, which may come the way of undergraduates. C. S. Lewis' treatment of literary history in *The Discarded Image: An Introduction to Medieval and Renaissance Literature* (Cambridge: Cambridge University Press, 1964), and in the opening chapter especially of his *Oxford History of English Literature*, vol. 3 (Oxford: Clarendon, 1954) remains a model of clarity and scholarship for all Christian academics. Roland M. Frye's *Shakespeare and Christian Doctrine* (Princeton: Princeton University Press, 1963) is similarly a model for writers seeking distinctive Christian approaches to authors (some attempts are far from happy ones). He worries at the issues of literature and religion in a methodical way, especially in seeking to maintain the balance between the integrity of literature and the influence of religious faith and theological ideas, without secularizing them. Christian Shakespearian criticism can also be represented by Roy W. Battenhouse, *Shakespearian Tragedy: Its Art and Christian Premises* (Bloomington: Indiana University Press, 1969) and *Shakespeare's Christian Dimension* (Bloomington: Indiana University Press, 1994), which reprints abridged versions of ninety-two critical commentaries and contains a bibliography of more than 250 items. Incidentally, Wheaton College houses the Batson Shakespeare collection, which contains virtually everything that has been published on Shakespeare and Christianity.

Christian writers have been caught up in discussion on the general nature of tragedy and comedy. For example, Barbara Hunt, in *The Paradox of Christian Tragedy* (Troy, NY.: Whitston, 1985) arguing against Ryken and Edwards, claims the impossibility of Christian tragedy. Other works worth citing here are Frederich Buechner, *Telling the Truth: The Gospel as Tragedy, Comedy, and Fairy Tale* (San Francisco: Harper and Row, 1977); Melvin Vos, *The Drama of Comedy: Victim and Victor* (Richmond: John Knox, 1966); Ralph C. Wood, *The Comedy of Redemption:*

Christian Faith and Comic Vision in Four American Novelists (Notre Dame: Notre Dame University Press, 1988); and Conrad Hyers, *The Comic Vision and the Christian Faith: A Celebration of Life and Laughter* (New York: Pilgrim Press, 1981). Two recent British studies in the Studies in Literature and Religion series are also worth mentioning. In *Pity and Terror: Christianity and Tragedy* (Basingstoke: Macmillan, 1989), Ulrich Simon pleads positively for 'Christian tragedy and tragic Christianity'. His first six chapters deal with tragedy in the Bible; much of the rest of the book deals with Shakespearian tragedy, although there is an interesting chapter entitled 'Casterbridge and Geneva'. He very much posits Unamuno (as in *The Tragic Sense of Life*) over against Steiner (*The Death of Tragedy*). Max Harris, in *Theatre and Incarnation* (Basingstoke: Macmillan, 1990), holds more to the Nathan Scott approach of finding a reconciliation between the modern arts and the church. To do this, he tries to see incarnation and theatre as paradigms of each other. Karl Barth provides the main theological basis for his contention – a sensible and readable discussion.

Another book in this series is also worth citing, on modern literature. Robert Detweiler, *Breaking the Fall: Religious Readings of Contemporary Fiction* (Basingstoke: Macmillan, 1989) applies to postmodernism what Dyson argued for in modernism: that the creative act undermines both theory and nihilism. He bases much of what he has to say on the idea of a Christian reading community, and looks at kinds of texts that would inspire such a community – texts of pain, of love and of worship. He looks at contemporary literature, particularly fiction, to supply examples of such texts, though each set of texts is read from a different critical perspective. In other words, a sophisticated literary matrix is set up which presupposes a good working knowledge of modern theory. The book could be seen as a follow-up from Donald G. Marshall's chapter in this book in terms of community, and John Schad's in terms of postmodernist readings of contemporary fiction.

David Jasper and Colin Crowder have co-edited a Durham conference's offerings in *European Literature and Theology in the Twentieth Century* (Basingstoke: Macmillan, 1990). There are good papers by Edwards and Detweiler. Of other books by Christians on twentieth-century literature, Ruth Etchell's *Unafraid to Be* (London: IVP, 1969) was the first British evangelical reading of modern (non-Christian) literature and its implicit witness to Christian truth. D. Z. Phillips, *From Fantasy to Faith: The Philosophy of Religion and Twentieth-Century Literature* (Basingstoke: Macmillan, 1991), is a more recent survey, ranging from Frank Baum to Tom Stoppard. Ian Gregor and Walter Stein have edited *The Prose for God* (London: Sheed and Ward, 1973) which focuses on modern novelists and the status they may be seen to have as theologians. And lastly, I will mention William T. Noon, *Poetry and Prayer* (New Brunswick: Rutgers University Press, 1967).

I want to stress that the titles cited in this second section are selective and representative only. They have been mentioned to offer some idea of the multiplicity of books available to the Christian student. If nothing else, this should have finally convinced discerning Christian students of literature (if they needed convincing) that they are not alone. Libraries are full of Christian writers, Christian critics, and many others who perceive that the transcendence, the radiance, of literature point beyond its makers to their Maker.

Notes

1. What does literature do? Roger Pooley (pp. 15–35)

[1]W. H. Auden, 'In Memory of W. B. Yeats', *Collected Poems*, ed. Edward Mendelson (London: Faber, 1976), p. 197; P. B. Shelley, 'A Defence of Poetry', *Shelley's Poetry and Prose*, ed. Donald H. Reiman and Sharon B. Powers (New York: Norton, 1977), p. 508; W. Wordsworth and S. T. Coleridge, in Michael Mason (ed.), *Lyrical Ballads* (Harlow: Longman, 1992), p. 71.

[2]'The Choice', in W. B. Yeats, *Collected Poems* (London: Macmillan, 2nd edn., 1950), p. 278.

[3]Graham Swift, 'Postscriptive Therapy,' in Claire Boylan (ed.), *The Agony and the Ego: The Art and Strategy of Fiction Writing Explained* (Harmondsworth: Penguin, 1993), p. 25.

[4]Michael Edwards, *Towards a Christian Poetics* (Grand Rapids: Eerdmans; Basingstoke: Macmillan, 1984), pp. 2–7, bases a similar analysis on a formulation of Pascal's, about the *grandeur* and *misère* of humanity. *Cf.* Ps. 8:4–6, Rom. 7:21–24. Donald T. Williams examines *imago Dei* formulations in chapter 3 of this collection.

[5]Samuel Taylor Coleridge, *Biographia Literaria*, ed. James Engell and W. Jackson Bate (Princeton: Princeton University Press, 1983), vol. I, p. 304. See the discussion on pp. lxxxi–civ of the Editors' Introduction.

[6]Nicholas Berdyaev, *The Meaning of the Creative Act*, trans. Donald A. Lowrie (London: Gollancz, 1955), pp. 9, 99.

[7]Erich Auerbach, *Mimesis: The Representation of Reality in Western Literature*, trans. Willard R. Trask (Princeton: Princeton University Press, 1981), chapter 2, esp. pp. 40–48. For a recent treatment of the debt of the early novel to Christian ideas and storytelling relative to scepticism and other factors, see Michael McKeon, *The Origins of the English Novel, 1600–1740* (Baltimore: Johns Hopkins University Press, 1987).

[8]Derrida introduces the phrase, and much of his method, in *Of Grammatology*, trans. G. C. Spivack (Baltimore: Johns Hopkins University Press, 1976). For further guidance and reading, see Kevin Mills' chapter 7, 'Words and presences' in this collection.

[9]George Steiner, *Real Presences* (London: Faber, 1989), p. 1

[10]Geoffrey H. Hartman, *Criticism in the Wilderness* (New Haven: Yale University Press, 1980), p. 272.

[11]So, for example, bell hook's [sic] resounding call to confront 'the realities of sex,

race, and class' in order to reconcile them 'in the making of a feminist revolution, in the transformation of the world', is twice quoted approvingly in Margo Hendricks and Patricia Parker (eds.), *Women, 'Race' and Writing in the Early Modern Period* (New York and London: Routledge, 1994), pp. 14, 193.

[12]Martin Amis, 'Author, Author', *Granta* 47 (1994), p. 23.

[13]Hayden White, *The Content of the Form: Narrative Discourse and Historical Representation* (Baltimore: Johns Hopkins University Press, 1987), p. 24.

[14]T. R. Wright, *Theology and Literature* (Cambridge, MA. and Oxford: Blackwell, 1988), p. 83.

[15]John Navone, *Towards a Theology of Story* (Slough: St Paul Publications, 1977), p. 41.

[16]George Eliot, *Middlemarch*, ed. W. J. Harvey (Harmondsworth: Penguin, 1965), p. 230.

[17]John Berger, *Once in Europa* (New York: Pantheon, 1988), p. 39.

[18]John Berger, 'A Story for Aesop', *Granta* 21 (Spring 1987), p. 18.

[19]Samuel Johnson, *The Rambler*, ed. W. J. Bate and Albrecht B. Strauss (New Haven: Yale University Press, 1969), vol. 1, pp. 22–23; no. 4, March 1750.

[20]Erich Auerbach, *Literary Language and its Public in Late Latin Antiquity and the Middle Ages*, trans. Ralph Manheim (London: Routledge and Kegan Paul, 1965), pp. 35–52.

[21]Brendan Kennelly, *The Book of Judas* (Newcastle: Bloodaxe, 1991), p. 372.

[22]Stanley Fish, *Doing What Comes Naturally: Change, Rhetoric and the Practice of Theory in Literary and Legal Studies* (Oxford: Clarendon, 1989), p. 439.

[23]Richard Rorty, *Contingency, irony, and solidarity* (Cambridge: Cambridge University Press, 1989), pp. 141–143.

[24]R. Davenport-Hines, *Sex, Death and Punishment* (London: Fontana, 1991), pp. 226–227.

[25]Donald Davie, *A Gathered Church: The Literature of the English Dissenting Interest, 1700–1930* (London: Routledge, 1978), p. 106. For the earlier, 'heroic' period of nonconformist literature, see N. H. Keeble, *The Literary Culture of Nonconformity in Later Seventeenth-Century England* (Leicester: Leicester University Press, 1987).

[26]Paul Muldoon (ed.), *The Faber Book of Contemporary Irish Poetry* (Faber, 1986), p. 345.

[27]Roland Barthes, *Sade, Fourier, Loyola*, cited by Richard Brown in Paul Hyland and Neil Sammells (eds.), *Writing and Censorship in Britain* (London: Routledge, 1992), p. 255.

[28]D. H. Lawrence, 'Why the Novel Matters', in A. A. H. Inglis (ed.), *A Selection from Phoenix* (London: Peregrine, 1971), p. 188.

[29]Valentine Cunningham, *In the Reading Gaol: Postmodernity, Texts and History* (Cambridge, MA. and Oxford: Blackwell, 1994), p. 378.

[30]See David Lawton, *Blasphemy* (Hemel Hempstead: Harvester Wheatsheaf, 1993), pp. 5–6 and *passim*.

[31]Rick Simpson, *Blasphemy and the Law in a Plural Society* (Nottingham: Grove Booklets, 1993) argues that 'the answer to blasphemy is not to outlaw it, but to show by the quality of the church's life that it is not true' (p. 23).

[32]Oliver O'Donovan, *Resurrection and Moral Order: An Outline for Evangelical Ethics* (Grand Rapids: Eerdmans; Leicester: Apollos, 2nd edn. 1994), p. 171.

[33]Colin Gunton, *The One, the Three and the Many: God, Creation and the Culture of Modernity* (Cambridge: Cambridge University Press, 1993), p. 124.

[34]Gunton, p. 230; and *cf.* Jeremy Begbie, *Voicing Creation's Praise: Towards a Theology of the Arts* (Edinburgh: T. and T. Clark, 1991).

[35]Wallace Stevens, 'The Relations between Poetry and Painting', *The Necessary Angel* (New York: Vintage, 1951), p. 169.

[36]Matthew Arnold, *Culture and Anarchy*, ed. J. Dover Wilson (Cambridge: Cambridge University Press, 1966), p. 154. (First published 1869.)

[37]George Steiner, *Real Presences*, p. 141.

[38]David Jones, 'Art and Sacrament', in Nathan A. Scott, Jr (ed.), *The New Orpheus: Essays Towards a Christian Poetic* (New York: Sheed and Ward, 1964), p. 27. (The essay is also printed in Jones' *Epoch and Artist*.) Sidney's *Apology for Poetry* makes a similar point; Dorothy L. Sayers, in *The Mind of the Maker*, carries the analogy between the novelist and God as far as it can go, and probably further. See Donald T. Williams' discussion in chapter 3.6 of this collection.

[39]Flannery O'Connor, *Mystery and Manners: Occasional Prose*, ed. Sally and Robert Fitzgerald (London: Faber, 1972), p. 68. For a fuller bibliography, see chapter 3, n. 57.

[40]Augustine, *Confessions*, trans. R. S. Pine-Coffin (Harmondsworth: Penguin, 1961), p. 21.

2. Canons: Valentine Cunningham (pp. 37–52)

[1]Henry Louis Gates Jr, 'Canon Confidential: A Sam Slade Caper', in *Loose Canons: Notes on the Culture Wars* (New York and Oxford: Oxford University Press, 1992), chapter 1.

[2]Sandra M. Gilbert and Susan Gubar, 'Masterpiece Theatre: An Academic Melodrama', *Critical Inquiry* 17 (Summer 1991), pp. 693ff.

[3]'Bellow Brandishes his Pen Against Cultural Vigilantes', *The Times* (London, 17 March 1994), p. 12.

[4]John Updike, *Memories of the Ford Administration* (1992; Hardmondsworth: Penguin, 1993), pp. 197, 53–54.

[5]Matthew Arnold, 'Preface', *Culture and Anarchy*, ed. John Dover Wilson (Cambridge: Cambridge University Press, 1932), p. 6.

[6]Alastair Fowler, 'Genre and the Literary Canon', *New Literary History* 11 (1979–80), pp. 97–119; chapter 12 of Fowler, *Kinds of Literature: An Introduction to the Theory of Genres and Modes* (Oxford: Clarendon, 1982). Wendell V. Harris, 'Canonicity', *Publications of the Modern Languages Association* (*PMLA*) 106 (1919), pp. 110–121.

[7]See John Guillory, 'Canon', in Frank Lentricchia and Thomas McLaughlin (eds.), *Critical Terms for Literary Study* (Chicago: University of Chicago Press, 1990), pp. 233–249.

[8]Michel Bérubé, *Marginal Forces/Cultural Centers: Tolson, Pynchon, and the Politics of the Canon* (Ithaca and London: Cornell University Press, 1992), pp. 6, 8. Paul Lauter, *Canons and Contexts* (New York and Oxford: Oxford University Press, 1991), pp. 154–171.

[9]Gerald L. Bruns, 'Canon and Power in the Hebrew Scriptures', in Robert von Hallberg (ed.), *Canons* (Chicago: University of Chicago Press, 1984), p. 67.

[10]Chris Baldick, *The Social Mission of English Criticism 1848–1932* (Oxford: Clarendon, 1983), especially chapter 4, 'Literary-Critical Consequences of the War', pp. 86ff. George Sampson, *English for the English: A Chapter on National Education* (1921), edited and introduced by Denys Thompson (Cambridge: Cambridge University Press, 1970).

[11]John Henry Newman, *The Idea of a University Defined and Illustrated* (1852; New York and London: Longmans, Green & Co., 1927), pp. 233, 321, 324.

[12] A *Wall Street Journal* joke, quoted by James Atlas, *Battle of the Books: The Curriculum Debate in America* (New York and London: Norton & Co., 1993), p. 48.

[13] T. S. Eliot, *After Strange Gods: A Primer in Modern Heresy* (London: Faber, 1934).

[14] James Atlas, *Battle of the Books*, p. 34.

[15] *Ibid*. p. 40.

[16] See 'Canon' in Bruce M. Metzger and Michael D. Coogan (eds.), *The Oxford Companion to the Bible* (New York and Oxford: Oxford University Press, 1993).

[17] John Henry Newman, *An Essay on the Development of Christian Doctrine* (1845 – the edition reprinted in the edition of J. M. Cameron; Harmondsworth: Pelican, 1974).

[18] Frank Kermode, *The Classic: Literary Images of Permanence and Change* (1975; Cambridge, MA. and London: Harvard University Press, 1983), p. 80.

[19] The questions come from Paul Lauter, 'The Literature of America – A Comparative Discipline', in his *Canons and Contexts* (New York and Oxford: Oxford University Press, 1991), p. 55.

[20] See Jonathan Goldberg (ed.), *Queering the Renaissance* (Durham, NC. and London: Duke University Press, 1994).

[21] *Cf*. Mary Jacobus, 'Is There a Woman in this Text?', in *Reading Woman: Essays in Feminist Criticism* (London: Methuen, 1986), p. 83.

[22] Carolyn Heilbrun, 'Feminist Criticism: Bringing the Spirit Back to English Studies' (1979), in Elaine Showalter (ed.), *The New Feminist Criticism: Essays on Women, Literature and Theory* (London: Virago, 1986), pp. 21ff.

[23] 'Aspiring Dons Desert Tradition for Angela Carter', *The Independent* (London, 1 April 1994).

[24] Lisa Jardine, 'Saxon Violence', *The Guardian* (London, 8 December 1992).

[25] Stanley Fish, *There's No Such Thing as Free Speech: And It's a Good Thing Too* (New York and Oxford: Oxford University Press, 1994), pp. 54, 95. Dinesh D'Souza, *Illiberal Education: The Politics of Race and Sex on Campus* (New York: Free Press; New York and Oxford: Maxwell Macmillan International, 1991).

[26] Stanley Fish, *There's No Such Thing*, p. 95.

[27] Lillian S. Robinson, 'Treason Our Text: Feminist Challenges to the Literary Canon', in Showalter (ed.), *The New Feminist Criticism*, p. 112.

[28] T. S. Eliot, 'Tradition and the Individual Talent' (1919), in *Selected Essays* (London: Faber, 1932), p. 15.

[29] Barbara Herrnstein Smith, 'Contingencies of Value', in Hallberg (ed.), *Canons*, pp. 5–39; and *Contingencies of Value: Alternative Perspectives for Critical Theory* (Cambridge, MA. and London: Harvard University Press, 1988).

[30] See Valentine Cunningham, *In The Reading Gaol: Postmodernity, Texts and History* (Cambridge, MA. and Oxford: Blackwell, 1994), pp. 35–36, 50, 75, n. 133.

[31] Samuel Johnson, *The History of Rasselas, Prince of Abyssinia* (1759), chapter 10, 'A Dissertation Upon Poetry'.

[32] Matthew Arnold, 'On the Modern Element in Literature', *Selected Prose*, ed. P. J. Keating (Harmondsworth: Penguin, 1970), p. 72.

[33] Lisa Jardine, 'Saxon Violence'.

[34] Molly Hite, 'Except Thou Ravish Mee': Penetrations into the Life of the (Feminine) Mind', in Gayle Greene and Coppélia Kahn (eds.), *Changing Subjects: The Making of Feminist Literary Criticism* (New York and London: Routledge, 1993), pp. 123–124. Elisabeth Jay examines feminist views over canonicity in chapter 6 of this collection.

[35] Paul Lauter's case that Meridel LeSueur's story of a woman's violent loss of virginity in seedy circumstances is more potent than anything in the notorious two-

and-a-half-foot shelf of old Great Books has some force, but as big stories go this one is small potatoes by the side of the biblical big stories and grand narratives, and also some of the less grand ones including, of course, the stories of women's forced sexual encounters. Lauter, *Canons and Contexts*, pp. 252–253.

[36]Maurice Blanchot, 'Reading', in *The Space of Literature*, translated and introduced by Ann Smock (Lincoln, NB.: University of Nebraska Press, 1982), pp. 194–196. See Valentine Cunningham, *In the Reading Gaol*, pp. 393ff. *Cf.* Michel de Certeau, 'What We Do When We Believe', in *On Signs: A Semiotics Reader* (Oxford: Blackwell, 1985), pp. 192–202: 'The believer says: "I believe that you will (re)appear." '

[37]Newman, *The Idea of a University*, Discourse IX, p. 233.

[38]Stanley Fish, 'Milton, Thou Shouldst Be Living at This Hour', in *There's No Such Thing as Free Speech*, p. 272. The text, Hebrews 1:1, Authorized Version.

3. Christian poetics, past and present: Donald T. Williams (pp. 53–68)

[1]See H. Richard Niebuhr, *Christ and Culture* (New York: Harper and Row, 1951), Henry R. Van Til, *The Calvinistic Concept of Culture* (Philadelphia: Presbyterian and Reformed, 1959), and Leland Ryken, *Culture in Christian Perspective* (Portland: Multnomah, 1986).

[2]Augustine, *Confessions*, trans. William Watts. The Loeb Classical Library. 2 vols. (Cambridge: Harvard University Press, 1946), I.xvii (vol. 1, p. 51).

[3]*Ibid.*, I.xiii (vol. 1, pp. 39–40).

[4]*Ibid.*, III.ii (vol. 1, p. 103).

[5]*Ibid.*, III.ii (vol. 1, p. 101).

[6]*Ibid.*, III.iv (vol. 1, p. 109).

[7]*Ibid.*, III.iv (vol. 1, pp. 109f).

[8]Augustine, *Christian Education*, II.xxviii–xxxii, in George Howie (ed. and trans.), *St Augustine: On Education* (Chicago: Regnery, 1969), pp. 350–351.

[9]Augustine, *Confessions*, I.xvi (vol. 1, p. 149).

[10]See also *Confessions*, XI.xxvi (vol. 2, p. 267) for a discussion of how a knowledge of scansion helps us to understand the concept of time.

[11]Augustine, *Christian Education*, II.lvi–lxi (p. 364).

[12]*Ibid.*, II.liv (p. 360).

[13]*Ibid.*, IV.ii–xi (p. 369); *cf.* Henry Chadwick, *Augustine* (New York: Oxford University Press, 1986), who notes that 'Cicero's prose and Virgil's poetry were so profoundly stamped on Augustine's mind' that he could not write without a reminiscence or allusion (p. 4), and that in his old age he was still quoting Cicero (p. 10).

[14]Alex Preminger *et al.* (eds.), *Classical and Medieval Literary Criticism: Translations and Interpretations* (New York: Ungar, 1974), pp. 285–286.

[15]See J. R. R. Tolkien, 'Beowulf: The Monsters and the critics', and Marie Padgett Hamilton, 'The Religious Principle in *Beowulf*', both reprinted in Lewis E. Nicholson (ed.), *An Anthology of Beowulf Criticism* (Notre Dame: University of Notre Dame Press, 1963), pp. 51–103 and 105–135.

[16]The best edition of *The Divine Comedy* in English is Dorothy L. Sayers' translation with its wonderful introductions and notes (Baltimore and Harmondsworth: Penguin, 1949–62); the definition of allegory used here is from Thomas Sackville's 'Induction' to *The Mirror for Magistrates*, in Hyder E. Rollins and Herschel Baker

(eds.), *The Renaissance in England* (Lexington: D. C. Heath, 1954), p. 273.

[17]F. N. Robinson (ed.), *The Works of Geoffrey Chaucer* (Boston: Houghton Mifflin; London: Oxford University Press, 2nd edn. 1961), p. 265.

[18]See Donald T. Williams, 'John Calvin: Humanist and Reformer', *Trinity Journal* 5 (1976), pp. 67–68.

[19]Roger Ascham, *The Schoolmaster*, in Rollins and Baker, *The Renaissance in England*, p. 833.

[20]Richard Baxter, *The Practical Works of Richard Baxter*, vol. 1, *The Christian Directory* (London: George Virtue, 1838), pp. 56–57.

[21]Sir Philip Sidney, *The Defense of Poesy*, in Rollins and Baker, *The Renaissance in England*, p. 610. The best UK edition is that edited by G. Shepherd (Manchester: Manchester University Press, 1973).

[22]*Ibid.*

[23]*Ibid.*, p. 607.

[24]*Ibid.*, p. 608.

[25]F. E. Hutchinson (ed.), *The Works of George Herbert* (Oxford: Clarendon, 1941), p. 176. See also Donald T. Williams, ' "Thou Art Still My God": George Herbert and the Poetics of Edification', *Christian Scholar's Review* 19:3 (March 1990), pp. 271–285.

[26]For a masterful treatment of this point, see Barbara Kiefer Lewalski, *Protestant Poetics and the Seventeenth-Century Religious Lyric* (Princeton: Princeton University Press, 1979).

[27]John Milton, 'Areopagetica', in Merritt Y. Hughes (ed.), *John Milton: Complete Poems and Major Prose* (Indianapolis: Bobbs-Merrill, 1957), pp. 728–729.

[28]Milton, 'Of Education', in Hughes, *John Milton*, p. 631.

[29]*Ibid.*

[30]Milton, 'Areopagetica', in Hughes, *John Milton*, p. 720.

[31]*Ibid.*

[32]E. D. Hirsch, *Validity in Interpretation* (New Haven:Yale University Press, 1967).

[33]Milton, 'Areopagetica', in Hughes, *John Milton*, p. 728.

[34]Samuel Johnson, 'Preface to the Plays of William Shakespeare', in Geoffrey Tillotson *et al.* (eds.), *Eighteenth-Century English Literature* (New York: Harcourt, Brace and World, 1969), pp. 1066–1067.

[35]Important statements include Cleanth Brooks and Robert Penn Warren, *Understanding Poetry* (New York: Holt, Rineheart and Wilson, 3rd edn. 1960), Cleanth Brooks, *The Well-Wrought Urn* (New York: Harcourt, Brace and World, 1947), and other works by John Crowe Ransom, Allan Tate, *etc.*

[36]W. H. Gardner and N. H. MacKenzie (eds.), *The Poems of Gerald Manley Hopkins* (London: Oxford University Press, 4th edn. 1967), pp. xx–xxi.

[37]Norman Reed Cary, *Christian Criticism in the Twentieth Century* (Port Washington: Kennicat, 1975), pp. 35, 27.

[38]Michael Edwards, *Towards a Christian Poetics* (Grand Rapids: Eerdmans, 1984; Basingstoke: Macmillan, 1986), p. 12.

[39]*Ibid.*

[40]J. R. R. Tolkien , 'On Fairy Stories' (1938), in C. S. Lewis (ed.), *Essays Presented to Charles Williams* (Grand Rapids: Eerdmans; Oxford: Oxford University Press, 1966), pp. 38–89; and in *The Tolkien Reader* (New York: Ballantine, 1966), pp. 26–84. See also his fictional symbolization of the same ideas, 'Leaf by Niggle', in *The Tolkien Reader*, pp. 85–112. Both essay and story are also to be found in *Tree and Leaf* (London: Allen and Unwin, 1964). Citations in this essay are from *The Tolkien Reader*.

[41]*Ibid.*, p. 54. Superficial resemblances to Coleridge's language in *Biographia*

Literaria, chapter xiii, should not blind us to the fact that the conception is fundamentally different. Coleridge speaks of 'primary' and 'secondary' *imagination*, but they are not parallel to Tolkien's primary and secondary *creation*. Coleridge's primary imagination is a 'repetition' of God's act of creation in the 'finite mind'; Tolkien's primary creation *is* God's act of creation. Tolkien's exposition is more simple and direct, and closer in spirit to Sidney than to the Romantics. *Cf.* Coleridge, *Biographia Literaria*, ed. by George Watson for Everyman's Library (New York: E. P. Dutton; London: J. M. Dent, 1960), p. 167.

[42]Tolkien, *op. cit.*

[43]Dorothy L. Sayers, *The Mind of the Maker* (London: Methuen, 1941; San Francisco: Harper and Row, 1968); see also the many stimulating essays reprinted in *A Matter of Eternity* (Grand Rapids: Eerdmans, 1973) and *Christian Letters to a Post-Christian World* (Grand Rapids: Eerdmans, 1969); see also her *Creed or Chaos?* (London: Religious Book Club, 1947).

[44]C. S. Lewis, 'Christianity and Culture', in Walter Hooper (ed.), *Christian Reflections* (Grand Rapids: Eerdmans; London: Geoffrey Bles, 1967), pp. 12–36; *cf.* Leland Ryken's excellent summary and evaluation of the argument in *Triumphs of the Imagination: Literature in Christian Perspective* (Downers Grove and Leicester: IVP, 1979), pp. 225–227. For examples of Lewis' practical criticism, see *A Preface to Paradise Lost* (New York and London: Oxford University Press, 1942), or Walter Hooper (ed.), *Selected Literary Essays* (Cambridge: Cambridge University Press, 1969).

[45]Cary, *Christian Criticism*, p. 16.

[46]C. S. Lewis, 'First and Second Things', in *Undeceptions* (London: Geoffrey Bles, 1971), reissued as *First and Second Things* (London: Collins Fount, 1985); in the USA it is in *God in the Dock*, ed. Walter Hooper (Grand Rapids: Eerdmans, 1970), pp. 278–281; and 'Lilies that Fester', in *The World's Last Night and Other Essays* (New York: Harcourt, Brace and World, 1960), pp. 31–49, or in *They Asked for a Paper* (London: Geoffrey Bles, 1962), pp. 105–119.

[47]C. S. Lewis, 'On Three Ways of Writing for Children', in Walter Hooper (ed.), *Of Other Worlds* (New York: Harcourt, Brace, Jovanovich, 1964), p. 29, or in Hooper (ed.), *Of This and Other Worlds* (London: Collins, 1982), p. 56; *cf.* 'The Language of Religion', in *Christian Reflections*, p. 333; 'An Expostulation against Too Many Writers of Science Fiction', in *C. S. Lewis: Poems* (New York and London: Harcourt, Brace, Jovanovich, 1964), p. 58; and C. S. Lewis, *An Experiment in Criticism* (Cambridge: Cambridge University Press, 1969), p. 40.

[48]Lewis, 'Sometimes Fairy Stories Say Best What's to be Said', in *Of Other Worlds*, p. 37, or in *Of This and Other Worlds*, p. 71.

[49]Lewis, 'A Confession', in *Poems* , p. 1

[50]Lewis, 'On Three Ways of Writing . . .', p. 31

[51]Lewis, 'On the Reading of Old Books', in *God in the Dock*, pp. 200–207, or in Walter Hooper (ed.), *The Grand Miracle* (New York: Ballantine, 1970), pp. 122-128; *cf.* 'Is England Doomed?' in Hooper (ed.), *Present Concerns: Essays by C. S. Lewis* (San Diego: Harcourt, Brace, Jovanovich, 1986), pp. 27–31.

[52]Lewis, *An Experiment in Criticism*. Lewis argues that a book should be judged by the quality of reading it encourages over time, not that its *meaning* is a wax nose to be twisted into whatever shape the readers, in their ignorance, prefer.

[53]T. S. Eliot, 'Tradition and the Individual Talent' (1919), in *Selected Essays of T. S. Eliot* (New York: Harcourt, Brace & World, 1964), p. 6.

[54]Eliot, 'Shakespeare and the Stoicism of Seneca' (1927), in *Selected Essays*, p. 116.

[55]Eliot, 'Dante' (1929), in *Selected Essays*, p. 231.

[56]Eliot, 'Religion and Literature' (1935), in *Selected Essays*, p. 354.

[57]Flannery O'Connor, *Mystery and Manners: Occasional Prose*, ed. Sally and Robert Fitzgerald (New York: Farrar, Straus and Giroux, 1961; London: Faber, 1972); *cf.* Sally Fitzgerald (ed.), *The Habit of Being: Letters of Flannery O'Connor* (New York: Farrar, Straus and Giroux, 1979). Her fiction can be found in *Flannery O'Connor: The Complete Stories* (New York: Farrar, Straus and Giroux, 1974; London: Faber, 1990); for several of the short stories with two novelettes, see *Three by Flannery O'Connor* (New York: Signet, n.d.).

[58]Cary, *Christian Criticism*, pp. 3–4.

[59]Francis A. Schaeffer, *Art and the Bible: Two Essays* (Downers Grove: IVP; London: Hodder and Stoughton, 1973), p. 5. Schaeffer is known for his incisive discussions of the ways in which art reflects the worldview of the artist. This little pamphlet contains much sane discussion which would surprise readers who know Schaeffer only by reputation and caricature.

4. Reading and interpretive communities: Donald G. Marshall (pp. 69–84)

[1]In the National Gallery, Washington DC.

[2]See Michael Fried, *Absorption and Theatricality: Painting and Beholder in the Age of Diderot* (Berkeley: University of California Press, 1980), especially the chapter 'The Primary of Absorption', pp. 7–70.

[3]Other examples are Gerard Dou's portrait of Rembrandt's mother reading the Bible; Winslow Homer's 'The New Novel' (Museum of Fine Arts, Springfield, MA.) showing a woman alone in a landscape, lying on her side; Charles Sprague Pearce's 'Reading by the Shore' and Robert Reid's 'Reverie' (both in the Manoogian collection) show the American interest, as does Mary Cassatt's 'Woman Reading in a Garden'; Berthe Morisot's 'The Mother and Sister of the Artist' shows how the mother's absorption leads to the daughter's neglect.

[4]See Ian Watt, *The Rise of the Novel: Studies in Defoe, Richardson and Fielding* (London: Chatto and Windus, 1957; Berkeley: University of California Press, 1962), especially the chapter 'The Reading Public and the Rise of the Novel'.

[5]It could be seen that the withdrawal is not negative but allows the re-drawing of the borders between private and public, free from political or religious surveillance. See J. Habermas, *The Structural Transformation of the Public Sphere: An Inquiry into a Category of Bourgeois Society*, trans. Thomas Burger (Cambridge, MA.: MIT Press, 1989), pp. 14–26, 31–43.

[6]The new understanding of the human being as a finite, sensuous and imaginative creature is the theme of Ernst Cassirer's chapter, 'Fundamental Problems of Aesthetics', in his *The Philosophy of the Enlightenment*, trans. C. Fritz, A. Koellin and James Pettegrove (Boston: Beacon, 1955), pp. 275–360, which is placed as conclusion to his account of eighteenth-century philosophy.

[7]The statue is described in Jesper Svenbro, *Phrasikleia: an Anthropology of Reading in Ancient Greece*, trans. Janet Lloyd (Ithaca: Cornell University Press, 1993), pp. 10–11.

[8]*Ibid.*, p. 25.

[9]*Ibid.*, p. 24.

[10]*Ibid.*, p. 18.

[11]*Ibid.*, p. 46.

[12]Augustine, *Confessions*, VI.iii.3, p. 114. See M. T. Clanchy, *From Memory to*

Written Record: England 1066–1307 (London: Edward Arnold, 1979): 'Private reading must still have been a luxury, largely confined to retiring ladies and scholars. Books were scarce and it was ordinary good manners to share their contents among a group by reading aloud' (p. 198). Quoted in Susan Noakes, *Timely Reading: Between Exegesis and Interpretation* (Ithaca: Cornell University Press, 1988), p. 26, who suggests a notion of a 'reading-aloud culture'.

[13]See Wytold Rybczynski, *Home: a Short History of an Idea* (New York: Penguin, 1987). In his discussion of Jan Vermeer's 'The Love Letter' he relates the house to home as a site for 'rich interior awareness' (pp. 71–75).

[14]Charles Taylor, *Sources of the Self: The Making of the Modern Identity* (Cambridge, MA.: Harvard University Press; Cambridge: Cambridge University Press, 1989).

[15]René Descartes, *Philosophical Essays*. Of many editions, I am using Laurence Lafleur's translation (Indianapolis: Bobbs-Merrill, 1964). Citations are from 'Discourse on Method', but see the reformulation in 'Meditations Concerning First Philosophy', esp. pp. 75–82.

[16]'Discourse on Method', p. 5.

[17]*Ibid.*, p. 8.

[18]*Ibid.*, p. 10.

[19]*Ibid.*, p. 15.

[20]*Ibid.*, p. 24.

[21]A leading example of this quest for a reliable method is E. D. Hirsch, Jr, *Validity in Interpretation* (New Haven: Yale University Press, 1967) where he thinks the ideal of literary study is 'as a corporate enterprise and a progressive discipline' (p. 209) – obvious marks of modern science. See also his *The Aims of Interpretation* (Chicago: Chicago University Press, 1976). I feel he is misguided because it attempts a Cartesian solution to the problem of the isolated reader instead of questioning this modern picture and rethinking the nature of reading.

[22]See Phil. 2:12, 'Therefore, my beloved, as you have always obeyed, so now, not only as in my presence but much more in my absence, work out your own salvation with fear and trembling' (Revised Standard Version). Reformation theologians such as John Calvin did not take this to mean an individual's isolation from the church, but the risk of individualism in the Protestant Reformation did reach extreme conclusions from time to time, *e.g.* Ann Hutchinson's 'antinomianism' in the Boston colony in the 1630s.

[23]See, for example, John Bossy, *Christianity in the West 1400–1700* (Oxford: Oxford University Press, 1985), where the rise of indulgences and Reformation rejection of them are discussed on pp. 54–56 and 91–97.

[24]Thomas Paine, *The Age of Reason* (Secaucus, NJ.: Citadel, 1974), pp. 66–68. He traces both purgatory and indulgences back to the belief 'that one person could stand in the place of another, and could perform meritorious services for him'.

[25]Because he recognizes that human beings are essentially social, Aristotle sees that ethics concerns our relations to others, so that it would be strange to say someone has attained a good life in solitude (*Nichomachean Ethics*, I.vii.6.1097b.11; *cf.* IX.ix.3.1169b.20). Hence in discussing ethics he includes a chapter on friendship. In the *Politics*, Aristotle again asserts the priority of the community to the individual. A human being who cannot enter into social relations or is so self-sufficient that there is no need to do so must be either a beast or a god (I.i.12.1253a.25ff.).

[26]Pierre Bourdieu, *Distinction: a Social Critique of the Judgement of Taste*, trans. Richard Nice (Cambridge, MA.: Harvard University Press, 1984).

[27]Noakes, *Timely Reading*, p. 27.

[28]See the excellent account of the emergence of modern 'print culture' and its impact on authors and readers in Alvin Kernan, *Printing Technology, Letters and Samuel Johnson* (Princeton: Princeton University Press, 1987). The mechanical nature of printing makes the text seem even more free-standing. A manuscript more obviously bears the marks of its human producer's uniqueness. Manuscripts often end with a short remark by the scribe, recording his name, perhaps speaking about the hard labour of copying or expressing thanks to God for completing the task, sometimes dedicating the work. In religious works especially, this 'colophon', as it is called, may take the form of a prayer or a request that the reader pray for the scribe. Some books still conclude with a colophon giving some information about the typography, facts of publication, or the author.

[29]Stephen Carter, *The Culture of Disbelief: How American Law and Politics Trivialise Religious Devotion* (New York: Basic Books, 1993) provides a thought-provoking analysis of the destructive reduction of religion to a merely private affair in modern American life. British readers will see many parallels.

[30]John Milbank, *Theology and Social Theory: Beyond Secular Reason* (Oxford: Blackwell, 1990) addresses the need to rethink the 'church' as a critique of the modern concept of the 'social' so as to liberate Christianity from the private sphere to which modern social theory has banished it. Milbank's book is difficult but worthy of the most serious study.

[31]Josiah Royce, *The Problem of Christianity* (Chicago: University of Chicago Press, 1968).

[32]*Ibid.*, p. 62.

[33]*Ibid.*, p. 65.

[34]*Ibid.*, pp. 72–73.

[35]*Ibid.*, pp. 80–81.

[36]*Ibid.*, p. 94.

[37]*Ibid.*, p. 83.

[38]*Ibid.*, p. 84.

[39]*Ibid.*, p. 85.

[40]*Ibid.*, p. 108.

[41]*Ibid.*, p. 116.

[42]*Ibid.*, p. 119.

[43]*Ibid.*, p. 215.

[44]*Ibid.*

[45]*Ibid.*, p. 239.

[46]*Ibid.*, p. 243.

[47]*Ibid.*

[48]*Ibid.*, p. 245.

[49]*Ibid.*, p. 246.

[50]*Ibid.*, p. 247.

[51]*Ibid.*, p. 254.

[52]*Ibid.*, p. 253.

[53]*Ibid.*, pp. 255–256.

[54]*Ibid.*, p. 256.

[55]*Ibid.*, p. 265.

[56]*Ibid.*, p. 274.

[57]*Ibid.*, p. 284.

[58]*Ibid.*, p. 315.

[59]*Ibid.*, p. 317.

[60]*cf.* Stanley Fish, *Is There a Text in This Class? The Authority of Interpretive*

Communities (Cambridge, MA.: Harvard University Press, 1980). Fish thinks of interpretive communities in terms of rules which guide members and determine what counts as a correct interpretation within the community. This is a version of the classical theory of social contract. Its insoluble problem is why and how individuals form such communities. The only answer is some form of material gain, and Fish quite consistently eulogizes the profession of literary study as an end in itself which confers its rewards – a high salary, fame among the experts, and tenure at a leading university – on those who follow the rules with particular skill and flair. In his later *Doing What Comes Naturally: Change, Rhetoric, and the Practice of Theory in Literary and Legal Studies* (Durham, NC.: Duke University Press; Oxford: Clarendon, 1989), Fish tries to repair some of the defects of this conception by elaborating the concept of 'practice'. But he is unable to explain practice as temporally situated in relation to a past and to a specific future or aim. A tradition and an aim are, however, necessary to the constitution of a practice, which cannot be reduced merely to a body of rules. See Alan Jacobs' incisive review, 'The Unnatural Practices of Stanley Fish: a Review Essay', *South Atlantic Review* 55 (1990), pp. 87–97.

[61]Patrocinio Schweickart, 'Reading Ourselves: Toward a Feminist Theory of Reading' in Robyn R. Warhol and Diane Price Herndl (eds.), *Feminisms: An Anthology of Literary Theory and Criticism* (New Brunswick, NJ.: Rutgers University Press, 1991).

[62]*Ibid.*, p. 535.

[63]*Ibid.*, p. 539.

[64]*Ibid.*, p. 545, italics in original.

[65]*Ibid.*

[66]Implicit throughout this essay has been the issue of validity in interpretation. My argument has been that what makes interpretation valid and simultaneously makes untenable the claim (or fear) that interpretation is purely subjective, so that in it 'anything goes', is the realization that readers are always already embedded in a community, responding to those through whom the text has reached them and responsible to those with whom they want or believe it important to pass on both the text and their understanding of it. For a presentation of these views in the terms of Hans-Georg Gadamer's hermeneutic philosophy, see Donald G. Marshall, 'Reading as Understanding: Hermeneutics and Reader-Response Criticism' in *Christianity and Literature* 33 (1983), pp. 37–48.

5. *The turn to history: John D. Cox (pp. 85–102)*

[1]W. K. Wimsatt and Monroe C. Beardsley, *The Verbal Icon* (Lexington: University of Kentucky Press, 1954), p. x.

[2]Cleanth Brooks, *The Well Wrought Urn* (New York: Reynall and Hitchcock, 1947; repr. London: Dobson, 1960), p. 184.

[3]J. Hillis Miller, 'The Triumph of Theory, the Resistance to Reading, and the Question of the Material Base', *PMLA* 102 (1987), pp. 281–291.

[4]Louis Althusser and Etienne Balibar, *Reading Capital*, trans. Ben Brewster (New York: Pantheon Books, 1970), p. 17.

[5]Karl Marx and Frederick Engels, *Collected Works*, 46 vols. (New York: International Publishers, 1976–), vol. 29, pp. 262–263. Hillis Miller alludes to Marx's metaphor (whether he has it in mind or not) in his phrase 'the material base' (see above, n. 3).

[6]Hillis Miller, 'The Triumph of Theory', p. 289.

[7]Marx, *Collected Works*, vol. 5, p. 24.

[8]*Ibid.*, p. 5.

[9]Jonathan Dollimore and Alan Sinfield (eds.), *Political Shakespeare: New Essays in Cultural Materialism* (Manchester: Manchester University Press, 1985), p. viii.

[10]Jonathan Dollimore, *Radical Tragedy: Religion, Ideology and Power in the Drama of Shakespeare and his Contemporaries* (Durham, NC.: Duke University Press, 2nd. edn. 1992), pp. 1–19.

[11]Stephen Greenblatt, *Marvelous Possessions: The Wonder of the New World* (Chicago: University of Chicago Press, 1991).

[12]Marx, *Collected Works*, vol. 3, p. 175.

[13]Frederick Douglass, *Narrative of the Life of Frederick Douglass, an American Slave* (1845; Harmondsworth: Penguin, 1982), pp. 97–98.

[14]Marx himself became increasingly attracted to positivism as his philosophical career matured, and an important part of the Marxist tradition perpetuates that attraction. Strongly influenced by the linguistic turn, however, recent Marxists have insisted (I think rightly) that positivism is not inherent in historical materialism and may be a powerful aberration from it.

[15]John Milbank, *Theology and Social Theory: Beyond Secular Reason* (Oxford: Blackwell, 1990), pp. 177–205.

[16]Biblical quotations are from the Jerusalem Bible (1966).

[17]Nicholas Lash, *A Matter of Hope: A Theologian's Reflections on the Thought of Karl Marx* (Notre Dame: University of Notre Dame Press, 1982), pp. 135–152. I am indebted to Lash throughout this essay for my sense of how Christianity relates to Marxism.

[18]*Ibid.*, p. 138.

[19]For recent summaries of the division, see Craig M. Gay, *With Liberty and Justice for Whom? The Recent Evangelical Debate over Capitalism* (Grand Rapids: Eerdmans, 1991), and John P. Tiemstra, 'Christianity and Economics: A Review of the Recent Literature', *Christian Scholar's Review* 22 (1993), pp. 227–247.

[20]Maurice Blondel, *Action (1893): Essay on a Critique of Life and a Science of Practice*, trans. Olivia Blanchette (Notre Dame: University of Notre Dame Press, 1984); Ronald J. Sider, *Rich Christians in an Age of Hunger* (Dallas: Word, 3rd edn. 1990).

[21]Francis Fukuyama, *The End of History and the Last Man* (New York: Macmillan, 1992).

[22]E. M. W. Tillyard, *The Elizabethan World Picture* (London: Chatto and Windus, 1943; New York: Macmillan, 1944).

[23]*Shakespeare's History Plays* (London: Chatto and Windus, 1944; New York: Macmillan, 1946).

[24]Millbank, *Theology and Social Theory*, p. 1.

[25]Stephen Greenblatt, 'Invisible Bullets', in *Shakespearean Negotiations* (Berkeley and Los Angeles: University of California Press, 1988), pp. 21–65. Greenblatt published the same essay in slightly different forms in other places before 1988.

[26]*Ibid.*, p. 53.

[27]*Ibid.*, p. 22.

[28]*Ibid.*, p. 33.

6. The woman's place: Elisabeth Jay (pp. 103–119)

[1]There are of course critics who believe that once feminism 'enters the literary studies as critical discourse it is just one more way of talking about books'. See K. Ruthven, *Feminist Literary Studies: An Introduction* (Cambridge: Cambridge University Press, 1984), p. 8.

[2]Audre Lorde, 'The Masters Tools Will Never Dismantle the Master's House', in C. Moraga and G. Anzaldua (eds.), *This Bridge Called My Back: Writings by Radical Women of Color* (Watertown, MA.: Persephone Press, 1981), pp. 98–101.

[3]For a discussion of the place a feminist analysis should occupy within Christian theology today see E. Storkey, *What's Right with Feminism* (London: SPCK, 1985).

[4]Marge Piercy's novel, *Vida* (London: The Women's Press, 1980), provides a graphic picture of this.

[5]Toril Moi believes that abandoning the feminist stage of defending women *as* women is politically dangerous, and should not be wholly abandoned in favour of Kristeva's final goal of deconstructing the metaphysics of gender identity. *Sexual/ Textual Politics* (New York and London: Methuen, 1985).

[6]For further discussion of this problem see below, E. R. Clarke, 'How feminist can a handmaid be?', p. 240.

[7]A remark made by Anne Seller, University of Kent, at the Higher Education Foundation Conference held at St John's College, Oxford, Easter 1993.

[8]See *Men in Feminism* ed. Alice Jardine and Paul Smith (New York and London: Routledge, 1987) for a fuller discussion of men's relation to feminism. For Mary Eagleton, however, the title of this book is itself controversial: 'To some extent the whole problem of men's relation to feminism can be interpreted as a problem of prepositions and conjunctions'. Like Irigaray (see below n. 19), Eagleton hopes for a new discourse that will liberate us from the double bind of the political and semantic constraints inherent in man-made, male-oriented language. (*Feminist Literary Criticism* ed., Mary Eagleton, New York and London: Longman, 1991, pp. 20–21.)

[9]*Cf.* Margaret Atwood's declared intentions. See below, Clarke, p. 237.

[10]*Coming to Terms: Feminism, Theory, Politics*, ed. E. Weed (New York and London: Routledge, 1989), p. xxiv.

[11]Actually, such criticism seems based to me upon a misunderstanding of the complex relation of realism to the world held by many of the great novelists working within this tradition. George Eliot's *Middlemarch* would be an apposite novel to examine here as a text, often seen as the high point of the 'realist' tradition, which, by deploying its narrative strategies to enact opposition to 'the limiting concept of selfhood', also constitutes a critique of that tradition. Eliot's desire to substitute humanism tinged with religious traditions for Christianity might, in turn, provide a salutary warning that a concept of 'selfhood' may prove an essential constituent part of a Christian understanding.

[12]Patrocinio Schweickart, 'Reading Ourselves: Towards a Feminist Theory of Reading', *Speaking Gender* (New York and London: Routledge, 1989), p. 27.

[13]Daphne Hampsen, *Theology and Feminism* (Oxford: Basil Blackwell, 1990). For some exemplars of feminist readings of biblical texts see below note 1 to E. R. Clarke's essay.

[14]For a fascinating essay outlining the problematics of a variety of feminist attempts to recuperate myth see Diane Purkiss, 'Women's Rewriting of Myths', in Carolyne Larrington (ed.), *The Feminist Companion to Mythology* (London: Pandora, 1992), pp. 441–457.

[15]Cf. Zelda Austen, 'Why the Feminists are Angry with George Eliot', *College English* 37 (1976), pp. 549–561.

[16]Julia Kristeva, 'Talking about Polylogue', trans. Sean Hand, in Toril Moi (ed.), *French Feminist Thought: A Reader* (Cambridge, MA. and Oxford: Blackwell, 1987), pp. 110–117.

[17]This very abbreviated account of the implications of French feminism's use

of Freudian and Lacanian theory necessarily raises another discussion as to whether feminism can properly have anything to do with such male-centred discourses.

[18]In practice, however, as Margaret Atwood's commentary illustrates, it has proved difficult for women writers to celebrate the pre-linguistic. Offred may acclaim the sheer physicality of words, but she remains desperate to re-enter the symbolic world and the handmaids only have recourse to bodily language after they have been denied access to the abstract order. See below, Clarke, pp. 238–239 and 245–246.

[19]For a fuller discussion of the theological implications of recent attempts at inclusive language and, in particular, Luce Irigaray's challenge to the homosexuality of Lacan's theory of language, see G. Ward, 'In the Name of the Father and of the Mother', *Literature and Theology*, vol. 8, No. 3 (September 1994), pp. 311–327.

[20]'Stabat Mater', in Toril Moi (ed.), *The Kristeva Reader* (Oxford: Basil Blackwell, 1986), pp. 161–185.

[21]'Difficult Joys', in Helen Wilcox, Keith McWatters, Ann Thompson and Linda R. Williams, (eds.), *The Body and the Text: Hélène Cixous, Reading and Teaching* (New York and London: Harvester Wheatsheaf, 1990), p. 23.

[22]*Ibid.*, p. 29.

[23]Jeanette Winterson's *Written on the Body* (London: Jonathan Cape, 1992) might be cited as a recent English example of the attempt to realize the mute language of bodily desire that Luce Irigaray characterizes as *la paroles des femmes*. For an analysis of the various ways in which Winterson's strategies for evading the language and structures of binary opposition lead her instead into reproducing the self-same traditional power structures she was seeking to destroy, see a review by Helen Barr in *The English Review*, 3/4 (April 1994), pp. 22–23.

[24]See Margaret Whitford (ed.), *The Irigaray Reader* (Cambridge MA. and Oxford: Basil Blackwell, 1991), p. 138.

[25]Nina Baym, 'The Madwoman and her Languages: Why I Don't Do Feminist Literary Theory', (1984), Robyn R. Warhol and Diane Price Herald (eds.), *Feminisms: An Anthology of Literary Theory and Criticism* (New Brunswick: Rutgers University Press, 1991), pp. 154–167. For a discussion of the ways in which evangelicalism empowered some eighteenth- and nineteenth-century women to find a way out of this impasse, see C. L. Krueger, *The Reader's Repentance: Women Preachers, Women Writers, and the Nineteenth-Century Social Discourse* (Chicago: University of Chicago Press, 1993).

[26]Susan Sellers, 'Learning to Read the Feminine', in Wilcox *et al.* (eds.), *The Body and the Text: Hélène Cixous, Reading and Teaching*, p. 193.

7. Words and presences: the spiritual imperative: Kevin Mills (pp. 121–136).

I would like to thank David Jasper and David Barratt for their incisive and productive comments on earlier drafts of this essay, and Royden Morgan and Julie Reynard for being discerning readers.

[1]T. Hawkes, 'General Editor's Preface' to the 'New Accents' series, published by Routledge.

[2]J. Derrida, *Of Grammatology*, trans. G. C. Spivak (Baltimore: Johns Hopkins University Press, 1976), p. 24.

[3]*Ibid.*, p. 39.

[4]*Ibid.*, p. 24.

[5]*Ibid.*, pp. 7, 23.

[6]*Ibid.*, p. 65.

[7]J.–F. Lyotard, *The Postmodern Condition: A Report on Knowledge*, trans. G. Bennington and B. Massumi (Minneapolis: University of Minnesota Press; Manchester: Manchester University Press, 1984), p. xxiv.

[8]J. Baudrillard, *Selected Writings*, ed. M. Poster (Cambridge: Polity Press, 1989), p. 172. For an anti-postmodern appraisal see Christopher Norris, 'Lost in the Funhouse: Baudrillard and the Politics of Postmodernism', *Textual Practice* 3 (1989), pp. 360–387.

[9]Baudrillard, *Selected Writings*, p. 173.

[10]*Ibid.*, p. 169.

[11]*Ibid.*, p. 173.

[12]C. S. Lewis, 'Christianity and Literature', in *Rehabilitations and Other Essays* (Oxford: Oxford University Press, 1939), pp. 181–197, p. 191; T. S. Eliot, 'Tradition and the Individual Talent', in J. Hayward (ed.), *Selected Prose* (Harmondsworth: Penguin, 1953), pp. 21–30.

[13]T. R. Wright, *Theology and Literature* (Cambridge, MA. and Oxford: Blackwell, 1988), p. 32.

[14]K. Hart, *The Trespass of the Sign: Deconstruction, Theology and Philosophy* (New York and Cambridge: Cambridge University Press, 1990), pp. 64–70; K. Mills, review of R. Schwartz (ed.), *The Book and the Text*; Daniel Boyarin, *Intertextuality and the Reading of Midrash*; Kevin Hart, *The Trespass of the Sign*, in *Textual Practice* 6/2 (1992), pp. 338–347.

[15]P. Ricoeur, *The Rule of Metaphor*, trans. R. Czerny with K. McLaughlin and J. Costello (Toronto: University of Toronto Press, 1977).

[16]The contrary case is argued by Susan Handelman in *The Slayers of Moses: The Emergence of Rabbinic Interpretation in Modern Literary Theory* (New York: State University of New York Press, 1982).

[17]S. Mitchell, 'Post-structuralism, Empiricism and Interpretation', in S. Mitchell and M. Rosen (eds.), *The Need for Interpretation* (London: Athlone, 1983), pp. 54–89, quotation from p. 85.

[18]B. Smalley, *The Study of the Bible in the Middle Ages* (Oxford: Blackwell, 3rd edn., 1983).

8. The Bible and literary study: Leland Ryken (pp. 139–153)

[1]Northrop Frye, *The Educated Imagination* (Bloomington: Indiana University Press, 1964), pp. 110–111.

[2]'General Introduction', Robert Alter and Frank Kermode (eds.), *The Literary Guide to the Bible* (Cambridge, MA.: Harvard University Press, 1987), pp. 2–3.

[3]C. S. Lewis, *The Literary Impact of the Authorized Version* (Philadelphia: Fortress, 1967), p. 33.

[4]C. S. Lewis, *Reflections on the Psalms* (New York: Harcourt, Brace and World, 1958), p. 3.

[5]For a fuller account of the current landscape, see L. Ryken, 'The Bible as Literature: A Brief History', in Ryken and Tremper Longman III (eds.), *A Complete Literary Guide to the Bible* (Grand Rapids: Zondervan, 1993), pp. 49–68.

[6]Jonathan Culler, *Structuralist Poetics* (Ithaca: Cornell University Press, 1975), p. 136.

[7]Lewis, *Reflections on the Psalms*, p. 3.

[8]H. L. Mencken, *Treatise on the Gods* (New York: Aldred A. Knopf, 1946), p. 286.

[9]John Sider, 'Nurturing Our Nurse: Literary Scholars and Biblical Exegesis', *Christianity and Literature*, 32/1 (1982), pp. 19–20.

[10]For a fuller account of the history of literary interest in the Bible, see Ryken, 'The Bible as Literature'; and David Norton, *A History of the Bible as Literature*, (Cambridge: Cambridge University Press, 1993).

[11]Augustine, *On Christian Doctrine*, to be found *inter alia* in Robert M. Hutchins (ed.), *Great Books of the Western World* (Chicago: Encyclopaedia Britannica, 1952), vol. 18, p. 678.

[12]Barbara Lewalski, *Protestant Poetics and the Seventeenth-Century Religious Lyric* (Princeton: Princeton University Press, 1979).

[13]*The Reason of Church Government*, in Douglas Bush (ed.), *The Complete Poetical Works of John Milton* (Boston: Houghton Mifflin, 1965), p. xxix.

[14]Erich Auerbach, *Mimesis: The Representation of Reality in Western Literature*, trans. Willard Trask (Princeton: Princeton University Press, 1953), pp. 3–23.

[15]The quoted statements come, respectively, from T. R. Henn, *The Bible as Literature* (New York: Oxford University Press,. 1970), p. 258; and Northrop Frye, *Anatomy of Criticism* (Princeton: Princeton University Press, 1957), p. 316.

[16]C. S. Lewis, *The Literary Influence of the Authorized Version*, p. 15.

[17]Northrop Frye, *Anatomy of Criticism*, p. 135.

[18]*Ibid.*

[19]Francis A. Schaeffer, *Art and the Bible* (Downers Grove: IVP, 1973), pp. 60–61.

[20]Northrop Frye, *On Teaching Literature* (New York: Harcourt, Brace, Jovanovich, 1972), p. 13.

[21]Michael Edwards, 'The Project of a Christian Poetics', *Christianity and Literature*, 39/1 (1989), p. 73.

9. Shakespeare and Christianity: Rowland Cotterill (pp. 155–175)

[1]References to *King Lear* are taken from the New Cambridge text, ed. Jay L. Halio (Cambridge: Cambridge University Press, 1992).

[2]References to all Shakespeare plays other than *King Lear* and *Richard III* are taken from William Shakespeare, *The Complete Works*, ed. Stanley Wells and Gary Taylor (Oxford: Clarendon, 1986).

[3]Quotations from the Bible in this chapter are taken from the New English Bible (1970).

[4]*Antony and Cleopatra*, I.i.17.

[5]*Antony and Cleopatra*, V.ii.303–304.

[6]*Antony and Cleopatra*, IV.xvi.31ff.

[7]*Antony and Cleopatra*, V.ii.302, 310.

[8]For example, Mk. 10:17ff.

[9]William Cowper, 'God moves in a mysterious way'.

[10]*Richard II*, IV.i.82–91, 105–140.

[11]Winchester appears in *Henry VI Part I* and *Henry VI Part II*, Pandulph in *King John*, Southwell and Hume in *Henry VI Part II*, the Archbishop of York in *Henry IV Parts I* and *II*. The line quoted is *Henry IV Part II*, IV.i.54.

[12]*Hamlet*, V.ii.168.

[13]*King Lear*, V.ii.11.

[14]*The Tempest*, IV.i.156–157.

[15]In The Arden Shakespeare, *King Richard III*, ed. Antony Hammond (London: Routledge, 1981). Subsequent references to the play are to this edition.

[16]*Ibid.*, p. 109.

[17]E. M. W. Tillyard, *Shakespeare's History Plays* (New York: Macmillan; London: Chatto and Windus, 1944).

[18]Hammond, pp. 107–108.

[19]*Ibid.*, p. 110.

[20]*Richard III*, II.i.96–135.

[21]Hammond, p. 109.

[22]Fundamental is the chapter cn the play in J. Holloway, *The Story of the Night* (London: RKP, 1961) and the astringent arguments of W. Elton, *'King Lear' and the Gods* (San Marino: The Huntington Library, 1966, reprinted 1988). Stephen Greenblatt's essay, 'Shakespeare and the Exorcists', in P. Parker and G. Hartman (eds.), *Shakespeare and the Question of Theory* (New York and London: Oxford University Press, 1985) gives an important new direction to the issues. The sections 'The Theatres of Exorcism' and 'The Theatre of the Bible' in Halio's New Cambridge edition (pp, 8–9, 12–14) are helpful guides.

[23]Halio, p. 226, note on *King Lear*, IV.v.168.

[24]Compare Stanley Cavell, *Disowning Knowledge in Six Plays of Shakespeare* (Cambridge: Cambridge University Press, 1987), p. 28: 'It is my view that no-one knows from outside whether a marriage exists . . . whether the gift is accepted, a legitimate bond conferred.'

[25]Halio, p. 236, note on *King Lear*, IV.vi.36.

[26]*Ibid.*, p. 243, note on *King Lear*, V.ii.9–11.

[27]*Ibid.*, p. 22–23.

[28]William Empson, *The Structure of Complex Words* (London: Chatto and Windus, 1969), pp. 144–145.

[29]*Ibid.*, pp. 154–155.

[30]*Ibid.*, p. 154.

[31]Walter Stein, *Criticism as Dialogue* (Cambridge: Cambridge University Press, 1969), p. 145.

[32]*King Lear*, IV.vi.11–24, 42–74.

[33]For example, in *The Messingkauf Dialogues*, trans. John Willett (London: Methuen, 1965).

[34]Dorothy L. Sayers, *The Man Born to be King* (London: Gollancz, 1943), p. 19.

[35]I owe a debt here to the production of *The Winter's Tale* by Tom Hill at the Warwick Arts Centre, June 1990, and to discussion with Mark Fraser, who played Leontes.

[36]*King Lear*, I.i.85.

[37]*The Winter's Tale*, I.ii.335–343.

[38]Cavell, *Disowning Knowledge*, pp. 206, 204.

[39]I allude here to Jas. 3:18, Heb. 11:1, Mk. 10:26; 2 Cor. 5:19.

[40]W. B. Yeats, 'Sailing to Byzantium'.

[41]In the production mentioned above (n. 35), the same actress played all three roles.

[42]*The Winter's Tale*, IV.iv.88.

[43]Cavell, *Disowning Knowledge*, p. 218.

[44]I have not dwelt, in connection with *The Winter's Tale*, on the theme of

'forgiveness'. This is not because it seems to me unimportant, but because it is so important as to be invisible.

10. Reading Paradise Lost: U. Milo Kaufmann (pp. 177–193)

[1]William Butts (ed.), *Conversations with Richard Wilbur* (Jackson, MS. and London: University Press of Mississippi, 1990), p. 229. The full statement runs: 'When I teach Milton, for example, I deal with him in all respects, spending a lot of time on matters of technique. You have to with a great technician, with the greatest verse architect in history: you cannot understand "L'Allegro" and "Il Penseroso" are serious poems unless you worry the structure to death and discover the ideas implicit in the structure. And so I and the students wrestle for several days until we've found the structure of the two poems.'

[2]For this and all later quotations from *Paradise Lost* I have used the text included in Merritt Y. Hughes (ed.) *John Milton, Complete Poems and Major Prose* (New York: Odyssey Press, 1957). No modern text has matched this for the quality of the annotation, and it is still available.

[3]Interestingly, in modern romance–fantasy and science fiction – the epic form has a remarkable flowering. Vast public action is the norm, as in early epic, but in a work such as Frank Herbert's *Dune* one finds a joining of broad external action with profound internal action. Northrop Frye has commented on an element of science fiction in *Paradise Lost*, alluding no doubt to the technology employed by the rebel angels in the war in heaven. The tables have now been turned, for today it is scientific romance which is most likely to accommodate immense epic action, metaphysical or religious concerns, and the true heroes of modern western culture, namely scientists, inventors, explorers and bright mavericks.

[4]John Hick, *Evil and the God of Love* (1966).

[5]Dennis Danielson, *Milton's Good God* (Cambridge: 1982).

[6]Zwi Werblowsky, *Lucifer and Prometheus: A Study of Milton's Satan* (London: RKP, 1952).

[7]William Lynch, *Christ and Prometheus: A New Image of the Secular* (Notre Dame: University of Notre Dame Press, 1970).

11. Romantic poetry and the Wholly Spirit: J. R. Watson (pp. 195–217)

[1]T. E. Hulme, 'Romanticism and Classicism', in Herbert Read (ed.), *Speculations* (London: RKP, 1936), p. 118.

[2]M. H. Abrams, *Natural Supernaturalism* (New York: 1971), p. 12.

[3]*Biographia Literaria* in James Engel and W. J. Bate (eds.), *The Collected Works of Samuel Taylor Coleridge*, vol. 7 (Princeton and London: Princeton University Press, 1983).

[4]K. W. F. Solger, *Vier Gesprache uber das Schone und die Kunst* (1815), quoted in Kathleen Wheeler, *Sources, Processes and Methods in Coleridge's Biographia Literaria* (Cambridge: Cambridge University Press, 1980), p. 65.

[5]William Blake, *The Laocoon* (engraved *c.* 1820, with inscriptions). Reproduced with notes in G. E. Bentley Jr (ed.), *William Blake's Writings* (Oxford: Oxford University Press, 1978), I.663, 743.

[6]Mikhail Bakhtin, 'The Problem of Speech Genres', reprinted in extracts in G. S.

Morson (ed.), *Bakhtin, Essays and Dialogues on His Work* (Chicago: Chicago University Press, 1986), p. 92.

[7] Biblical quotations in this chapter are from the Authorized Version (1611).

[8] All quotations from *The Prelude* are from the 1805 text.

[9] See Owen C. Watkins, *The Puritan Experience* (London: RKP, 1972).

[10] *The Autobiography of Leigh Hunt*, ed. J. E. Morpurgo (London: Cresset Press, 1949).

[11] Alicia Ostriker, *Vision and Verse in William Blake* (Madison and Milwaukee: University of Wisconsin Press, 1965), pp. 213–214.

[12] D. W. Winnicott, *Playing and Reality* (1971: Harmondsworth: Penguin, 1980), p. 62.

[13] Abrams, *Natural Supernaturalism*, p. 13.

[14] *The Letters of John Keats*, ed. H. E. Rollins (Cambridge, MA.: Harvard University Press, 1958), II.103.

[15] *A Vision of the Last Judgment*, in Geoffrey Keynes (ed.), *The Complete Writings of William Blake* (Oxford: Oxford University Press, 1966), pp. 605–606.

12. Time for Hardy: Jude and the obscuring of Scripture: David Barratt (pp. 219–234)

[1] All page references from *Jude the Obscure* are from the Penguin Classics edition (Harmondsworth, 1985), ed. C. H. Sisson.

[2] Erich Auerbach, *Mimesis: The Representation of Reality in Western Literature* (Princeton: Princeton University Press, 1953).

[3] *The Return of the Native*, ed. George Woodcock (Harmondsworth: Penguin, 1985), to which all page references are made.

[4] *Ibid.*, p. 54.

[5] *Ibid.*

[6] *Ibid.*, p. 55.

[7] *Ibid.*, p. 473.

[8] Such as Pss. 78; 80; 89; 105–107; 135–136.

[9] Stephen Hawking, *A Brief History of Time* (London: Bantam, 1988).

[10] J. Hillis Miller, *Distance and Desire* (Cambridge, MA.: Harvard University Press; Oxford: Oxford University Press, 1970).

[11] *Jude*, p. 350.

[12] *Ibid.*, p. 366.

[13] *Ibid.*, p. 190.

[14] Barry Qualls, *Secular Pilgrims of Victorian Fiction* (Cambridge: Cambridge University Press, 1981).

[15] *Jude*, p. 50.

[16] *Ibid.*, p. 53.

[17] Hardy himself stated that 'an object or mark raised or made by man on a scene is worth ten times any such formed by unconscious Nature. Hence clouds, mists and mountains are unimportant besides the wear of a threshold, or the print of a hand.' Florence Hardy, *Life of Thomas Hardy* (London: Macmillan, 1928–30), p. 116. For a fuller discussion, see D. Barratt, 'Landmarks on the Spiritual Landscape', in *Proceedings of the English Association North*, 4 (1989), pp. 28–39.

[18] *Jude*, pp. 229, 200, 303, 305, 338.

[19] *Ibid.*, pp. 277, 354, 482, etc.

[20] *Ibid*, pp. 187, 191, 210.

[21]*Ibid.*, p. 252.

[22]*Ibid.*, p. 357.

[23]*Ibid.*, p. 216.

[24]*Ibid.*, p. 231, *cf.* p. 391.

[25]*Ibid.*, p. 247.

[26]For an excellent discussion of biblical parody and antitype in *Jude*, see Eleanor McNees, 'Reverse Typology in *Jude the Obscure*', *Christianity and Literature* 39/1 (Autumn 1989), pp. 35–49.

[27]See Madan Sarup, *An Introductory Guide to Post-Structuralism and Postmodernism* (Hemel Hempstead: Harvester Wheatsheaf, 2nd edn. 1993), pp. 146, 181.

13. How feminist can a handmaid be? Margaret Atwood's The Handmaid's Tale: *Elizabeth Clarke (pp. 235–250)*

[1]See the treatments of the story in Phyllis Trible, *Texts of Terror: Literary-Feminist Readings of Biblical Narratives* (Philadelphia: Fortress; London: SCM, 1984), pp. 9–35; Renita J. Weems, *Just a Sister Away: A Womanist Vision of Women's Relationships in the Bible* (San Diego: Luramedia, 1988), pp. 1–19. See Lucy M. Freibert, 'The Politics of Risk in Margaret Atwood's *The Handmaid's Tale*', in Judith McCombs (ed.), *Critical Essays on Margaret Atwood* (Boston: G. K. Hall, 1988), p. 282, for biblical and non-biblical sources for the role of handmaid in Israelite history.

[2]Arnold E. Davidson, 'Future Tense: Making History in *The Handmaid's Tale*', in Kathryn van Spanckeren and Jan Garden Castro (eds.), *Margaret Atwood: Vision and Forms* (Carbondale and Edwardsville: Southern Illinois University Press, 1988), p. 117.

[3]Margaret Atwood, *The Handmaid's Tale* (London: Virago, 1987), p. 26.

[4]Elizabeth Schussler Fiorenza, *Bread Not Stone: The Challenge of Feminist Biblical Interpretation* (Edinburgh: T. and T. Clark, 1990), pp. 60–61: Rosemary Radford Ruether, *Sexism and God-talk* (London: SCM, 1983).

[5]Dorota Filipczak, in 'Is There No Balm in Gilead? Biblical Intertext in *The Handmaid's Tale*', *Journal of Literature and Theology*, 7/2 (June 1993), pp. 169–185, argues that Margaret Atwood is 'pointing to the dangers lurking in the process of institutionalization of the sacred text' (p. 169).

[6]Davidson, 'Future Tense: Making History in *The Handmaid's Tale*', p. 116.

[7]Le Anne Schreiber, interview with Margaret Atwood, *Vogue* (23 January, 1983), pp. 208–209, quoted in Gayle Greene, *Changing the Story: Feminist Fiction and the Tradition* (Bloomington and Indianapolis: Indiana University Press, 1991), p. 205. See also *Quill and Quire* 51/9 (September 1985): 'Margaret Atwood: "There's nothing in the book that hasn't already happened",' quoted in Freibert, 'The Politics of Risk in Margaret Atwood's *The Handmaid's Tale*', p. 290.

[8]*The Handmaid's Tale*, p. 195.

[9]*Ibid.*, pp. 201–202.

[10]*Ibid.*, p. 131.

[11]*Ibid.*, p. 279.

[12]T. Mark Ledbetter, 'An Apocalypse of Race and Gender: Body Violence and Forming Identity in Toni Morrison's *Beloved*', in David Jasper (ed.), *Postmodernism, Literature, and the Future of Theology* (Ipswich: Macmillan, 1993), p. 80.

[13]See Diane Purkiss, 'Women's Rewriting of Myth', in Carolyne Larrington (ed.), *The Feminist Companion to Mythology* (London: Pandora, 1992), pp. 441–458.

[14]Brian Stableford, 'Is There No Balm in Gilead? The Woeful Prophecies of *The Handmaid's Tale*', *Foundation: The Review of Science Fiction*, 39 (Spring 1987), p. 99.

[15]Gayle Green, *Changing The Story: Feminist Fiction and the Tradition* (Bloomington and Indianapolis: Indiana University Press, 1991), p. 206.

[16]*The Handmaid's Tale*, p. 181.

[17]*Ibid.*, p. 143.

[18]*Ibid.*, p. 144.

[19]*Ibid.*, p. 322.

[20]For further discussion of this issue, refer back to Elisabeth Jay's chapter 'The woman's place', especially the first section, 'Caveat Lector'.

[21]Freibert, 'The Politics of Risk in *The Handmaid's Tale*', pp. 280–281.

[22]*The Handmaid's Tale*, p. 144.

[23]*Ibid.*, p. 255.

[24]*Ibid.*, pp. 256, 262.

[25]*Ibid.*, p. 279.

[26]Margaret Atwood, *Second Words: Selected Critical Prose* (1982), p. 353, quoted in van Spanckeren and Castro (eds.), *Margaret Atwood: Vision and Forms*, p. 102.

[27]Hélène Cixous, 'The Laugh of the Medusa', in Elaine Marks and Isabelle de Courtivron (eds.), *New French Feminisms: An Anthology* (Amherst: University of Massachusetts Press, 1980), p. 258.

[28]Roberta Rubenstein, 'Nature and Nurture in Dystopia', in van Spanckeren and Castro (eds.), *Margaret Atwood: Vision and Forms*, p. 105.

[29]*The Handmaid's Tale*, pp. 72–73.

[30]*Ibid.*, pp. 83–84.

[31]Julia Kristeva, 'Talking About Polylogue', in Toril Moi (ed.), *French Feminist Thought: A Reader* (Oxford: Blackwell, 1987), pp. 110–117: see particularly p. 113.

[32]See Chris Weedon, *Feminist Practice and Poststructuralist Theory* (Oxford: Blackwell, 1987), p. 166. Julia Kristeva's response to this practice is extremely negative: 'It is unfortunately the case that some feminists persist in adopting sulking, and even obscurantist, attitudes; those, for example, who demand a separate language for women, one made of silence, cries or touch, which has cut all ties with the language of so-called phallic communication.' Toril Moi (ed.), *French Feminist Thought*, p. 116.

[33]*The Handmaid's Tale*, p. 149.

[34]*Ibid.*, p. 196.

[35]In a letter to a friend, Hopkins talks about the artist's 'most essential quality': 'masterly execution, which is a kind of male gift, and especially marks off men from women, the begetting of one's thought on paper, on verse, or whatever the matter is . . . the mastery I speak of is not so much in the mind as a puberty in the life of that quality. The male quality is the creative gift.' *The Correspondence of Gerard Manley Hopkins and Richard Watson Dixon*, ed. C. C. Abbott (1933), p. 133, quoted in Sandra M. Gilbert and Susan Gubar, *The Madwoman in the Attic: The Woman Writer and the Nineteenth-Century Literary Imagination* (New Haven and London: Yale University Press, 1975), p. 3.

[36]*The Handmaid's Tale*, p. 279.

[37]*Ibid.*, p. 144.

[38]*Ibid.*, p. 43.

[39]Weedon, *Feminist Practice and Poststructuralist Theory*, chapter 4: 'Language and Subjectivity', particularly pp. 105–106.

[40]Linda S. Kauffman, 'The Long Goodbye: Against Personal Testimony, or, An Infant Grifter Grows Up', in Gayle Greene and Coppélia Kahn (eds.), *Changing the*

Subject: The Making of Feminist Literary Criticism (New York and London: Routledge, 1993), p. 132.

[41]Davidson, 'Future Tense', p. 117.

[42]*Ibid.*, p. 115.

[43]The best work on a feminist literary reading of the Bible is that of Phyllis Trible. See her *God and the Rhetoric of Sexuality* (London: SCM, 1978); *Texts of Terror: Literary-Feminist Readings of Biblical Narratives* (London: SCM, 1984).

[44]For Christian feminist rewritings of the Bible, see Weems, *Just a Sister Away*, and the work of Sara Maitland, particularly *Daughter of Jerusalem* (London: Virago, 1981).

[45]*The Handmaid's Tale*, p. 204.

[46]Diane Purkiss, 'Women's Rewriting of Myth', p. 158.

14. Why wait for an angel? Thomas Pynchon's The Crying of Lot 49: John Schad (pp. 251–262)

[1]J.–F. Lyotard, *The Postmodern Condition*, tr. G. Bennington and B. Massumi (Minneapolis and Manchester: Manchester University Press, 1984), p. xxiv.

[2]All references to the Bible are to the Authorized Version.

[3]For a fuller summary see Tony Tanner, *Thomas Pynchon* (London: Methuen, 1982), pp. 56–57.

[4]Thomas Pynchon, *The Crying of Lot 49* (London: Picador, 1979), p. 72.

[5]*Ibid.*, p. 73.

[6]*Ibid.*, pp. 74, 6, 10.

[7]*Ibid.*, p. 24.

[8]*Ibid.*, p. 14.

[9]*Ibid.*, p. 62.

[10]*Ibid.*, p. 124, my italics.

[11]Philippa Berry, 'Deserts of the Heart', *Times Higher Educational Supplement* (28 December 1990), p. 7.

[12]See John Schad, ' "Hostage of the Word": Poststructuralism's Gospel Intertext', *Religion and Literature* 25 (1993), pp. 1–16; Valentine Cunningham, *In the Reading Gaol* (Cambridge, MA. and Oxford: Blackwell, 1994), pp. 363–410; Kevin Hart, *The Trespass of the Sign* (Cambridge: Cambridge University Press, 1989); and Philippa Berry and Andrew Wernick (eds.), *Shadow of Spirit: Postmodernism and Religion* (London: Routledge, 1992).

[13]Roland Barthes, 'Death of the Author' in Stephen Heath (ed.), *Image–Music–Text* (London: Fontana, 1977), p. 147.

[14]*The Crying of Lot 49*, p. 126.

[15]*Ibid.*, p. 45.

[16]See Edward Mendelson, 'The Sacred, the Profane, and *The Crying of Lot 49*', in Kenneth Baldwin and David K. Kirby (eds.), *Individual and Community* (Durham, NC.: Duke University Press, 1975), p. 208.

[17]*The Crying of Lot 49*, pp. 45, 81, 82.

[18]It is important to note that for the early Greeks, in particular Heraclitus, the *logos* does not necessarily have this meaning: as John D. Caputo comments, 'the [Heraclitean] *logos* does not refer to some kind of systematic principle which imposes a unity of order upon things'. *Heidegger and Aquinas:* (New York: Fordham University Press, 1982), p. 195. Perhaps, then, *Lot 49*'s 'epileptic Word' recovers something of the earlier, Heraclitean meaning of *logos*.

[19]*The Crying of Lot 49*, p. 15.

[20]*Ibid.*, p. 12.

[21]*Ibid.*, p. 61.

[22]*Ibid.*, p. 89.

[23]*Ibid.*, pp. 15, 19, 84.

[24]David Seed, *The Fictional Labyrinths of Thomas Pynchon* (London: Macmillan, 1988) p. 132.

[25]In John's Gospel the *Logos* speaks *logoi*; thus the same word is used to describe both Christ and utterance, or speech.

[26]Foucault argues that ' "Truth" is linked in a circular relation with systems of power which produce and sustain it'. Michel Foucault, *Power/Knowledge*, ed. Colin Gordon (Brighton: Harvester Wheatsheaf).

[27]*The Crying of Lot 49*, p. 15 (my italics).

[28]*Ibid.*, p. 56.

[29]*Ibid.*, p. 46.

[30]*Ibid.*, p. 31.

[31]See Jn. 5:1–9.

[32]*The Crying of Lot 49*, p. 127.

[33]*Ibid.*, p. 20.

[34]*Ibid.*

[35]*Ibid.*, p. 84.

[36]*Ibid.*

[37]For a good summary of the debate surrounding this possibility see Terry Eagleton, *The Ideology of the Aesthetic* (Oxford: Blackwell, 1990), pp. 403–405.

[38]*The Crying of Lot 49*, p. 62.

[39]*Ibid.*, pp. 81–82.

[40]*Ibid.*, p. 83.

[41]*Ibid.*, pp. 107–108.

[42]*Ibid.*, pp. 117–118.

[43]*Ibid.*, p. 127.

[44]For many cultural theorists the cultural imperialism of America is a crucial aspect of postmodernism – see Peter Brooker (ed.), *Modernism/Postmodernism* (London: Longman, 1992), p. 24.

[45]*The Crying of Lot 49*, p. 126.

[46]*Ibid.*

[47]*Ibid.*, p. 110.

[48]*Ibid.*, p. 27.

[49]*Ibid.*, p. 85.

[50]*Ibid.*, p. 57.

[51]*Ibid.*, p. 88.

[52]*Ibid.*, p. 62.

[53]*Ibid.*, p. 127.

[54]*Ibid.*, p. 80.

[55]*Ibid.*, p. 81.

[56]*Ibid.*, p. 85.

[57]*Ibid.*, p. 83.

[58]It is, of course, the Anglican *Book of Common Prayer* that refers to the eucharist as a 'perpetual memorial'. In the portion of *Lot 49* that was first published in *Esquire* magazine our 'heroine' was called Oedipa *Mass*.

[59]*The Crying of Lot 49*, p. 15.

[60]*Ibid.*, p. 46.

[61]*Ibid.*, p. 68.

[62]*Ibid.*, p. 126.

[63]Mendelson, 'The Sacred, the Profane', p. 192.

[64]*The Crying of Lot 49*, p. 84.

[65]*Ibid.*, p. 83.

[66]*Ibid.*, p. 123.

[67]*Ibid.*, p. 15, my italics.

[68]Mendelson, 'The Sacred, the Profane', p. 190.

[69]Jacques Derrida, *The Post Card*, trans. Alan Bass (Chicago: University of Chicago Press, 1987), p. 123.

[70]*The Crying of Lot 49*, p. 80.

[71]Jacques Derrida, *Writing and Difference*, trans. Alan Bass (London: Routledge, 1978), p. 82.

General Index

No attempt has been made to index the commonest terms, such as 'literature', 'criticism', 'language', 'text' *etc*. Only the most significant references to other common terms, such as 'discourse', 'Bible', 'tradition', have been given.

Index of Scripture Passages

I. The Old Testament

II. The New Testament